BRITISH ORDERS AND AWARDS

BRITISH ORDERS
AND AWARDS

A description of all Orders, Decorations, Long
Service, Coronation, Jubilee and Commemoration Medals, together with historical details
concerning knighthood, service ranks and
similar information.

KAYE & WARD
LONDON

First edition 1959
Second entirely revised edition 1968
Kaye & Ward Limited
194–200 Bishopsgate, London E.C.2

Revised edition © 1968 Kaye & Ward Limited

SBN: 7182 0766 1

PRINTED IN GREAT BRITAIN BY
RICHARD CLAY (THE CHAUCER PRESS) LTD.
BUNGAY, SUFFOLK

CONTENTS

PART I

ORDERS OF KNIGHTHOOD

THE MOST NOBLE ORDER OF THE GARTER
Motto: Honi soit qui mal y pense (Evil be to him who Evil Thinks)

This Order is one of the most ancient of all orders of knighthood in Europe. It was founded by Edward III, though the exact year of its institution is not certain. All authorities agree that is was established at Windsor in 1348. The reason for the institution of the Order has never been established.

There is a story, which may or may not be fictitious, that Edward III picked up a garter dropped by the Countess of Salisbury at a ball and, placing it round his leg below the knee remarked to his courtiers, "Honi soit qui mal y pense", which afterwards became the motto of the Order.

There is a tradition which dates back to the time of Henry VI that the Order owed its origin to the fair sex.

It was founded in honour of the Holy Trinity, the Virgin Mary, St George and St Edward the Confessor. St George, then as now, the patron saint of England, was considered its patron and protector.

The Order originally consisted of twenty-five knights and the sovereign, twenty-six in all. The number remained the same until the reign of George III who decreed that princes of the royal blood and certain foreigners might receive the Order as supernumeraries to the original number.

The Military Knights of Windsor are an adjunct to the Order of the Garter. This charity, originally known as the Poor Knights of Windsor or Alms Knights, was founded by Edward III soon after the institution of the Order of the Garter, to maintain twenty-four (afterwards raised to twenty-six) poor individuals who had rendered distinguished military service. The change in title was made by William IV in 1833.

There are six officers to the Order of the Garter: Prelate, who is always the Bishop of Winchester; a Chancellor, the Marquess of Salisbury; a Registrar, the Dean of Windsor; Garter King-of-Arms; a Gentleman Usher of the Black Rod and a Secretary.

The original dress of the Order was a mantle, tunic and hood, all of blue cloth; those of the knights companions were lined with miniver, those of the sovereign in ermine. These garments were embroidered with garters of blue and gold, that of the mantle being larger than the others. The collar and the George as now worn were added by Henry VII. The last alteration was made by Charles II who instituted the wearing of the mid-blue ribbon over the left shoulder from which the Lesser George, worn on the right hip, is suspended.

From the first institution of the Order it was the practice to admit ladies. The queen and other important ladies were given their robes and hoods by the king, as well as the Ensign of the Garter. They were termed "Dames de la Fraternite de St George". Jean Froissart, a fellow countryman of Edward II's wife, Philippa of Hainault, and a reliable chronicler of the times, wrote eulogistically about the appearance of the queen at the feast of the Order.

The appointment of ladies to the Order fell into abeyance for some years. Charles I tried to revive the practice but nothing came of his efforts. When, however, Queen Anne attended a thanksgiving service at St Paul's in 1702, and again in 1704, she wore the Garter set with diamonds, as Sovereign of the Order, round her left arm.

There are nine insignia to the Order, as follows:

The Garter is of dark blue velvet about 1 in. wide edged with gold, bearing the motton of the Order *Honi soit qui mal y pense* in gold letters. It is worn by ladies above the left elbow, by knights below the left knee.

The Mantle of blue velvet has the badge of the Order embroidered on the left breast.

The Hood is made of crimson velvet.

The Surcoat is of crimson velvet lined with taffeta.

The Hat of black velvet, is lined with white taffeta, to which is fastened a plume of white ostrich feathers with a tuft of black heron's in the centre. The plume is fastened to the hat by means of a diamond band.

The Collar, with the George, is of gold weighing thirty ounces, troy weight. It is composed of twenty-six pieces representing buckled garters and in the centre of each is a red rose, alternating with knots made of gold cord.

The George, of gold enamel, represents the figure of St George, in armour and in his right hand a spear which was piercing the throat of a Dragon, and is worn pendant from the Collar.

The Badge (or Lesser George) of gold is oval and consists of the device on the George surrounded by the motto of the Order. It is worn on the right hip suspended from a dark blue sash worn over the left shoulder.

The Star consists of an eight-pointed star in the centre of which is the red cross of St George encircled by a blue garter bearing the motto of the Order, and is worn on the left breast.

The Ribbon, which was originally believed to be black, was changed by various sovereigns through numerous shades of blue until George VI changed it yet again, in 1950, to the 'Garter" blue, known today. It is worn over the left shoulder.

The full regalia is only worn on special occasions or by Royal Command. The Collar and Ribbon are never worn at the same time.

In the case of the three senior orders of knighthood, no ribbon is worn on the tunic in uniform.

THE MOST ANCIENT AND MOST NOBLE ORDER OF THE THISTLE

Motto: *Nemo me impune lacessit* (No one provokes me with impunity)

The origin of this Order is somewhat obscure. It is difficult to believe in its existence prior to the reign of James VII of Scotland and II of England unless we take what is legendary as fact. Whether it existed before then or not, it is certain that all orders of knighthood after the Restoration were considered by Scotsmen as relics of popery so that the Order fell into desuetude.

The Warrant signed by James II bears the date Windsor, 29th May, 1687; but though eight knights were appointed, the patent never bore the Great Seal. It was at this time that St Giles' Cathedral, Edinburgh, was designated the Chapel of the Order and continues so to be.

On the abdication of James II in 1688, the Order again fell into abeyance until finally revived on the lines of the Garter, by Queen Anne's instructions on 31st December, 1703.

The Warrant of James II stated that the Order should consist of twelve knights (an allusion to Our Lord and the Twelve Apostles) Queen Anne ordained the same number though it was not completed for some time. The number of eight stood till 17th July, 1821, when George IV increased it to twelve; and in 1827 the number was extended to the sovereign and sixteen brethren, though this number may be increased by members of the Royal Family.

As originally instituted, none but Scottish nobles were admitted, but since the reign of George I, it has been conferred on English peers, though not for many years. No foreigners had been admitted to the Order until King Olav V of Norway was admitted as an Extra Knight in October, 1962.

It was ordered by George I that vacancies should be filled by election in a Chapter of the Order. It is, however, usual practice for the sovereign to fill vacancies without summoning the Chapter.

There are four officers of the Order: the Dean, the Chancellor, the Lion King-of-Arms and the Usher of the Green Rod.

The four insignia of the Order are as follows:

The Mantle of green velvet is tied with green and gold tasselled cords. On the left the Star of the Order is embroidered.

The Collar is of gold, enamelled in proper colours, with alternating devices of thistles and sprigs of rue, the ancient symbols of the Picts and Scots.

The Badge (or Jewel) consists of the golden figure of St Andrew carrying a white enamelled Cross before him, is surrounded by golden rays, which were added to the Badge on the orders of George I in 1715, and is worn suspended from the collar. When the collar is not worn, a Gold Badge is suspended in such a way that the Badge itself rests on the right hip.

The Star is in the shape of a St Andrew's Cross, with rays issuing from between the arms of the cross. In the centre is a green thistle on a gold field surrounded by a green circlet bearing the motto in golden letters: this is worn on the left breast.

THE MOST ILLUSTRIOUS ORDER OF ST PATRICK

Motto: Quis separabit? (Who shall separate?)

This Order was founded by George III on 5th February, 1783, and named after the patron saint of Ireland as it was intended to assign it as a national knighthood to that country. The original number of brethren was fifteen but was subsequently increased by six in 1821 and by a further four in 1831.

The insignia of the Order are as follows:

The Mantle of sky-blue satin, lined with white silk was fastened by blue and gold cords, with the Star of the Order embroidered on the left side.

The Collar was of gold, composed of five roses and six harps placed alternately and connected with knots of gold. The harps and roses are arranged in such a way that a harp is immediately in the centre with the others alternating outwards. From this centre harp, which is surmounted by a gold Imperial Crown, hangs the Badge.

The Badge was gold and oval in shape, in the centre of which is a red enamelled Cross of St Patrick charged with a green trefoil, having an Imperial Crown on each of its leaves. Around this, on a sky-blue enamel band is, at the top, the motto, *Quis separabit*; around the bottom half is the date "MDCCLXXXIII".

When the Collar is not worn the Badge is suspended from a wide sky-blue ribbon worn over the right shoulder in such a way that the Badge rests on the left hip.

The Star was of silver with eight points in the centre of which is the red enamelled Cross of St Patrick charged with a green trefoil bearing an Imperial Crown on each leaf. This is surrounded by a blue enamelled circle bearing the motto and date as on the Badge.

The Order is now moribund.

THE MOST HONOURABLE ORDER OF THE BATH

Motto: Tria juncta in uno (Three joined in one)

This order receives its name from the ancient custom of bathing prior to the installation of knights.

The first mention of an order of knights expressly called Knights of the Bath, is at the coronation of Henry IV in 1399, and there seems little doubt that this is when the Order was instituted.

Froissart, writing of this king, says:

"The Saturday before his coronation he departed from Westminster, and rode to the Tower of London with a great number; and that night all such esquires as should be made knights the next day, watched, who were the number of forty-six. Every squire had his own bayne (bath) by himself; and the next day the Duke of Lancaster made them all knights at the masstime. Then had they long coats with strait sleeves, furred with mynever like prelates, with white laces hanging on their shoulders."

It subsequently became the practice for kings to create Knights of the Bath on the occasion of their coronation, or at some occasion peculiar to the Royal Family.

From the time of the coronation of Charles II the Order was discontinued until revived as a regular military order by George I by a Warrant dated 18th May, 1725, to consist of thirty-six knights.

The Prince Regent, on 2nd January, 1815, in order to commemorate what he called "the auspicious termination of the long and arduous contests in which the empire has been engaged", decreed that henceforth the Order should be considerably enlarged and be composed of three classes, differing in their ranks and degrees of dignity. The first class to consist of knights grand crosses; the second of knights commanders; the third of companions.

On 14th April, 1847, Queen Victoria extended the Order to include civil Knights and civil Companions.

The officers appointed to the Order are, in addition to the Great Master, the Dean, the Bath King-of-Arms, the Genealogist, the Registrar and Gentleman of the Scarlet Rod, the Usher and the Secretary.

The insignia of the Order are not the same for the Civil and Military Divisions so will be given separately.

Military. Knight Grand Cross (G.C.B.). Statute permits 68 *appointments*.

The gold Collar weighing thirty ounces troy weight is composed of nine Imperial Crowns and eight roses, thistles and shamrocks issuing from a gold sceptre, enamelled in their proper colours, tied or linked together by seventeen gold knots, enamelled white, from which the Badge hangs.

The Badge is composed of a rose, thistle and shamrock issuing from a sceptre between three imperial crowns, surrounded by the motto *Tria juncta in uno* in gold letters on a red enamelled ground, this, in turn, is surrounded by a green enamelled laurel wreath, below is a dark blue enamel scroll bearing the words *Ich dien* (I serve) in gold letters.

The Star is in the form of silver rays (in the form of a star) on which is a gold Maltese cross in the centre of which is a similar design to that on the Badge, excepting that only the three Imperial Crowns are depicted, also the gold lions are omitted; this is worn on the left.

Civil. Knight Grand Cross (G.C.B.). Statute permits 27 *appointments*.

The Collar is similar to that of the Military Division.

The oval filigree Badge of gold has the same device in the centre as the military Badge. Around this is a gold band bearing the motto of the Order in gold letters.

The Breast Star of silver with eight points has as its central device three crowns on a silver field surrounded by a red circlet bearing the motto. Similar to the Military Division this is worn on the left side.

Military. Knight Commander (K.C.B.). Statute permits 173 *appointments*.

The Badge is smaller than that of the G.C.B. suspended from a crimson ribbon and worn round the neck.

The Breast Star is similar to that of the G.C.B. as regards the central device (the gold Maltese cross being omitted) which is mounted on a cross patté formed of silver rays. This is worn similarly to the G.C.B.

Civil. Knight Commander (K.C.B.). Statute permits 112 *appointments.*

The Badge is smaller than that of a G.C.B. suspended from a crimson ribbon worn round the neck.

The Breast Star is similar to the military K.C.B. but the central device is the same as in the civil G.C.B. This is also worn on the left.

Military and Civil Companions (C.B.). Statute permits 943 *appointments* (M). Statute permits 555 *appointments* (C).

Companions wear a small-sized Badge suspended from a crimson ribbon worn round the neck.

THE MOST EXALTED ORDER OF THE STAR OF INDIA

Motto: Heaven's light our guide

This Order was instituted by Queen Victoria on 23rd February, 1861, to reward her subjects who performed particularly valuable service in India, or towards her Indian Empire. The original limitations as regards membership were extended in 1866, 1875 and 1876, but as the Order is no longer bestowed it is unnecessary to go into the details as regards the numbers of each of the categories. No appointment for the Order has been made since 1947 when India gained her independence.

The insignia for these Crosses of the Order are:

G.C.S.I. Knights Grand Commander. 36 *appointments.*

The Mantle was of light blue satin lined with white and fastened with a cord of white silk with silver and blue tassels. On the left side is a representation of the Star.

The Collar was composed of six lotus flowers, five red and white roses and ten sprays of palm. In the centre is an Imperial Crown from which the Badge of the Order is suspended.

The Badge consists of an onyx cameo of Queen Victoria's effigy set in a gold and ornamental oval, bearing the motto of the Order in diamonds on a pale blue ground. The whole is surmounted by a gold star inlaid with diamonds.

The Star was composed of golden rays in the form of a ball of fire having in its centre another star of diamonds on a light blue enamelled circular band tied at the bottom and bearing the motto of the Order. This is worn on the left breast.

Knights Commander. 85 *appointments.*

A K.C.S.I. wears a silver Star similar in design to that of the G.C.S.I. on his left breast and the Badge suspended from a 2-in. wide ribbon of light blue edged with white worn round his neck.

Companions. 170 *appointments.*

A C.S.I. wears the Badge suspended round his neck from a 1½-in. wide ribbon of light blue with white edges.

THE MOST DISTINGUISHED ORDER OF ST MICHAEL AND ST GEORGE

Motto: Auspicium melioris ævi (Token of a better age)

This Order was instituted by the Prince Regent on 27th April, 1818, as an award of appreciation for services rendered by the inhabitants of the Ionian Islands which, in 1815, had been formed into an independent state under the protection of Great Britain. In 1879, and again in 1902, the limitations concerning the awarding of the Order were extended to include valuable service in any of the Colonies.

The Order like the Bath is divided into three classes, the insignia for which are:

The Mantle is of Saxon blue satin lined with scarlet silk. The Star of the Order is embroidered on the left side.

The Hat (or Chapeau) of blue satin lined with scarlet silk is surmounted with black and white ostrich feathers.

The Collar of gold* has a complicated design. In the centre, at the bottom are two winged lions facing inwards, passant guardant, each holding a book and seven arrows in his forepaw. Surmounting them is the Imperial Crown. Going round the Collar to the left (facing) are the above-mentioned winged lion, the letters S.M., a Maltese cross, a lion of England, the letters S.G. Going to the right, after the winged lion are the letters S.G., a Maltese cross, a lion of England, the letters S.M. This information appears twice on each side before reaching the back of the Collar where there are two exactly similar lions as those at the bottom of the front. The whole is of gold* except for the Maltese crosses which are enamel white and edged, also emblem is linked to the Collar by small gold chains.

The Badge consists of a gold* cross of seven arms each with V-shaped extremities; the whole thing being faced with white enamel surmounted with an Imperial Crown. In the centre, on the one side is depicted the Archangel St Michael holding a flaming sword in his right hand and encountering Satan; on the other St George on horseback and in armour encountering the Dragon. These illustrations are surrounded by a dark blue circlet on which is the motto of the Order.

The Star is of seven silver rays with a smaller gold one in between each and overall is the red enamelled cross of St George. In the centre the design is the same as that on the badge depicting the Archangel St Michael and Satan, surrounded by a blue enamel ribbon bearing the motto in gold.

When the Collar is not worn a G.C.M.G. wears the badge on the left hip suspended from the broad Saxon-blue ribbon 4-in. in width with a scarlet central stripe worn over the right shoulder, with the Star on the left breast.

*Now of silver gilt.

Knights Commanders. 38 *appointments.* **Companions.** 1435 *appointments.*

A K.C.M.G. wears the badge suspended from a 2-in. wide ribbon worn round the neck as do Companions. In the case of the G.C.M.G. and K.C.M.G. the ribbon is threaded through a ring on the top of the crown surmounting the Badge; the Badge of a Companion was, prior to 1917, fitted with a straight gold* suspender through which the ribbon was passed. It is now suspended from a ring.

THE MOST EMINENT ORDER OF THE INDIAN EMPIRE

Motto: Imperatricis auspiciis (Under the auspices of the Empress)

This Order was instituted by Queen Victoria on 31st December, 1877, as the Order of the Indian Empire of which there was only one class. On 2nd August, 1886, the original Warrant was abrogated and the Order opened as a junior to that of the Star of India, and to have three classes of recipients; at the same time the title was altered to that given at the heading.

The insignia of the Order are as follows:

The G.C.N.G. Collar composed of elephants, lotus flowers, Indian roses and peacocks, the whole linked together by golden chains. In the centre is an Imperial Crown from which the Badge is suspended.

The Badge consists of a gold, fine petalled rose, enamelled crimson and with a green barb between each petal. In the centre an effigy of Queen Victoria on a gold ground with a purple circle edged with gold, on which is the motto of the Order in gold letters, surmounted by an Imperial Crown in gold.†

The Star of the first class has five rays of gold upon five of silver, forming ten points, issuing from a gold centre similar to that of the Badge.

The Mantle is of imperial purple satin lined with white silk. Purple and gold tassels are attached to it by a cord of white silk. On the left side is embroidered a first class Star of the Order.

There are some of the early types of this badge with brooch fittings, but I am not prepared to say whether these had been altered privately or original.

THE ROYAL VICTORIAN ORDER

Motto: Victoria

This Order, of which there are now five classes, and a medal in three grades—silver gilt, silver and bronze, was instituted on 21st April, 1896, by Queen Victoria as a personal reward to those who rendered special services to the Sovereign and Royalty. There are no limitations as to the number of appointments.

There are the following insignia to the Order:

*Now of silver gilt.
†The first type had a letter from the word INDIA on each of the petals.

G.C.V.O. Knights and Dames Grand Cross

The Mantle of dark blue silk, edged with red satin, lined in white silk and fastened by dark blue silk and gold cords, tasselled. On the left side is a representation of the Star of the Order.

The Collar composed of blue octagonal pieces ornately framed with a rose in the centre. In the centre of the Collar is a blue and red octagonal device bearing the Queen's effigy from which the Badge is hung.

The Badge is in the form of a white enamelled Maltese cross, with an oval device in the centre bearing the cypher "V.R.I." on a red enamel ground, and surrounded by a blue enamelled band bearing the single word VICTORIA in gold letters; above this is the Imperial Crown in its proper colours.

The Star is of chipped silver with eight points having a representation of the Badge in the centre; this is worn on the left breast.

The Knights Commanders' badge is slightly smaller than that of a G.C.V.O. and suspended from a similar ribbon but 1¾ ins. wide and worn round the neck. Dames Commanders wear the same badge but this is worn from a ribbon tied in a bow on the left shoulder. They also wear the same Star.

THE MOST EXCELLENT ORDER OF THE BRITISH EMPIRE

Motto: For God and the Empire

There are five classes to the Order whose members are known as: (1) Knights (or Dames) Grand Cross, (II) Knights (or Dames) Commanders, (III) Commanders, (IV) Officers, (V) Members.

This Order was instituted during the First World War (17th June, 1917) as a reward to those who rendered special service to the Empire other than of a military nature. Then, in 1918, it was divided into two divisions—Military and Civil. The Order is open to both sexes in both divisions.

The insignia of the Order are as follows:

A Mantle of pale pink satin lined with grey silk and fastened by a pearl-grey silk cordon with pink and silver tassels. The Star of the Order is embroidered on the left side.

The Badge is in the form of a cross patonce enamelled pearl-grey, surmounted by the Imperial Crown, in the centre of which are the conjoint busts of H.M. George V and Queen Mary, facing left. Around these busts, on a crimson circlet, is the motto of the Order. A bow for the ladies and a smaller Breast Star.

The Star of chipped silver rays, of eight points, with the same device in the centre as the Badge.

The ribbon for a K.B.E. is 1¾ ins. wide from which the Badge is suspended worn round the neck.

The ribbon of the C.B.E. is the same as that for a K.B.E. and the Badge is worn round the neck.

The Badge of the O.B.E. is smaller than that of a C.B.E. and is of silver-gilt. It is worn from a ribbon 1½ ins. wide on the left breast with other decorations and medals.

The Badge of a Member is of silver and worn as the O.B.E.

From the date of its inception till 1937 the central device of the Badge represented Britannia holding a trident and seated beside a shield depicting the Union Jack. George V ordered that it should be changed to that representing the effigies of himself and Queen Mary and was not to be again altered.

Prior to 1937 the colour of the ribbon was purple with a narrow scarlet stripe down the centre for military recipients. It was at Queen Mary's request that the colours were altered. The ribbon now being rose-pink, edged with pearl-grey. Military recipients wear a narrow pearl-grey stripe down the centre of the ribbon.

It was announced on 14th January, 1958, that by command of the Queen, Elizabeth II, future appointments to, or promotions in, the Order of the British Empire and awards of the British Empire Medal, when granted for gallantry would be so stated in the announcement.

They will be distinguished by the wearing of a silver oak-leaf emblem on the ribbon. When the ribbon only is worn the emblem will be in miniature. This ruling will apply to both the military and civil awards.

The emblem referred to is a very simple design consisting of two crossed oak leaves.

The title of this Order is somewhat misleading for Canada has no knighthoods, to give only one example. The term "Empire" is also rather out of date.

BADGES OF BARONET AND KNIGHT BACHELOR

BARONET'S BADGE

Oval gold and enamel badge.

Description: The Arms of Ulster (a red left hand) on a silver shield surmounted by an Imperial Crown in its proper colours within an oval pierced wreath composed of roses, thistles and shamrocks according to whether the baronetcy is of England, Scotland or Ireland. Baronets other than these had a badge with a wreath composed of these three emblems in alternation. Since 1801, the year of the Irish Union, all baronets created are of the United Kingdom.

This rank owes its origin to the poverty of James I who wanted money to improve the conditions in Ulster. He hit upon the idea of creating a new dignity, which was to be granted to all who paid the sum of £1,095 which was estimated to be the amount required to maintain thirty infantrymen for three years. This sum, based on the figure of 8d. per man per day, was paid into the Exchequer. The dignity gave rank, precedence and title without privilege. The new baronet still remained a commoner.

The first patent is dated 22nd May, 1611, and stipulates that the number of baronets should never exceed two hundred; and that there would be no replacements to make up the number—in other words, the title was to work its own way to extinction through the death of the original recipients.

We need not go into the details concerning the precedence granted to the holders but it is worth mentioning that they were allowed to bear, either on a canton or in an escutcheon on their shield of arms, the arms of Ulster, which, being a bloody hand, could hardly have been more symbolical of the state of the province at the time. Another attraction to pay this sum is worth quoting in full as it either shows that James I had an impish sense of humour, or did all in his power to make the new dignity an outstanding success from the time of its receipt to, literally the grave. It reads, "The King, to ampliate his favour, this dignity being His Majesty's own creation, and the work of his hands, does grant that every baronet, when he has attained the age of twenty-one years, might claim from the King the honour of knighthood; that in armies they shall have place near about the Royal Standard; and, lastly, that in their funeral pomp they shall have two assistants of the body, a principal mourner, and four assistants to him, being a mean betwixt a baron and a knight."

To make quite sure that this commodity (surely we cannot call it more) became known, commissioners (we would now call them travellers) were sent out who were to see that they only did business with those who could prove that they had an annual income of £1,000. To avoid any suggestion that the dignity had been obtained through wealth, the recipient had to swear on oath that he had paid no more than the £1,095.

One, or is it only I, can almost hear these commissioners going round calling, "Walk up, walk up, a baronetcy and a slap up funeral all for a thousand quid. What more do you want?"

On 22nd May, 1611, eighteen gentlemen "of the first quality" were admitted, but it was not until 1622 that the full quota was reached. Charles I thought it an excellent scheme and found 458 "gentlemen of the first quality" thus increasing his pocket by over £501,000 and in the rush of business appears to have forgotten all about the conditions in Ulster. Since Charles II this "deposit" has been remitted.

The first baronet created was Sir Nicholas Bacon whose descendant is styled Primus Baronettorum Angliæ. The first Irish baron, created in 1619, was Sir Francis Blundell. Sir Robert Gordon was created, in 1625, the first of the baronets of Nova Scotia, with whom we deal next.

The wearing of the badge, instituted by Charles I from an orange tawny ribbon, went into disuse. In August, 1835, the Baronets of England made a petition that a badge should be designed and allowed to be worn, but it was not granted and nothing was done till 1929 when the badge described was allowed to be worn suspended from the neck on a 1.75-in. wide orange ribbon with dark-blue edges, neither of which are worn in undress uniform.

BARONETS OF NOVIA SCOTIA (1624)

Description: A gold oval shield enamelled white on which is the Cross of St Andrew. In the centre is a small gold shield charged with the Scottish Lion, rampant displayed, in red enamel. This shield is surmounted by the Imperial Crown in gold. The whole is surrounded by a blue enamel border bearing the words, in gold lettering, FAX MENTIS HONESTAE GLORIA. The badge, which is double-sided, with the same design on both sides, is approximately 2 ins. by 1·5 ins., has a ring for suspension from a 1·75-in. wide yellow ribbon with dark-blue edges.

In the same way as James I had established the order of English baronets to raise money to help Ulster, so he decided to do the same for encouraging the prosperity of Nova Scotia. He died before anything had been done about it but his successor adopted the scheme and, in 1625, commenced to grant land in Nova Scotia with which went the rank, style and title of baronet of that province. Among additional privileges granted them was the right to wear "a ribbon and medal, with badge and insignia of the order". A baronet added the arms of Nova Scotia to his coat-armour.

The original number was to be 150 but this was exceeded, till 1707 when the creation ceased.

BARONETS OF IRELAND (1620)

These were instituted by James I in the same way as those already dealt with. The money was paid into the Irish exchequer.

I have been unable to trace any details of their badge, or even if they had one, so that further reference to them will be out of place.

BADGE OF A KNIGHT BACHELOR (1926–   ).

Description: An oval badge of vermilion enamel with an upright sword in the centre between two spurs surrounded by a sword belt, all in gilt. It measures approximately 3 ins. by 2ins.

Knight Bachelor is the most ancient Order of Knights in the Kingdom. Henry III added the word Bachelor to signify that the title dies with the person. The title ranks below that of baronet, though both carry the prefix "Sir".

The Order, though the oldest, is not a Royal Order. The Register, originated by James I, was not maintained. In, or about 1908, Edward VII ordered that a voluntary association be formed under the title of "The Society of Knights" (now "The Imperial Society of Knight Bachelor" by Royal Command). Its object was to collate the information contained in all the old registers and, to henceforth maintain a register of all knights subsequently created.

Royal approval was granted in 1926 for a badge to be worn by Knights Bachelor, a description of which is given above, and is worn similarly to that of a Star of an Order.

ORDERS

THE ORDER OF MERIT

Limited in number to 24—an unlimited number of foreign honorary members may be appointed.

This Order was instituted by Edward VII on 23rd June, 1902, to be a personal award from the sovereign to those who won distinction in either of the military services, in literature, in science, or in art. The first recipient was Lord Roberts and the second Viscount Wolseley. Only one lady ever received this award. This was Miss Florence Nightingale in November, 1907.

The Badge is of circular design consisting of a gold cross patté surmounted by a Tudor crown on top of which is a ring for suspension. The centre of each limb is red and the edges are of blue enamel. In the centre within a laurel is a blue enamel circle bearing the words *For Merit* in gold letters. The centre of the reverse, also within a laurel wreath is the Royal Cypher in gold.

Orders awarded for military service carry two crossed swords of silver, with gold hilts plated diagonally between the angles of the cross.

The Badge is worn round the neck suspended from a 2-in. wide ribbon, half blue (to the left, facing wearer) and half crimson.

The order is unusual in that there is no miniature, as ruled by Edward VII in 1903, but the blue and crimson ribbon may be won on undress uniform.

THE ORDER OF THE COMPANION OF HONOUR

This Order like the Order of Merit carries no title or rank and was instituted by King George V on 4th June, 1917. It serves very much the same purpose as the Order of Merit in that it is awarded to those who perform some special service of national importance. The membership is open to both men and women though limited to a total of 50 altogether.

The badge is oval surmounted by an Imperial Crown enamelled in its proper colours. The centre piece is a rectangular medallion depicting a knight in armour mounted on a horse standing by an oak tree on which is a shield of the Royal Arms. The central medallion is surrounded by a blue enamel border on which is the motto, In Action Faithful and in Honour Clear.

The ribbon is carmine with an in-and-out gold threaded border; 1½-ins. wide.

The Badge is worn suspended from the neck by men and from a ribbon in the form of a bow on the left shoulder by women.

Again like the Order of Merit this Order is not worn in miniature, but the ribbon may be worn on undress uniform.

THE DISTINGUISHED SERVICE ORDER

This Order was instituted on 6th September, 1886, for rewarding meritorious or distinguished service in war. The recipient must hold a commission in the Army, Navy, R.A.F. or R.M. It is not open to civilians as such but, in time of war officers of the Merchant Navy are eligible.

The Badge consists of a gold cross patté, 1·56-in. diameter, enamelled white, edged with gold having in the centre of the obverse, within a wreath of laurel enamelled green, a gold Imperial Crown, upon a red enamelled field. On the reverse, within a similar wreath and on a similar red field is the Royal Cypher surmounted by a small crown.

The cross is suspended from a gold bar ornamented with laurel. The ribbon is 1·125 ins. wide; crimson with blue borders, it hangs from a similar gold bar.

The original crosses were of gold and enamel but that has now given place to silver gilt.

Subsequent acts for which the Order is awarded are denoted by a gold bar worn on the ribbon; in undress uniform a silver rosette is worn on the ribbon for each award of the Order after the original.

THE IMPERIAL SERVICE ORDER ✓
THE IMPERIAL SERVICE MEDAL

This Order was instituted on 8th August, 1902, by King Edward VII to reward long and praiseworthy service of members of the Civil Service at home and abroad. The normal minimum length of service to qualify is twenty-five years at home and periods of sixteen or more in countries with severe climates though these periods were not taken into account when the Order was to be awarded for a particular piece of meritorious service. It may also be awarded for meritorious acts irrespective of qualifying service.

The Order has only one class and carries no knighthood and has no motto. Recipients of the Order are known as Companions. The Badge consists of a gold circular plaque with the Royal Cypher in the centre surrounded by the inscription FOR FAITHFUL SERVICE, both in dark blue enamelled letters.

The plaque is really the basis of the badge which, in the case of male recipients, is surrounded by—or mounted on—a seven-pointed silver star surmounted by a crown. The badge for women is enclosed in a silver laurel wreath instead of a star.

There is also an Imperial Service Medal which may be awarded under the same conditions as the Order and when first issued during Edward VII's reign and the early part of George V's reign it was very similar to the badge just described, except that the centre plaques were of silver and the surrounding stars or wreaths were of bronze. The present form is that of a silver medal with the crowned head of the sovereign on the obverse and the inscription FOR FAITHFUL SERVICE on the reverse.

The recipient's name is engraved on the edge.

The Badge and Medal each have a ring suspension and are worn by men on the left breast as a medal; women wear them suspended from a bow on the left shoulder.

The ribbon is 1½ ins. wide, in watered red-blue-red of equal width stripes.

THE ORDER OF BRITISH INDIA

This Order was instituted on 17th April, 1837, to be awarded to senior Indian officers (subadars and jemadars) for long and honourable service. Two classes were approved, each with its own insignia. A member of the second class could be appointed to the first, in which case he handed in his badge and received that of the higher class. The two could not be worn simultaneously.

The Badge of the first class (title "Sardar Bahadur") is an eight-pointed gold star. In the centre a gold lion statant guardant on a half-inch light blue enamel field surrounded by a dark blue enamel band containing the words ORDER OF BRITISH INDIA in gold. This is surrounded by a laurel wreath also in gold. A crown between the two top points is fitted with a ring which in turn is connected to another 0·35 in. wide and 0·8 in. high of ribbed gold through which the ribbon is threaded and from which the decoration is worn round the neck.

The Badge of the second class (title "Bahadur"), being slightly smaller, is also an eight-pointed gold star with the limbs of different shape. The ring for suspension is fitted direct on the top of the uppermost limb as there is no crown. The field in the centre is of dark, instead of light, blue.

The ribbons are 2 ins. and 1½ ins. wide respectively. They were both originally of light blue, but were altered to crimson in 1838.

This is the only decoration that I recall having a different ribbon for wear in undress uniform. In this case members of the first class differentiate from those of the second by wearing a ribbon with two thin pale blue stripes down the centre; the ribbon of the second class has one stripe.

INDIAN ORDER OF MERIT (1813)

This, in my opinion, is one of the most interesting decorations which have been awarded.

It has one outstanding incongruity—if I may use that term—in that its title infers that it is for merit whereas, in reality, it was for valour. I could understand the title better if it had been named like the Prussian Order of Military Merit as in that title the word "merit" is qualified but that word without qualification means, to me at any rate, something quite different from heroism.

A clause in the General Order concerning its conception states that the widow of the recipient would be able to draw the pension for three years and adds that in the case of plurality of wives—a nice expression—the first would have preference.

The Order is divided into three classes which are of the step-ladder variety in that a recipient cannot gain a higher class unless he has previously held the lower. In fact, therefore, the ownership of a second class corresponds to a bar; that of the first class to two bars. On promotion, the lower Order has to be surrendered prior to the issue of the higher.

All the classes had a direct bearing on the pay of the recipient in that he received a third of his pay extra for the third class; two-thirds for the second class; and double pay for the first class. The same remarks applied to pension.

The details concerning the Badges of the three classes are as follows:

FIRST CLASS

Obverse: A gold eight-pointed star, 1½ ins. diameter. In the centre a 0·5 in. diameter blue circle on which are two gold swords in saltire, around them in gold lettering REWARD OF MERIT. Around this central circle is a raised wreath of laurel.

Reverse: "1st Class Order of Merit."

Suspension: By a delicate curved V-shape suspender attached to a ring at the top of the star.

Ribbon: 1·5 ins. wide. Dark blue with red edges.

SECOND CLASS

Obverse: The central device is identical with the above but the star itself is of silver.

The measurement is the same.

Reverse: "2nd Class Order of Merit."

Suspension: As for the First Class but in silver.

Ribbon: As for the First Class.

THIRD CLASS

Obverse: Similar to the foregoing except that silver replaces gold for the swords, wording and wreath.

Reverse: "3rd Class Order of Merit."

Suspension: As for the Second Class.

Ribbon: As for the First Class.

All the classes were awarded unnamed though they are found with the recipient's name engraved on the reverse.

All three classes are worn on the left breast.

THE ORDER OF BURMA

This Order was established in 1938 for award by the Governor to a limited number of his commissioned officers of the military forces and police.

There is only one class to the Order which carries no precedence.

The Badge is in the form of a gold star with, in the centre, a blue circle on which is a peacock; around this are the words, in golden letters, ORDER OF BURMA.

The ribbon, worn round the neck, from which the Badge is suspended is

1½ ins. wide of dark green with light blue edges.

This Order is obsolete.

THE GRAND PRIORY IN THE BRITISH REALM OF THE MOST VENERABLE ORDER OF ST JOHN OF JERUSALEM, abbreviated to ORDER OF ST JOHN

This ancient Order originated with the Hospitallers of St John of Jerusalem, a body of military monks which in turn owed its origin to an even earlier body of non-military monks who founded a hospital in Jerusalem.

Its military character started sometime in the twelfth century when, after the capturing of Jerusalem by the Moslems, they endeavoured to defend Acre. After being driven out they went to Cyprus and in the fourteenth century migrated to Rhodes. In 1522 this island was captured by the Turks. The Knights Hospitallers, after many wanderings, were given the island of Malta by Charles V, in 1530, which they governed until its capture by Napoleon on 12th June, 1798.

La Valetta, the capital, or Valetta as it is now called, was founded by J. P. Valette in 1566 and still contains many relics of the occupation by the Knights of Malta.

The Order was given its Charter by Queen Victoria in May, 1888, and granted the title of Venerable in 1926.

It is, as regards Great Britain, divided into five classes whose members are styled Bailiffs, or Dames Grand Cross; Knights or Dames; Commanders; Officers; and Serving Brothers and Sisters.

The sovereign is the Sovereign of the Order, next in order are the Grand Prior, Sub-Prior, Titular Bailiff of Egle, Honorary Bailiffs and then the grades of members as stated.

Selection for admission to the Order is made by the Chapter General, and then the name of the candidate, if approved by the Grand Prior is submitted by him to the sovereign.

The insignia of the Order are as follows:

The Grand Prior has a mantle of black velvet with the Badge of the Order in white silk embellished in gold.

The Bailiffs and Dames Grand Cross wear a silk mantle.

The Badge consists of a Maltese cross of white enamel embellished between the arms alternately with a unicorn and lion either in gold or silver according to classes.

Members of the first class wear the Badge on the left hip from a sash over the right shoulder and a white enamelled star set in gold without embellishments on the left breast.

Members of the second class wear the Badge round the neck. Commanders wear the Badge round the neck (women from a bow on the left breast). Officers wear the Badge on the left breast. Serving Brothers and Sisters wear a circular medal which bears the cross of the Order in white enamel on a black enamel background.

Knights and Dames of Justice wear a plain white enamel star set in gold. Knights and Dames of Grace wear an enamel star set in silver.

ORDERS AWARDED TO
LADIES ONLY

THE ROYAL ORDER OF VICTORIA AND ALBERT

This Order was instituted on 10th February, 1862, just six months before the death of the Prince Consort. It was a personal award from the Queen and her husband to some forty-five ladies who received one of the four classes of the Order according to rank.

The only insignia consists of a heavily jewelled Badge which varies with the classes as follows:

First Class—awarded to senior Royal Ladies, an oval Badge approximately 2 ins. by 1½ ins., with the busts of Queen Victoria and Prince Albert in the centre. The oval is most beautifully set in diamonds and surmounted by an Imperial Crown, also richly jewelled. At the top of the crown is a narrow flat ring set at right-angles through which the 1½-in. wide ribbon of white watered silk made up in a bow is threaded. The Badge is worn on the left shoulder.

Second Class—also awarded to Royal Ladies, an oval Badge similar to the last but less ornate and set in pearls instead of diamonds.

Third Class—awarded to titled ladies, a large and wider Badge than the last with a circlet at the edge quartered with four diamonds with five pearls in each quarter.

Fourth Class—awarded to ladies, consists of the monogram "V" and "A" surmounted by an Imperial Crown. The letters are most beautifully set in graduated pearls. On the top of the crown is a plain gold ring for taking the ribbon in the same manner as just detailed.

THE IMPERIAL ORDER OF THE CROWN OF INDIA

This Order was instituted by Queen Victoria on 1st January, 1878, to commemorate her assumption of the title of Empress of India.

It had only one class composed of the Royal Princesses, wives of Indian princes, the Vicerene, and other ladies whose husbands held high office in India.

The sole insignia consists of an oval Badge of approximately 1¼ ins. by 1¾ ins. surmounted by an Imperial Crown. In the centre is the Imperial Cypher, V.R.I., with the "V" and "R" studded with diamonds, the "I" studded with turquoises. Around this is an oval band quartered with four large pearls with ten smaller ones in each quarter.

It is worn on the left shoulder suspended from a bow of light-blue watered silk ribbon, edged white, 1½ ins. wide.

The last appointments to the Order were the Queen, Elizabeth II, and Princess Margaret in June, 1947.

The Order is now obsolete.

THE ROYAL RED CROSS

This Order was instituted by Queen Victoria on 23rd April, 1883, as a reward to women of whatever nationality who nurse the sick and wounded of the armed forces.

In addition to the above ladies, who earned it by their service, it may also be worn by the Queen Regnant, Queen Dowager and Queen Consort. As originally instituted there was only one class but in 1917 a second was added. A holder of the first class is known as a member and is entitled to the letters R.R.C. after her name; a recipient of the second class is an associate and uses the letters A.R.R.C. A bar may be awarded to both classes of the Order for subsequent service.

The decoration consists, for the first class, of a gold cross patté*, of 1·37 ins. across; the centre of each arm is of crimson enamel. Reading clockwise from the top the limbs are embossed FAITH, CHARITY, 1883, and HOPE respectively. In the centre is a gold circle on which is the Royal and Imperial Effigy facing left. The reverse bears the Royal and Imperial Cypher and Crown.

The second class decoration is of the same size as that of the first class in silver, with the effigy of the sovereign in the centre of the obverse while the reverse is like the obverse of the first class except that the Royal Cypher and Crown replace the effigy of the sovereign. Elizabeth II issue bear the year of issue below date of institution.

The ribbon is 1-in. wide; blue with crimson borders.

*The first class decorations were of gold, but are now of silver gilt. The second class are of silver and enamel. In the case of both classes, awards made during the reign of Elizabeth II bear on the obverse the date of award under that of its institution, i.e. 1883.

DECORATIONS

VICTORIA CROSS (1856–   )

Description: A bronze cross patté and not a Maltese cross as erroneously described in the Warrant of institution and by most people ever since.

Obverse: A lion statant guardant standing on the Royal Crown; and below, on a scroll, the words FOR VALOUR. The cross has a raised edge, $\frac{3}{16}$ in. wide, with a beading of the same width and at that distance running round inside.

Reverse: A raised circle in the centre and the same beaded edges and lining as the obverse.

Size: 1·375 ins. across.

Ribbon: 1·5 ins wide. The colour was originally dark blue for the Navy, and crimson for the Army. In 1918 the colour for the Army was adopted for all awards irrespective of the service of the recipient.

Suspension: A loop at the top of the cross is joined by a ring to a Roman V which is part of a straight flat suspender ornamented with laurel leaves. The ribbon is threaded through a slot at the top of the suspender.

Designer: It is said to have been designed by the Prince Consort.

Naming: The recipient's name, rank and unit are engraved at the back of the suspender; the date of the act which gained the award is engraved in the circle at the centre of the reverse.

This cross, the most prized award that any British subject can earn, was instituted by a Royal Warrant dated 29th January, 1856.

The object of the award was so that the sovereign could give a mark of distinction to junior officers and other ranks in the Services who, prior to its inception, went unrewarded for acts of valour. The third class of the Most Honourable Order of the Bath (Companionship, or C.B. as it is generally called) was only given to senior officers. Though the Meritorious Service Medal had been in existence since 1845 its purpose was to award good, in addition to long, service and had nothing to do with bravery. It was not available to junior officers who might serve long, well, and bravely yet receive nothing to show for it.

It was Queen Victoria's special wish that the crosses should be made from cannon captured during the Crimean War, and for this purpose a gun captured at Sebastopol was brought home. Messrs. Hancock who still make all Victoria Crosses state that bronze from Crimean cannon is still used.

On 28th July, 1959, the Prime Minister announced in Parliament that an annuity of £100, tax free, would be granted to all holders of the Victoria Cross, irrespective of rank and private means, for whom the Government was responsible. This would replace the previous scheme whereby holders below warrant rank in the Navy and commissioned rank in the Army and Royal Air Force received an annuity of £10 a year and a further payment of £75 per annum to those handicapped from earning a living through various causes.

I doubt whether the reader would be interested in reading every word of every Royal Warrant that has been issued concerning this award so I will take them in their order, give their dates, pick out the important points of each and give them together with a few amplifying remarks.

1856

1. It was ordained that the distinction should be designated the "Victoria Cross" and would consist of a Maltese cross of bronze.
2. A registry of all recipients to be kept by the Secretary of State for War.
3. The award to be for some single act of valour or devotion to their country in the presence of the enemy and that a bar would be attached to the ribbon for every subsequent act of bravery that would have earned the Cross had the doer not already been in possession of it. The ribbon was to be blue for the Navy and red for the Army.
4. For a joint act of outstanding gallantry performed by not less than fifty men of any service the Cross could be awarded to one officer, one petty officer or non-commissioned officer, and two seamen or private soldiers or marines, by ballot. This was later amended increasing the number of crosses which could be granted.
5. If the recipient be subsequently convicted of treason, cowardice, felony, or any other infamous crime, the Cross and the financial emoluments that go with it, can be forfeited. It is, however, expressly stated that such forfeiture lies solely at the discretion of the sovereign who, in like manner, may restore them.

Interesting items are contained in paragraphs 1 and 3.

It is strange that nobody bothered to look up to see that the shape intended was really Maltese. I can recall many instances when the title of the bar has not agreed with the Order that authorized it, but I know of no other case in which the shape of the proposed award as stated in the Order signifying its institution has not been adhered to.

The different coloured ribbons for the two services is interesting though difficult for the reason to be understood. The ribbons to the Orders worn by the two services were the same so why not those for a decoration obtainable by both? The dark blue ribbon to the Navy must have been somewhat inconspicuous against the blue uniform; that to the Army was almost identical in colour to the Long Service ribbon, which had not then got the white edges as it has now. One must remember, when discussing the possible confusion of ribbon colours, that the tiny replica now worn on the ribbon was not introduced till 1920.

1858 (10th August)

In this year the award was extended to those who, "May perform acts of conspicuous courage and bravery under circumstances of extreme danger,

fire on board ship, shipwreck, and any other occasion on which exceptional
bravery saved life and public property". This clause was probably inspired
by the gallantry of the 54th regiment during the burning of the *Sarah Sands*
though their courage on this occasion was not rewarded by the grant of any
Victoria Cross.

This extended the award to occasions when brave deeds were done at
times other than in the presence of an enemy.

1858 (13th December)

A special Order was issued to the effect that civilians who volunteered to
fight the mutineers in Lucknow and elsewhere would be considered eligible.
In this connection one recalls the act of Mr Kavanagh who, disguised as a
native, left Outram's besieged garrison to guide in the relieving force under
Sir Colin Campbell.

1867

In this year it was found that members of the local forces in New Zealand
were not eligible for the Cross so a special Warrant was issued to include
them and make the award open to all forces throughout the Empire.

1881

Apparently some confusion had arisen as to the translation of the original
Warrant so, in this year, a special one was issued to say that the Cross would
only be awarded for bravery when in face of the enemy. In this year, too,
another was published making members of the Indian Ecclesiastical Establishments eligible and it was as a result of this Warrant that the Cross was
conferred on the Rev. J. W. Adams for his outstanding bravery in rescuing
wounded during the Afghanistan Campaign, 1878–80.

1902

In this year it was decreed that the Cross would be given to the next of
kin of those who died before receiving their Cross. Prior to this, though the
recipient's name was entered in the registry, no award was made to relatives
so that the gaining of the distinction became no more than a paper entry.

1911

In this year the Cross was made available to all ranks of the Indian Army
on precisely the same basis as for Europeans.

1918

In this year the blue ribbon for the Navy was abolished and the present
colour was adopted for all the Services.

1920

In this year all the previous Rules and Ordinances affecting the award
were rewritten, varied and extended.

While all that has already been mentioned was included, the following
items concerning eligibility, etc., appear:

1. Members of the Merchant Marine (now styled the Merchant Navy) become eligible while serving under Naval or Military Authority.
2. Matrons, sisters, nurses and the staff of the Nursing Services pertaining to hospitals and nursing, and civilians of both sexes, while serving regularly or temporarily under the orders or direction of either of the three services.
3. When only the ribbon is worn a replica of the Cross in miniature shall be affixed to the centre of the ribbon. In the case of a subsequent award a further such miniature shall be added. In the case of all other decorations a silver rose is worn on the ribbon for every subsequent award to the first so that in the case of the Victoria Cross two emblems, on the ribbon denote one bar.
4. The date and place of the act is inscribed on the bar awarded for the second occasion on which the Cross is won.

The following facts concerning the Victoria Cross may be of interest.

1. The Cross may be awarded, and has been, for a series of acts and it is for this reason that more than one date, or an inclusive period, is, in such cases, mentioned on the centre of the reverse.
2. There have been six awards of the Cross for bravery when not in the presence of the enemy.
3. The Cross was awarded to Surgeon W. D. Maillard, R.N., for endeavouring to save the life of Seaman Arthur Stroud who had been wounded by the insurgents on the island of Crete during the insurrection of Mohammedan refugees in Candia. The award is interesting in that it was gained during operations to quell a riot and not against a declared enemy, or during operations of a protracted nature.
4. The first act for which the Cross was awarded was that performed by Lieutenant Charles Davis Lucas, R.N., who threw a live shell overboard while his ship, H.M.S. *Hecla*, was bombarding the forts at Bomarsund, in the Baltic, on 20th June, 1854. He was at the time only eighteen years old and was promoted to the rank of Lieutenant on the next day. He did not receive his Cross till the investiture on 26th June, 1857. The ruling for a long time has been that the award shall be made as soon as possible after the Gazette; I believe that Lucas's case represents the longest interval, though one must remember that at the time of his act the Cross had not been instituted. This brings out the point that if some such award had not been available his gallantry would have gone unrewarded.
5. Three Crosses were awarded to members of the crew of H.M.S. *Euryalus* for their bravery at the capture of a Japanese fort in the Straits of Simono Saki on 5th September, 1864.

The events that led up to our operations in that country are interesting and very little known.

Until 1854 Japan had forbidden any foreigner to land but in this year the Americans had obtained a trade agreement and another was concluded between Japan and Great Britain in 1862. The Japanese, however, declined to play with the result that a fleet under Admiral Kuper was sent to oil the wheels of trade—Victorian fashion. Having flattened everything in sight from the seaward, parties were landed to demolish anything that had been overlooked.

Trade was resumed at the beginning of the next year.

GEORGE CROSS (1940–   )

Description: A silver St George's cross.
Obverse: A representation of St George and the Dragon surrounded by the words FOR GALLANTRY. The Royal Cypher is in the angle of each limb.
Reverse: Plain.
Size: 1·375 ins. across.
Ribbon: 1·5 ins. wide, dark blue. Although described in the Warrant as "dark blue" the ribbon is in fact "Garter Blue".
Suspension: A ring connects the Cross with a straight flat suspender ornamented with laurel leaves.
Naming: The recipient's name and the date of the act are inscribed on the reverse.

The original Warrant instituting the Cross was dated 24th September, 1940, but this was cancelled by another dated 24th June, 1941, to which amendments were promulgated on 3rd November, 1942.

It is intended primarily for civilians but members of all the Services are equally eligible in cases when a military award is not normally given.

A bar is awarded for a subsequent act of heroism that gains the Cross, and a small replica is worn on the ribbon in a similar manner as with the Victoria Cross.

On the introduction of this Cross the Empire Gallantry Medal of 1917 was made obsolete and those in possession of the medal were asked to return it and receive a George Cross in exchange.

The award is open to any member of the British Commonwealth of Nations irrespective of sex, colour or creed. It ranks immediately after the Victoria Cross and immediately before all Orders of Knighthood.

While the actions which earn the Victoria Cross are, of necessity, somewhat similar in each of the Services those that have gained this Cross are incredibly varied and make fine reading and show the heights to which human bravery can ascend and the depths of depravity and beastial torture to which certain races boasting of the prefix "human" can descend.

Holders of the George Cross now receive an annuity of £100 per year.

CONSPICUOUS SERVICE CROSS (1901–14)

See Distinguished Service Cross which follows immediately.

DISTINGUISHED SERVICE CROSS (1914–   )

Description: A silver convexed cross patté.
Obverse: The crowned Cypher within a plain circle.
Reverse: Plain.

B

Size: 1·65 ins. across.
Ribbon: 1·375 ins. wide, white between blue in three equal stripes.
Suspension: By a ring.
Naming: The crosses are awarded unnamed.

The Conspicuous Service Cross was conferred for meritorious or distinguished service before the enemy performed by Warrant Officers, Acting Warrant Officers, or subordinate Naval Officers providing that his name had been mentioned in despatches.

In October, 1914, the title, Conspicuous Service Cross was changed to Distinguished Service Cross and eligibility opened to Naval Officers of the rank of Lieutenant-Commanders, and to Majors of the Royal Marines.

In December, 1939, the rank of Commander was also included. Since 1931 officers of the Merchant Navy have also been eligible as are members of the Women's Royal Naval Service and those of the Royal Air Force when serving with the Fleet Air Arm. In fact awards were made to officers of the Merchant Navy during the War of 1914–18.

Bars are awarded for further acts gaining the award.

MILITARY CROSS (1914–   )

Description: An ornamental silver cross.
Obverse: In the centre is the Royal Cypher superimposed on a raised cross. There is a Royal Crown on each arm.
Reverse: Plain.
Size: 1·72 ins. across.
Ribbon: 1·35 ins. wide, violet between white in three equal stripes.
Suspension: By a ring connected to a plain flat suspender.
Naming: The crosses are awarded unnamed. George VI and later issues have the year engraved at the bottom of the reverse.

This decoration was instituted by a Royal Warrant dated 31st December, 1914, in which it states that it would be awarded to officers of, and below, the rank of Captain, and to Warrant Officers. This was altered by another of 5th February to include the rank of Major.

Bars are awarded for subsequent awards—the maximum number of which I have heard is three. This indicates that the recipient had earned the Cross four times, which makes one wonder whether there should not be a limit to the number of bars awarded to a decoration. It is reasonable to suppose that anyone who has shown such consistent bravery as to win the Military Cross four times is more worthy than another officer who has been considered somewhat lucky to have got the Distinguished Service Order once.

The award of a bar is indicated by a silver rosette worn on the ribbon when the Cross is not worn. When the Cross is worn a bar bearing an Imperial Crown in the centre is attached to the ribbon.

It is, I imagine, the only article in the whole Commonwealth of Nations which shows the Imperial Crown upside down as is done on the bottom arm of the Cross. It seems rather unnecessary to show four crowns in any case.

DISTINGUISHED FLYING CROSS (1919–)

Description: A silver cross flory terminated in the horizontal and base bars with flaming bombs, the upper bar terminating with a rose, etc.

Obverse: In the centre is a Tudor rose on which are the initials R.A.F. surmounted by an Imperial Crown within a laurel Wreath tied at the bottom with a tasselled cord.

Reverse: The Royal Cypher above the date 1918.

Size: 2·188 ins. across.

Ribbon: 1·25 ins. wide, violet and white in alternate diagonal* stripes running downwards left to right.

Suspension: A straight suspender supported by two sprays of palm leaves.

Naming: Unnamed.

This decoration was instituted on King George V's birthday, 3rd June, 1918, though not gazetted till 1919.

It is awarded to Officers and Warrant Officers for acts of valour performed while flying in active operations against the enemy.

The bombs incorporated in the design seem unnecessary as the award is not confined to Bomber Command.

Eligibility for the award was extended to the Fleet Air Arm on 9th April, 1941.

The award of a bar is indicated by a rosette worn in the centre of the ribbon when the Cross is not worn, and by a straight bar with an eagle in the centre attached to the ribbon when it is.

AIR FORCE CROSS (1919–)

Description: A silver cross which almost defies description in detail but is said to be a "thunderbolt in the form of a cross, the arms conjoined by wings, etc."

Obverse: The uppermost point terminates in an Imperial Crown, the others in points. Reading clockwise, each arm has one of the following letters G, I, V and R. The "V" is, for some inexplicable reason, upside down. In the centre is a representation of Hermes, holding a wreath in his outstretched right hand, while riding a hawk.

Reverse: The Royal Cypher above the date 1918.

Size: 1·65 ins. across.

Ribbon: 1·25 ins. wide, red and white in alternate diagonal stripes.

Suspension: By a straight suspender supported by two sprays of palm leaves.

Naming: The crosses are awarded unnamed.

This Cross is awarded to officers and warrant officers for acts of courage, etc., when not in the presence of the enemy. It is also, in spite of its name, open to civilians and members of the other Services who perform a service, or services, furthering the cause of aviation.

Deeds performed prior to the institution of the Cross were included as it

*The original R.A.F. ribbons had horizontal stripes which were altered in June, 1919, to the present diagonal.

was given to Mr Hawker and Commander Grieve, R.N. who made a gallant attempt to cross the Atlantic from West to East in May, 1919, but fell into the sea. The suspense concerning their whereabouts when they became overdue on the 19th was terrific. In the end the world was relieved to learn that they had been rescued by a ship that was not fitted with wireless. I believe that they were the first two to receive the Cross from His Majesty.

Bars are awarded and the appropriate emblems worn in the same way as those for the Distinguished Flying Cross.

KAISAR-I-HIND MEDAL (1900–47)

Description: An oval badge.
Obverse: The Imperial Cypher with an ornamental border surmounted by the Imperial Crown.
Reverse: The words KAISAR-I-HIND on a scroll upon a floral background; around this is a band bearing FOR PUBLIC SERVICE IN INDIA.
Size: 1·75 by 1·375 ins.
Ribbon: 1·5 ins. wide, slate blue.
Suspension: A ring connects the top of the Crown to a plain wire suspender.
Naming: This applies to the first issues. Subsequent ones had G.VI. R.I., G.VI. R. or E.II. R. according to the reign of issue.

This medal, though in view of its shape, decoration would seem to be the better word, was instituted by a Royal Warrant dated 10th April, 1900, which was amended by another dated 8th July, 1902, to be awarded to those who "performed important and useful service in the advancement of the public interest in India".

There were three classes. The first class medal is of gold and was awarded by the sovereign on the recommendation of the Secretary of State for India. The second class medal is of silver and was awarded by the Governor-General. The third class medal is of bronze and was also awarded by the Governor-General.

All classes were open to either sex, any nationality and those of all colours and creeds, and clasps may be awarded.

ALBERT MEDALS (1866–   )

Description: There are four distinct Albert Medals, all oval badges known as:
   1. Albert Medal in Gold for Gallantry in saving life at sea.
   2. Albert Medal in Gold for Gallantry in saving life on land.
   3. Albert Medal for Gallantry in saving life at sea.
   4. Albert Medal for Gallantry for saving life on land.
The original titles, changed to the above in 1917 were respectively:
   1. Albert Medal (Sea) First Class.
   2. Albert Medal (Land) First Class.
   3. Albert Medal (Sea) Second Class.
   4. Albert Medal (Land) Second Class.

For saving life at sea, first class.

Obverse: A gold oval badge enamelled in dark blue, with the letters "V" and "A" in the form of a monogram, interlaced with an anchor erect, in gold, surrounded by a bronze garter bearing in raised gold lettering, FOR GALLANTRY IN SAVING LIFE AT SEA. The whole surmounted by a representation of the crown of H.R.H. the late Prince Consort, and edged with gold.

Reverse: The recipient's name and details of the act of gallantry.

Size: 1·5 by 1·25 ins.

Ribbon: The original was ⅝ in. wide, dark blue with two white stripes; in 1867 the width was increased to 1⅜ in. and in 1904 two extra white stripes added. It is now, therefore, dark blue, with four white stripes.

Suspension: By means of a ring fitted to the top of the crown.

For saving life at sea, second class.

Description: The badge is the same as that of the first class, except that it is entirely of bronze. The ribbon, originally ⅝ in. wide, is now 1⅜ ins. wide with two white stripes.

For saving life on land, first class.

Obverse: A gold oval badge enamelled in crimson, with the letters "V" and "A" in the form of a monogram, in gold, surrounded by a bronze garter bearing in raised gold lettering, FOR GALLANTRY IN SAVING LIFE ON LAND. The whole surmounted by a representation of the crown of H.R.H. the late Prince Consort, and edged with gold.

Reverse: The recipient's name and details of the act of gallantry.

Size: 1·5 by 1·25 ins.

Ribbon: Exactly the same as the previous except that the word "crimson" must be substituted for blue.

Suspension: By means of a ring fitted to the top of the crown.

For saving life on land, second class.

Description: The badge is exactly the same as that of the first class, except that it is entirely of bronze. The ribbon is the same.

The most extraordinary thing about this medal is, in my opinion, the low position it holds in the order of seniority of awards for bravery. We have already noted that the George Cross was instituted to be to those who perform heroic deeds out of action what the Victoria Cross is to those who perform their brave deeds in the presence of the enemy. The preamble to the Royal Warrant of 7th March, 1866, would infer that it was to be—to use a modern twist to an old expression—"the mariner's V.C."

There have been several Royal Warrants published on the subject of this decoration but I think it will suffice if I give the dates and salient details of those which materially affected the medal.

The original Warrant of 7th March, 1866, which instituted the decoration, refers to it as having only one class and that it was only for heroism at sea.

The second, dated 12th April, 1867, cancelled the first and made two classes. The first was for extreme and heroic daring in life saving from shipwreck and other perils of the sea; the second, for deeds of a similar kind but of lesser merit.

A Warrant dated 30th April, 1877, introduced the two medals whose details have been given for saving life on land. It also decreed that subsequent awards would be indicated by a bar.

The award is open to members of the Services in the same way as is the George Cross. The recommendation for the Albert Medal is made by the President of the Board of Trade to the Sovereign's Principal Secretary of State for the Home Department. Recommendations in cases of members of the Royal Navy and Royal Marines are made by the Lords Commissioners of the Admiralty to the Principal Secretary of State for the Home Department.

The final decision as to its award rests with the sovereign, as does that of its forfeiture in the event of the recipient disgracing himself.

DISTINGUISHED CONDUCT MEDAL (1862–   )
1862

Obverse: Military trophy, with shield of the Arms of Queen Victoria in the centre.

Reverse: Inscription in four lines, FOR DISTINGUISHED CONDUCT IN THE FIELD.

Size: 1·42 ins. dimater.

Ribbon: 1·25 ins. wide, crimson, with a ⅜ in. wide blue stripe down the centre.

Suspension: By an ornate scroll bar suspender.

Designer: Designed and engraved by B. Pistrucci.

Naming: The recipient's rank, name and regiment were indented on the edge in Roman capitals on the early issues, the later ones were engraved. I have also seen them with the date of the deed that won the medal added.

1902 et seq.

Obverse: The effigy of the reigning sovereign.

Naming: In indented capitals.

All other particulars: The same as for 1862.

I note that it is frequently stated that this medal was instituted in 1854 which, in my opinion, shows that a confusion has existed between the grant of a pecuniary award for distinguished conduct and the award of a medal.

As this medal is so well known, I think it would be best if I give the Royal Warrant of 1854 in full and another of 1862 which is the first in which the words "For Distinguished Conduct in the Field" are mentioned.

Royal Warrant, 4th December, 1854.

Victoria R.

Whereas by Our Royal Warrant of the 4th June, 1853, We were pleased to extend the rewards to Sergeants of Our Army for distinguished service from £2,000 a year to £4,000 a year, by an annual progression at the rate of £250 a year, or such other rate as might be decreed most expedient by our Secretary at War; and whereas We deem it expedient to mark Our sense of the distinguished gallant and good conduct of the Army serving in the East under the command of Field-Marshal Lord Raglan, Our Will and Pleasure is, that one sergeant in each regiment of cavalry and infantry, and of each battalion of the Foot Guards, and of the Rifle Brigade, serving in the East, in the Crimea, or elsewhere, under the command of Field-Marshal Lord Raglan, shall be selected by the commanding officer and recommended to Us for the grant of an annuity not exceeding £20, provided that the aggregate of grants now made, and to be made, shall not exceed £4,000 in any one year.

The annuity so granted is to be at the disposal of such Sergeant, although he may be still in Our Service.

It is also Our will and pleasure, to extend the Provisions of Our Royal Warrant of 13th April, 1854, and with the special view of marking our sense of the distinguished service and gallant conduct in the field of our Army now serving in the East, in the Crimea, or elsewhere, under the command of Field-Marshal Lord Raglan, to order and direct that the commanding officer of each regiment of cavalry shall be allowed to recommend one sergeant, two corporals and four privates, and the commanding officer of each regiment of infantry and of each battalion of Foot Guards and of the Rifle Brigade shall be allowed to recommend one sergeant, four corporals and ten privates, to receive a Medal and a gratuity of

For a sergeant	£15
For a corporal	£10
For a private	£5

The gratuity to be placed in the Regimental Savings' Bank, there to remain in deposit at interest until his discharge from Our Service, and to be deemed to be his personal property, in conformity with the terms of our Royal Warrant of 13th April, 1854.

After reading that one is inclined to wonder whether parsimony and gallantry have ever been so closely associated. One is also entitled to speculate what would have happened if the gallantry of the Army had exceeded the money in the kitty, and to ponder why the Foot Guards, infantry and the Rifle Brigade were allowed a bigger share of it than the cavalry.

However, what I would ask the reader to do is to see if he can find any mention of a Distinguished Conduct Medal in that Warrant. I agree that he will see the word "Medal" mentioned but that medal was the Meritorious Service Medal which, until 1862, was awarded for service that included bravery. This fact is, surely, made abundantly clear in the first paragraph of the following Royal Warrant, as is the institution of the Distinguished Conduct Medal in the second.

Royal Warrant, 30th September, 1862

Victoria R.

Whereas with a view to reward distinguished and meritorious service, and of promoting good conduct in Our Army, We have been pleased to declare that a certain fixed sum may be granted in annuities to Sergeants in Our Service, and that the Sergeants selected for the same shall be entitled to receive and wear a Silver Medal, bearing on one side the Royal Effigy, and on the other the words "For Meritorious Service", the name and rank of the Sergeant being inscribed thereon—

It is Our Royal Will and Pleasure that a Silver Medal, bearing on it the words "For Distinguished Conduct in the Field", shall in certain cases where specially recommended, be issued to Sergeants with annuity, subject, however, to the conditions and limitations now in force as to the grant of annuities.

And further, that a like Medal be granted without annuity or gratuity to Sergeants, Corporals and Privates of Our Army, where specially recommended by the General Commanding-in-Chief, and approved by Our Secretary of State for War, for individual acts of distinguished conduct in the field in any part of the world.

There is no doubt, however, that a medal for "Distinguished Conduct" was actually given for acts of gallantry before 1862. A number were awarded for the Crimean War and also, but rather sparingly, for the Indian Mutiny. In his book, *Medals of the British Army*, published in 1861, Thomas Carter not only describes this medal but it is actually illustrated with the familiar red and blue ribbon and the obverse of the same design as that of the Long Service and Good Conduct Medal.

The authority for the award of a bar was dated 7th February, 1881, and it is interesting to note that only seven were awarded in Queen Victoria's reign, and that one of these was for an act performed in 1880.

I leave the reader to form his own opinions as to how this number compares with the 501 bars that were awarded for the First World War, 1914–18, and pass on to some more particulars concerning the medal.

By a Royal Warrant dated 24th May, 1894, special Distinguished Conduct Medals were introduced for the Colonial Forces. The obverses were the same as those already described; the reverses bore the name of the appropriate colony above the usual wording. Though the Colonies adopted their particular ribbons for their Long Service and Meritorious Service Medals they all used the same as the Home Forces for their Distinguished Conduct Medals, i.e. crimson, with a blue central stripe.

The Colonies and Forces which had their own D.C.M. are the following:

Canada	New Zealand
Cape of Good Hope	Natal
New South Wales	West African Frontier Force*
Queensland	King's African Rifles*
Tasmania	

Bars could be awarded to all these medals which, except for the last two, are now obsolete.

*The reverses of these two medals are different in that the applicable name of the unit surrounds the wording FOR DISTINGUISHED CONDUCT IN THE FIELD. The ribbon in each case is dark blue with a central maroon stripe, down the centre of which is a narrow green one.

The award of a bar is indicated by a silver rosette affixed to the ribbon when the medal is not worn, and a bar on the ribbon when it is. The date of the act is inscribed on the bar.

The greatest number of bars awarded to any one recipient is, to my knowledge, two.

There are many extraordinary coincidences in the story of all awards but, I know of a case where a father and his two sons received the D.C.M. in the First World War. This must be a rare family honour but in this case the long arm of coincidence is stretched even further because the two sons performed their deeds on the same day, one on the Gallipoli Peninsula and the other in France.

The D.C.M., unlike the Military Medal, is not available to women, but is to members of the Navy and Royal Marines when serving under immediate military command as, for instance, the members of the Royal Naval Divisions during the First World War.

There is a certain amount of doubt as to when a member of one service should receive the award of another and while I doubt whether a hard and fast rule could be laid down, there is a sort of guiding principle. If a sailor is a member of a landing-party and serving entirely under naval officers he would get a naval award, as he would be recommended by his own senior naval officer. If, however, a sailor was one of a small party of seamen serving under a military officer commanding the operation, the recommendation would be forwarded by that officer and the chances are that the sailor would get the D.C.M. or M.M. There are several cases in which the converse has happened, i.e. when soldiers have received what are normally considered to be purely naval awards. A man of the Royal Marines was awarded both the Distinguished Conduct Medal and the Conspicuous Gallantry Medal during the China War of 1900.

CONSPICUOUS GALLANTRY MEDAL (1874–   )

Obverse: The diademed head of Queen Victoria and legend VICTORIA REGINA. Subsequent issues have the head of the reigning sovereign and appropriate legend.

Reverse: The words FOR CONSPICUOUS GALLANTRY, in three lines, within a wreath of laurels; above a crown.

Size: 1·42 ins. diameter.

Ribbon: 1·25 ins. wide, blue with central white stripe ⅜ in. wide. In 1921 this was changed to a white ribbon with blue edges, the ribbon of the old Naval General Service Medal.

Suspension: A plain straight suspender.

Designer: W. Wyon.

Naming: The early issues were engraved, the later impressed.

If parsimony was the right word for me to use to describe the attitude towards the original Distinguished Conduct Medals I wonder what description to give the genesis of this award.

I will not risk boring the reader by making him wade through pages of "whereas" and "whereof" so will try and predigest their contents for him.

In 1855 it was realized that the Army sergeants and below were getting pecuniary awards for meritorious and/or distinguished conduct but the Royal Navy and Marines nothing. By a Warrant dated 8th February, 1855, it was decided to grant to one or two sergeants of the Royal Marines the same boon [sic]. To allow for this extra strain on the £250 per annum allowed for rewarding bravery, a further £50 per annum was granted.

On 13th August, 1855, the Lords Commissioners of the Admiralty petitioned the Queen to grant to the Navy and Marines the equivalent awards as conferred on the Army. This petition, which was granted contained the following:

"We do therefore most humbly submit that Your Majesty may be graciously pleased by Your Order in Council to authorize us to confer Rewards, by the grant of Medals and Gratuities, on any Petty Officers, Seamen and Royal Marines who shall, whilst so serving, particularly distinguish themselves in action with the enemy, . . ."

Now for the medal!

The medal awarded to soldiers for meritorious service was used which, you will recall, has FOR MERITORIOUS SERVICE on the reverse. The last two words were filed off and CONSPICUOUS GALLANTRY engraved in their stead.

The particulars given at the head of this medal do not, therefore, include this strange issue which had the usual scroll suspender with one of the three words on the reverse embossed and the other two engraved.

Of the eleven C.G.M.s awarded for the Crimean campaign six of the recipients were subsequently awarded the Victoria Cross for the same acts of gallantry but it does not appear that they were required to surrender their C.G.M.s. Groups are known to exist containing both awards.

The medal which we now know was instituted by an Order in Council dated 7th July, 1874. There is no mention concerning the award of a bar for subsequent acts of bravery which accounts for the fact that I have a note dated May, 1911, to the effect that two of these medals were in a group of Crimean medals to David Barry.

CONSPICUOUS GALLANTRY MEDAL
ROYAL AIR FORCE (1943-   )

In 1943 it was announced that airmen of non-commissioned rank, glider pilots, observers and other Army personnel would be eligible for the award of the Conspicuous Gallantry Medal. This medal is, in all respects, similar to the Naval award but is worn with a ribbon of light blue with dark blue edges.

GEORGE MEDAL (1940-   )

Obverse: The effigy of the sovereign and the usual inscription.
Reverse: St George slaying the Dragon and words THE GEORGE MEDAL.

Size: 1·42 ins. diameter.
Ribbon: 1·25 ins. wide, red with five narrow blue stripes.
Suspension: By a ring fitted to an ornate claw.
Designer: S. Gooden, adapted by G. C. Gray.
Naming: Impressed on the edge.

This medal was instituted at the same time as the George Cross, 24th September, 1940. The circumstances that govern its award are similar to those of the George Cross and it is awarded for acts which are not considered to merit the Cross.

DISTINGUISHED SERVICE MEDAL (1914–   )

Obverse: The effigy of the reigning sovereign.
Reverse: The words FOR DISTINGUISHED SERVICE within a wreath of laurel and surmounted by an Imperial Crown.
Size: 1·42 ins. diameter.
Ribbon: Dark blue with a white central stripe down the centre of which is one of dark blue.
Suspension: By a plain straight suspender.
Naming: In the case of awards for the First World War, the names were impressed on the edge together with the name of the recipient's ship and the date, all in thin block capitals. If the medal was awarded for bravery at sea the name of sea is also stated, viz. VIOLA. ADRIATIC. 1915.

Those awarded for the Second World War gave only rank, name and number.

This medal was instituted on 14th October, 1914, for courage displayed by petty officers and ratings, and to their equivalents in the Royal Marines. Members of the Fleet Air Arm and Women's Royal Naval Service are also eligible. In 1942 eligibility was extended to the Merchant Navy. It is, of course, also open to all corresponding ranks in the various naval and other reserves while called up for service. Some awards of this decoration were made to men of the Royal Artillery serving in the Maritime anti-aircraft regiment.

Bars may be awarded for subsequent acts and are indicated on the ribbon by a silver rosette when the medal itself is not worn; by an ornamental rectangular bar on the ribbon, the same as with other decorations, when the medal is worn.

INDIAN DISTINGUISHED SERVICE MEDAL (1907–47)

Obverse: The crowned and robed bust of the king, with a palm branch below, and the wording EDWARDVS VII KAISAR-I-HIND. Those awarded in the reign of George V and George VI bore the sovereign's head crowned.
Reverse: The words FOR DISTINGUISHED SERVICE surrounded by a wreath of laurel.

Size: 1·42 ins. diameter.
Ribbon: 1·25 ins. wide, dark blue with a 0·5 in. wide central crimson stripe.
Suspension: By a scroll suspender.
Designer: G. W. De Saulles.
Naming: In engraved script.

This decoration was instituted on 25th June, 1907, to reward "the distinguished services of Indian commissioned and non-commissioned officers and men of the India Regular Forces, including the Reserve of the Indian Army, Border Militia and Levies, the Military Police and Imperial Service Troops when employed under the orders of the Government of India, who have distinguished themselves in peace or on active service".

On 6th July, 1917, a further Warrant was published extending the awarding of the medal to Indian non-combatants when on active service.

Bars were awarded, and indicated, in the same way as with the Distinguished Conduct Medal.

The award became obsolete on the partition of India in 1947.

MILITARY MEDAL (1916–)

Obverse: The effigy of the reigning sovereign and appropriate legend.
Reverse: The words FOR BRAVERY IN THE FIELD surmounted by the Royal
  Cypher and Crown encircled by a wreath.
Size: 1·42 ins. diameter.
Ribbon: Dark blue with three white and two crimson stripes down the centre.
Suspension: By an ornate scroll suspender.
Naming: In impressed capitals.

This medal was instituted by a Royal Warrant dated 4th April, 1916, for award to non-commissioned officers and men of the Army on the recommendation of the Commander-in-Chief, for acts of bravery. The Warrant does not specify that the act should be performed in the presence of the enemy but it seems to be generally understood that the medal is only awarded for bravery while on active service.

By another Warrant dated 21st June, 1916, women, both British and foreign, were made eligible for the award for acts of bravery and devotion to duty under fire, and several have been gained by them.

It is a little strange that the expression "under fire" or its equivalent, is not used when referring to the qualifications necessary in the case of men but expressly stated in the case of women yet the wording on the reverse mentions "in the field".

Bars are awarded as with other occasions and are indicated by a rosette on the ribbon, or a bar when the medal itself is being worn.

The medals awarded during the reign of George V normally showed him in military uniform but a few were also issued with the crowned head on the obverse.* I cannot say how many such medals were issued, but, judging by their rarity, it cannot have been very many.

*The first of these were awarded in, or about, 1930.

I know of a case where two Military Medals were given to the same man—the second instead of the authorization to wear a bar. This isolated—or at any rate faulty—occasion does not signify that two ribbons, or two medals, could be worn. I can only assume that the man had retired (or been demobilized) by the time the second medal was received so that there was never an occasion when he had to appear on parade. There is, too, the possibility that one, or both, of the awards were made posthumously.

DISTINGUISHED FLYING MEDAL (1919–)

Obverse: The sovereign's effigy and appropriate legend.
Reverse: The helmeted, seated, figure of Athene releasing a hawk with the words FOR COURAGE under her outstretched right arm.
Edges: Both sides have beaded edges.
Size: Oval, 1·5 by 1·3 ins.
Ribbon: 1·25 ins. wide, with alternating diagonal stripes of violet and white, $\frac{1}{16}$ in. wide.
Suspension: The suspender is in the form of outstretched wings attached to the top of the piece by an elaborate claw.
Naming: In impressed lettering.

This medal was instituted on 5th December, 1919, to be awarded to non-commissioned officers and men of the Royal Air Force for acts of gallantry against the enemy. It is to the ranks mentioned, what the Distinguished Flying Cross is to officers, and the same rules apply to both.

I should be interested to know why a representation of Athene was chosen as I have always been under the impression that she was the patroness of the elegant and useful arts, or, as some writers state, of wisdom and knowledge. She is also represented as a virgin of divinity, whose heart is inaccessible to the passion of love. It seems to me that a fellow who can show all these qualifications deserves a medal.

AIR FORCE MEDAL (1919–)

Obverse: The sovereign's effigy and appropriate legend.
Reverse: The figure of Hermes riding on a hawk while holding a wreath.
Edges: Both sides have beaded edges.
Size: Oval, 1·5 by 1·3 ins.
Ribbon: 1·25 ins. wide, with alternating diagonal stripes of crimson and white, $\frac{1}{16}$ in. wide.
Suspension: The suspender is in the form of outstretched wings, attached to the top of the piece by an elaborate claw.
Naming: In impressed lettering.

This medal was instituted on 5th December, 1919, for acts of courage and devotion to duty when not in the presence of the enemy. It is awarded to non-commissioned officers and men of the Royal Air Force and, since April,

1941, to the equivalent ranks in the Fleet Air Arm. The same rules concerning the award of bars apply as with other decorations.

BURMA GALLANTRY MEDAL (1937-47)

Obverse: The king's effigy.
Reverse: A wreath of laurel within which is BURMA FOR GALLANTRY.
Size: 1·42 ins. diameter.
Ribbon: 1·25 ins. wide, dark green with central crimson stripe.
Suspension: By a scroll suspender.
Naming: In impressed lettering.

This medal was awarded to all ranks of any of the military forces in Burma on the authority of the Governor-General. As the country became an independent state as from 17th October, 1947, the medal automatically became, like those awarded to the Indian Army, obsolete.

BRITISH EMPIRE MEDAL (1917-)

Obverse: The seated figure of Britannia holding a trident in her right hand and supporting a shield with her left hand with the motto FOR GOD AND THE EMPIRE. In the exergue FOR MERITORIOUS SERVICE.
Reverse: The Royal Cypher of the reigning sovereign surmounted by a crown and the words INSTITUTED BY KING GEORGE V.
Size: 1·42 ins. diameter.
Ribbon: 1·25 ins. wide, rose pink with pearl-grey edges, with the addition of a vertical grey stripe in the centre in the case of recipients of the military medal of the Order. But see ribbon of O.B.E.
Metal: Silver.
Naming: In impressed lettering. Those awarded during the reign of George VI and later are engraved with rank, name and number.
Bars: Awarded for further worthy deeds.
Suspension: By a clasp ornamented with oak leaves. (The E.G.M. clasp was ornamented with laurel leaves.) See also next para.

In 1917 there was a medal bearing a representation of Britannia on one side and the Imperial Cypher as described above on the other which was worn from a purple ribbon 1 in. wide. In 1918 the recipients were divided into two classes, military and civil. The former wore a red stripe down the centre of the ribbon: suspension was by means of a ring.

This medal was made obsolete in 1922 on the introduction of two medals known as "The Medal of the Order of the British Empire for Gallantry" (The Empire Gallantry Medal), and "The Medal of the Order of the British Empire for Meritorious Service".

In September 1940, the George Cross was instituted and the E.G.M. was abolished. Those who had qualified for it were instructed to apply to the Central Chantry for exchange. In March 1941 the title of the remaining medal for meritorious service was changed to that of the British Empire Medal with the two divisions, military and civil. The holder was permitted to put the letters B.E.M. after his name. On the occasions when this medal was awarded for gallantry, this was distinguished by the wearing of a silver emblem of crossed oak leaves on the ribbon.

MERITORIOUS SERVICE MEDAL (ARMY) (1845–)

Obverse: The diademed head of Queen Victoria and legend VICTORIA REGINA. On some the date 1848 is under the bust.
Reverse: The words FOR MERITORIOUS SERVICE, in three lines, within a wreath of laurel surmounted by a crown.
Size: 1·42 ins. diameter.
Ribbon: 1·25 ins. wide, crimson. Since 1917 maroon with white edges and central white stripe.
Suspension: A scroll suspender.
Designer: W. Wyon.
Naming: Found indented and engraved.

This medal was instituted by Royal Warrant dated 19th December, 1845, as a reward to sergeants for distinguished or meritorious service on the recommendation of the Commander-in-Chief. The number of awards was governed by the sum of money allocated for the annuity which accompanied the medal, which was given to sergeants only. It thus earned the name "The Sergeants' Medal". Recipients must now (A.O. 1956) complete twenty-seven years' service with twenty-three years' colour service but may now receive the medal without having to wait for the annuity to be available.

In 1917 the qualifications for the award of the M.S.M. were extended for all other ranks for specially meritorious service or acts of gallantry not in the presence of the enemy. It was, however, still awarded under the old conditions. Awards under this new Warrant are usually termed "Immediate Awards". A search of the *London Gazette* (not such an arduous task as it may appear) will usually reveal if the award is an immediate one. Entries are generally prefixed "for services with the Army in France", "valuable services with the Waziristan Force" or something similar.

Obverses have of course changed with the sovereign. King Edward VII and King George V are depicted in the uniform of a Field-Marshal though some of the medals to the Army bear the coinage head of King George V.

In spite of the belief of many old soldiers who received an Immediate Award, this medal should always be worn after the Long Service and Good Conduct Medal.

MERITORIOUS SERVICE MEDAL
(ROYAL MARINES) (1849–1947)

Obverse: Queen Victoria—as Army medal subsequently—sovereign in uniform of Admiral of the Fleet or George VI and Queen Elizabeth II crowned head.

The award of the M.S.M. to the Royal Marines was instituted on 16th

January, 1849. The ribbon is dark blue. In 1919 Immediate Awards were approved for the Royal Marines in the same way as for the Army and these awards were worn with the Army ribbon. The grant of Immediate Awards to the Royal Marines ceased in 1933 and in 1947 the award of the M.S.M. to this Corps was entirely discontinued.

MERITORIOUS SERVICE MEDAL
(ROYAL NAVY) (1919–33)

The award of the M.S.M. was extended to the Royal Navy in 1919 at the same time as to the Royal Marines. The obverse bore the bust of King George V in the uniform of an Admiral of the Fleet but there exists a medal to a Chief Writer of the Royal Navy which bears the effigy of the sovereign in the uniform of a Field-Marshal. The medal was worn with the Army ribbon. Awards to the Royal Navy were discontinued in 1933 after approximately some 1,062 awards had been made. Medals to the Royal Navy are inscribed on the rim with the words "services during war".

MERITORIOUS SERVICE MEDAL
(ROYAL AIR FORCE) (1918–28)

Obverse: Classic or coinage head of King George V.
Reverse: As Army medal.
Size: 1·42 ins. diameter.
Ribbon: Dark blue and crimson with white edges and a central stripe of white.
Suspension: By a scroll suspender.
Naming: In impressed lettering.

The *London Gazette* of 26th June, 1918, contains the following entry: "His Majesty the King has approved the adoption of the Medal for Meritorious Service by the Royal Air Force for valuable services in the field . . . as distinct from actual flying service . . .". Rather curiously the announcement of the first awards was published in the *Gazette* of 3 June 1918. No mention is made of a special ribbon for the Royal Air Force but an Air Ministry Order stated that it would be as described above. Some 860–900 awards of the M.S.M. were made to the Royal Air Force before it was discontinued in 1928. Unlike the Army medal the Royal Air Force M.S.M. is worn before that for Long Service but I do not think that there is any particular significance in this.

MERITORIOUS SERVICE MEDAL
(COLONIAL FORCES) (1894–1930)

Description: The first issues bore the crowned and veiled head of Queen Victoria and legend, VICTORIA REGINA ET IMPERATRIX. The reverses bore the name of the colony above the crown. In all other respects they were the same as those awarded to the Home Forces. Subsequent issues were the same as for the Home Forces with the additional name of the appropriate colony on the reverse.

These medals were introduced by Royal Warrant dated 24th May, 1894. The following ten issues were made during the thirty-six years of their existence:

Colony	Colour of Ribbon
Canada	Crimson, central white stripe
Cape of Good Hope	Crimson, central orange stripe
Natal	Crimson, central yellow stripe
New South Wales	Crimson, central dark blue stripe
New Zealand	Crimson, central light green stripe
Queensland	Crimson, central light blue stripe
South Australia	Crimson, no stripe
Tasmania	Crimson, central pink stripe
Victoria	Crimson, two dark green central stripes
Australian Commonwealth	Crimson, two dark green central stripes

MERITORIOUS SERVICE MEDAL
(SOUTH AFRICAN PERMANENT FORCES)
(1929–39)

Description: The obverse of this medal was the same as that for the Home Forces. The ribbon was crimson with blue edges, and central blue stripe bordered by those of white.

This medal was instituted in January, 1929, and discontinued in December, 1939, when the Union adopted the present Territorial Efficiency award.

NEW ZEALAND CROSS (1869)

Description: A silver cross patté surmounted by a gold crown.
Obverse: A gold wreath of laurel surrounding a central circlet on which are the words NEW ZEALAND. On each arm is a gold six-pointed star.
Reverse: A central circle bearing the date 1863. Around this is a circlet the top half of which bears the recipient's name; the bottom, the word DEFENCE.
Size: 1·5 ins. across; 1·9 ins. high to the top of the crown.
Ribbon: 1·5 ins. wide. Crimson.
Suspension: A small silver ring, fitted at right-angles, attaches the top of the crown to the V of a silver bar which is ornamented with a gold sprig of laurel.
Designer: The designing of the award was entrusted to a commission whose recommendations were submitted by the Governor to the Queen who approved of them.
Naming: In engraved block capitals on the circlet on the reverse.

This is one of the most interesting and rare of all our decorations and the only one which was not instituted by the sovereign. Queen Victoria's approval for its award was obtained after the Governor of New Zealand had issued an Order in Council sanctioning its bestowal on members of the local forces and constabulary. By the time the Queen knew anything about it it had already been given to ten members so that, without putting the Governor into an extremely delicate situation, to say the least, it is difficult to see how she could have done otherwise than to approve.

It bears, as already stated, the date 1863 though awarded to a total of twenty recipients for acts of courage performed against the Maoris between 1863 and 1870. Provision was made for a second award but there were no recipients of a bar.

It is the usual practice to give a detailed description of a new award in the Order that institutes it but, here again, this decoration has the distinction of being different.

The regulations, dated 10th March, 1869, that gave the terms of the award mentioned that it would be a silver cross bearing the name of the Colony and that of the recipient, and that it would be suspended from a crimson ribbon. It was another seventeen months before anything further was decided about the details.

Inspector McDonnell, for instance, did one brave deed in 1863 and another in 1866 which jointly gained him the Cross which he did not receive until 1886. Though campaign medals have been awarded fifty-three years after the action, I cannot recall any interval in the award of a decoration remotely approaching this. The first deed to win the Victoria Cross was performed by Lieutenant C. D. Lucas, R.N. on 20th June, 1854, but he did not receive his Cross till 26th June, 1857. For decorations other than the New Zealand Cross this is the longest interval that I can remember which was not caused on account of the recipient being a prisoner of war. There were, however, many occasions during the Second World War when the publication in the *London Gazette* was several years after the date when the deed of gallantry was performed.

Although the next two medals are not awards to the armed forces they are included as both may be awarded for gallantry.

KING'S POLICE MEDAL (1909–   )

Obverse: Head of sovereign.
Reverse: A watchman leaning on a sword and holding a shield inscribed "To GUARD MY PEOPLE", a fortified city in the background.
Ribbon: Dark blue with white central stripe and white stripes at the edges. (When the medal is awarded for gallantry each white stripe has a thin stripe of red.)

In 1909 a medal was established for award to police and fire-brigades for gallantry or distinguished service (not necessarily courage). After several amendments, in 1933 two distinct medals were authorized, one for gallantry with the words "For Gallantry" in the exergue on the reverse, the other bearing the words "For Distinguished Police Service" round the figure of the watchman. At the same time the thin red stripe was added to the ribbon of the gallantry award.

In 1954 it was ordained that separate medals should be awarded to the police and fire services. Both are of similar design as described above and medals for gallantry and distinguished service were retained for both services. On the Distinguished Service Medal for fire-brigades, however, the word "Fire" was substituted and a new ribbon was designed for it, the police continuing to wear the old ribbon. That for the fire services was a scarlet ribbon with narrow yellow edges and a central stripe of yellow. Each yellow stripe has a narrow stripe of blue when the medal is awarded for gallantry. In both services the award for gallantry is only made posthumously. It seems rather strange that a medal should be specially designed with a distinctive ribbon when the recipient would never be able to wear it.

NAVAL
LONG SERVICE MEDALS

As the medals that will be dealt with in this chapter were, or are still, awarded to members of a service about which the landsman knows very little, I trust that the following remarks will be of interest to them and skipped by all past and present members of the Royal Navy.

It seems to me to be just as wrong to know nothing about the service for which a Good Conduct Medal is awarded as to be ignorant of the action, or war, for which a campaign medal was given.

This, then, is my excuse for including these remarks which sketch, in brief outline, a summary of our Navy with, I admit, a few items that are not directly connected with medals.

Alfred the Great was the founder of the English navy as he was the first king to realize the necessity of a fleet to guard our shores against the pirates that infested the North Sea and English Channel. He too, originated the naval arms race which has caused such excitement and interest throughout the world ever since. He found that his galleys were no match for those of the pirates so built larger ones. He then found that his men were not so good as they might be at manning them, so he hired bigger and better pirates to man his fleet. Here, then, in about A.D. 897 was the genesis of what in a thousand and seventeen years' time was to become the largest navy the world has ever known.

Edgar carried on the good work of Alfred and felt so sure of himself that he adopted the title of Lord of the Ocean surrounding Britain which, with a little imagination, can be considered the first mention of a naval rank. This was in A.D. 965.

Ethelred II (known to most schoolboys as Ethelred the Unready) was the first to form a naval reserve. We shall mention when dealing with the Militia Long Service Medal how the early landowners had to supply a man for every so many hides of land they owned. Ethelred used this idea in the same way in that the owner of every 310 hides had to provide a ship. He also levied a contribution from every town. In A.D. 1007 he massed his fleet off Sandwich, reviewed it and dispersed it to various stations to ward off the impending attack of the Danes. Having credited him with holding the first naval review we had better omit the subsequent invasion and his flight and pass on to Richard I who, in 1191, issued the first naval laws which are now styled Admiralty Regulations.

In this jumping from prèmiere to prèmiere we have passed over the work of William the Conqueror who established the Cinque Ports and, in return for certain privileges insisted that they supplied him with 52 vessels, each with a

46

crew of 24, for 15 days when required to do so. Here, then, we may have the origin of the idea of using merchant vessels in time of war, not only as auxiliaries but as actual war vessels as was done in both the recent World Wars.

When Edward III, with 240 ships, was on his way to Flanders he encountered a French fleet of 400 sail with 40,000 men and completely defeated them off Sluys on 24th June, 1340, and thus fought the first naval action in our history.

The regular Navy is considered to have been started by Henry VII who, in 1488, built the Great Harry, a three-masted ship—the earliest man-of-war of any size—which was accidentally burnt at Woolwich five years later.

Henry VIII carried on the work of his father and instituted the Admiralty Office (and Trinity House) in 1512, and appointed commissioners to visit the ships to see that they were maintained in an efficient state. He also originated the giving of fixed salaries to both officers and men; and made service in the Royal Navy a profession. He also made laws reserving certain timbered areas so that the trees therein could be used to build ships. It was he, therefore, who instituted Crown Lands, that is, the cordoning off of areas for use by the Crown for war purposes.

On the outbreak of the Civil War Prince Rupert took over twenty-five vessels but Cromwell saw the necessity for a strong fleet and was the first to introduce what are termed Navy Estimates—in other words an estimated sum to keep the Navy going for a certain period. His first was for £400,000.

Naval uniform was first introduced in 1748 though there is a record dated 6th April, 1609, to show that James I had granted "liverie coats of fine red cloth" to six principal masters of the Navy.

The Navy continued to grow till the fall of Napoleon after which a sort of anticlimax set in and the quality of our ships, both in structure and armament fell behind that of continental powers. After the Wars of Napoleon a sort of apathy arose against any form of expenditure on armaments of any kind (as happened after both the recent World Wars); the people saw no sense in training for what could never happen again, so why spend money on ships and personnel when there was nobody to fight?

The imminence of a war with Russia brought people to their senses again with the result that a force known as Naval Coast Volunteers was started in 1853. In 1859 a brigade of coastal artillery was formed and, in the same year, the Naval Reserve. In 1875 a Royal Naval Artillery Volunteer Force was instituted by an Act of the same name. This must surely be the most parsimonious Act ever passed. It decreed that the force must entail no expense. Strange to say, a thousand volunteers enrolled in the first year. This prompted the voting of precisely £1,000 for their annual maintenance. The records show that by 1891 the strength had risen to 1,947 and their cost to the nation to £6,685. Whether this sum proved too much of a strain on the Naval Estimates, or whether the men were useless is not recorded but, the fact remains that the force was disbanded in 1891.

The Naval Forces Act, 1903, introduced the short service engagement whereby the last seven years of the contract could be spent in the Royal

Fleet Reserve. By this means the Navy, like the Army, assured itself of a considerable number of fully trained men immediately available.

Now let us consider the various medals which are awarded to men of the Royal Navy and its various reserve branches.

NAVAL LONG SERVICE MEDAL (1831-   )

1831

Obverse: An anchor within a wreath of oak leaves tied at the bottom with a bow.

Reverse: Between the edge and a beaded circle, FOR LONG SERVICE AND GOOD CONDUCT. The space in the centre is occupied by the recipient's name, rating and length of service.

Size: 1·34 ins. diameter.

Ribbon: Approximately 1 in. wide, plain dark blue.

Suspension: A small ring was fitted at the top when awarded though many are found with this removed and a wire suspender in its place.

Naming: Engraved in the centre of the reverse.

This medal was instituted by an Order in Council dated 24th August, 1831, to be awarded to petty officers or seamen, or non-commissioned officers and privates of Marines who, "having served above twenty-one years and behaved invariably well and be, in the captain's opinion, in every way deserving".

To be strictly accurate, the above remarks referred to the granting of a gratuity, for the Order goes on to say that, "All men receiving such Gratuity shall be afterwards entitled to wear a Silver Medal, the size of a Half Crown, at the third button of their Jackets, . . ."

It is unusual for the Order to specify the size of the medal to be awarded, and one might be excused for thinking that it would have been more tactful to have given the dimensions in inches rather than make such connection between the size and value.

However, having been so exact as regards the size, they were not so particular as regards quantity for it was not particularly unusual for a man to receive two medals.

John Midgeley received three medals, one during the reign of William IV and the other two during that of Queen Victoria. The periods of service on the reverses give, 21 years, 36 years and 39½ years respectively. As he also served seven years in the merchant service it seems that the sea must have had some attraction for him.

I have seen it stated that the original ribbon was of dark blue with white edges, as it is now, and I have also seen the first type suspended from such a ribbon but, though I can find no official Order to back me up, I am convinced that this is wrong. I have owned several of these medals and in every case when the ribbon has looked original it has been of the plain dark blue. I suggest that when they are found with a ribbon with white edges that this ribbon is a replacement however old and dirty it may be now.

The white edges to the Naval Long Service Medal were not introduced until 1848, and then on a ribbon 1·5 ins. wide. That 1·25 ins. wide with white edges was first issued with the second type of medal in Queen Victoria's reign, or about 1850.

1848

Obverse: The diademed head of Queen Victoria facing left with the designer's name on the truncation and legend VICTORIA REGINA.

Reverse: An old sailing man-of-war at anchor within a circle of cable tied with a reef-knot at the bottom; around the whole the legend, FOR LONG SERVICE AND GOOD CONDUCT.

Size: 1·42 ins. diameter.

Ribbon: The original was 1·5 ins. wide with white edges; in about 1850 it was altered to 1·25 ins. wide with white edges.

Suspension: By a plain straight suspender 1·5 ins. wide with the first type, and 1·25 ins. for the second as regards the opening for the ribbon.

Designer: W. Wyon.

Naming: In the case of the first type the recipient's name, rating and ship were engraved round the rim; in the second they were impressed in capital lettering.

I have been unable to trace any official Order authorizing the alteration of the design on the obverse so that the date 1848 must be considered as an approximation rather than fact. There is, however, one fact that leads me to believe that it is correct because the first issues of the new type bore that date on the obverse under the Queen's effigy. The type with the wide suspender is quite common so that it is reasonable to suppose that it was issued for a couple of years or so. To be on the safe side, the reader is advised to take the year 1850 as an approximation as well.

At about this time the period of service necessary to qualify for the medal was reduced to fifteen years.

Edward VII (1901–10)

Obverse: The bust of the King in naval uniform, and the legend EDWARDVS VII REX IMPERATOR.

Reverse: The same as the last issue.

Size: 1·42 ins. diameter.

Ribbon: 1·25 ins. wide, blue with white edges.

Suspension: By a plain straight suspender.

Designer: G. W. De Saulles.

Naming: The recipient's name, rank and ship are impressed on the edge.

George V (1910–36)

The particulars are identical with the above except, of course, with the reigning sovereign's effigy on the obverse.

The later issues had coinage head.

George VI (1936–52)

The same remarks as for the last issue apply.

Elizabeth II (1952–)

No alterations—except, of course, to the obverse—have been made.

ROYAL NAVAL RESERVE LONG SERVICE AND GOOD CONDUCT MEDAL (1908–)

Obverse: The bust of the King in naval uniform facing left; the legend EDWARDVS VII REX IMPERATOR.

Reverse: A representation of the first "dreadnought" in the world, H.M.S. *Dreadnought*; below DIUTERNE FIDELIS (Long and faithful service).

Size: 1·42 ins. diameter.

Ribbon: Until October, 1941, it was plain dark green; it was then altered to dark green with three white stripes.

Suspension: By a plain straight suspender.

Designer: Obverse, G. W. De Saulles; reverse, E. G. Gillick.

Naming: Impressed in capitals on the edge.

This medal was instituted by Admiralty Order in September, 1908, for award to men of the Royal Naval Reserve after fifteen years' service. The same medal was also awarded to men of the Royal Naval Volunteer Reserve after twelve years' service. In both cases the award was made on the recommendation of the Registrar-General of Shipping and Seamen. A bar is granted for the satisfactory completion of a second like period.

The same medal, with the appropriate alteration to the obverse has been awarded ever since. Those awarded during the latter part of the reign of George V had the classic head on the obverse.

In the reign of George V a separate ribbon (dark blue with a green central stripe bordered by two of red) was introduced for the Royal Naval Volunteer Reserve Medal.

The medal with the R.N.R. ribbon is awarded to qualifying members of the ROYAL NAVAL AUXILIARY SICK BERTH RESERVE.

The medal with the R.N.V.R. ribbon is awarded to qualifying members of the ROYAL NAVAL WIRELESS AUXILIARY RESERVE and the ROYAL NAVAL VOLUNTEER WIRELESS RESERVE.

ROYAL FLEET RESERVE LONG SERVICE AND GOOD CONDUCT MEDAL

The piece of this medal is identical with the above. It is suspended from a ring. The ribbon is white with a central wide dark blue stripe bordered with red. The qualifying period is fifteen years.

The later issues during the reign of George V had the classic head as did those of George VI.

ROYAL NAVAL RESERVE DECORATION (1908–   )

This consists of an oval silver badge with the Royal Cypher in the centre surmounted by a gilt crown. It is similar to the Territorial Decoration except that the wreath is replaced by a cable tied at the bottom. It is suspended from a ring through which the ribbon, 1·5 ins. wide, green with white edges, is threaded.

It is awarded to officers with fifteen years' service who have fulfilled certain necessary periods of training.

ROYAL NAVAL VOLUNTEER RESERVE DECORATION (1908–58)

This decoration is the same as the last. The qualifying period was twenty years. The ribbon is the same as for the men's medal but 1·5 ins. wide instead of 1·25 ins. It is dark blue with a green central stripe bordered by two of red.

ROYAL NAVAL VOLUNTEER RESERVE LONG SERVICE AND GOOD CONDUCT MEDAL (1908–58)

The piece of this medal is the same as the Royal Naval Reserve Medal; the ribbon is similar to that of the decoration except that the central green stripe is wider.

The requisite period of service was twelve years with a conduct not assessed below that of "Very good".

A bar was granted for each subsequent similar period designated by a silver rosette worn on the ribbon.

A recipient of this medal who was subsequently commissioned could gain a bar and then, if he completed the necessary further twenty years, obtain the decoration.

I had a group with both the decoration and the medal so, as the recipient would have been awarded a bar after twenty-four years' service, I presume he had to forego that. I can think of no other case where the gaining of a bar is cancelled.

The unusual thing about this medal is that service after the age of fifteen in an Army Cadet Force or Officers' Training Corps could count providing the cadet joined the Naval Reserve within six months of leaving. Again, I cannot recall another case where service as a boy is counted towards a medal for a man.

ROYAL NAVAL AUXILIARY SERVICE MEDAL (1965–   )

Obverse: Crowned effigy of the sovereign.
Reverse: A naval crown and fouled anchor (tilted to starboard) surrounded by oak leaves with an inscription in the surround reading ROYAL NAVY AUXILIARY SERVICE—LONG SERVICE.

Ribbon: $1\frac{1}{2}$ ins. wide—white, blue, white—each section defaced with a green vertical stripe $\frac{1}{16}$ in. wide.

This medal was instituted in 1965 (July) for officers and auxiliarymen (including women members of the Service) who complete twelve years' satisfactory service. The Royal Naval Auxiliary Service was formerly the Royal Naval Minewatching Service and previous service in this may be reckoned towards the requisite period.

ARMY AND ROYAL AIR FORCE
LONG SERVICE MEDALS

Long Service and Good Conduct Medals owe their origin to the private enterprise of the commanding officers of regiments who saw the advantage of encouraging good behaviour by the award of a visible token. Many regiments had done this prior to the institution of an official Long Service Medal but the credit for having originated the idea must go to the Royal Northumberland Fusiliers who, as early as 1767 had a medal for Merit. As a matter of fact they had three medals which were awarded after seven, fourteen and twenty-one years' service without a court martial.

It is interesting to note that the first official Long Service Medal was not given to the recipient until after he had retired from the Army. The qualifying period for those who served in the infantry was twenty-one years but only twenty in the case of the cavalry. The necessary period is now eighteen years.

There have been several different types of Long Service Medals since their inception which only have one item in common, namely, their size which has always been 1·42 ins, diameter, if circular.

The inscription on the reverse, FOR LONG SERVICE AND GOOD CONDUCT (in four lines) has always been the same but the size of the lettering has not.

The obverse of the original Army Long Service Medal—in fact all of those awarded during the reign of Queen Victoria—was the work of Benedetto Pistrucci. He incidentally, was an Italian engraver of gems who started his service with the Royal Mint in 1816. His original work is probably better known to coin collectors for it was he who introduced the idea of the designer having his initials, or name, on the dies. His first coins appeared in 1820.

It will, I think, be best if we deal with the Victorian issues by dates rather than types as it seems to me to be more logical to refer to a medal by date than by a type, or issue, especially when the period covered by the reign of Queen Victoria is sixty-four years.

Decorations awarded to officers for long service are included in this chapter as the term "decoration" is misleading. In this case it only signifies that the recipient has kept out of mischief as long as his men—which should not be very difficult for an officer.

The decoration does, like the appropriate medal to the man, signify that the recipient has given up much of his leisure time to the Service. It is debatable why an officer should get a decoration for doing so and a man only a medal as the personal sacrifice of both is identical. It seems a case of equal sacrifice and unequal reward. In addition to this an officer is allowed to use the initials T.D. (TERRITORIAL DECORATION) after his name whereas a man who might have considerably longer than the minimum service, has nothing.

One can quote numerous anomalies as regards the awarding of medals, and decorations for bravery too, but if an officer is allowed to use the initials T.D. after his name I cannot see any reason why the distinction of E.M. (Efficiency Medal) is not granted to those in the ranks on completion of the same number of years' service as required by an officer to get T.D., i.e. twenty years.

1830

Obverse: A military trophy having in the centre the arms of William IV with the Hanoverian inescutcheon.

Reverse: The inscription in four lines, FOR LONG SERVICE AND GOOD CONDUCT.

The Royal Warrant which authorized this medal is dated 30th July, 1830. It reads, "Discharged Soldiers receiving a gratuity for meritorious conduct shall be entitled to wear a Silver Medal, having on one side of it the words 'FOR LONG SERVICE AND GOOD CONDUCT'; and on the other side in relief the King's Arms, with the name and rank of the soldier, and the year, inscribed on the Medal. The Medal will be transmitted by the Adjutant-General to the Officer Commanding the Regiment, who will deliver it to the Soldier on the parade, with the parchment certificate of discharge, on which the grant will be recorded, as well as in the Regimental Orders, and in the Register of Soldiers' Services. If circumstances should prevent the Discharged Soldier from receiving the Medal at the Regiment, it will be delivered to him through the Adjutant-General at the Board of the Chelsea Commissioners."

The first issue numbered only 112 and was made in 1831. The pieces were fitted with crude steel clips through which passed a small ring, through which the ribbon was threaded. This ribbon, incidentally, was only 1 in. wide. It was, in fact, the Waterloo ribbon without the blue edges.

The name, rank and regiment of the recipient were impressed on the rim of the medals by the, then, new impressing machine invented by two Mint employees, Charles Harrison and Thomas Jerome. This machine was first used to name the Waterloo Medals.

The subsequent issues had a larger ring and a ribbon 1·25 ins. wide but I cannot trace the exact date on which these alterations were made.

1839

Obverse: The same as the foregoing except that the Hanoverian inescutcheon is omitted.

Reverse: The same as the foregoing.

This type, with its steel clip and ring, remained till 1846. The most common date is 1847. The date was often impressed on the rim.

The naming was done at the Mint by the machine, as already stated, which named the medals for Waterloo.

1850

The piece is identical with the foregoing; the difference being in the mode of suspension as in this year the scroll type of suspender was introduced for the Long Service Medal, i.e. the same type as on the Indian General Service Medals.

This date, 1850, is found on the obverse of medals which are named in impressed lettering and also in script. The reason being that in this year the medals were sent to the regiments unnamed with the result that almost an unlimited number of types of lettering are found. It was the regiment's responsibility to name the medals before they were awarded but that did not mean that all had to do it by stamping the names, or all by engraving them. A study of those awarded to the same regiment for a consecutive number of years will show what happened.

1874

The medals awarded on and after this year are all the same as the foregoing except that the lettering on the reverse is smaller.

Edward VII (1901–10)

The issues of this reign bear the effigy of the King in the uniform of a Field-Marshal on the obverse, with the legend EDWARDVS VII REX IMPERATOR. The medals had the same reverses and were suspended from the same 1·25 in. wide crimson ribbon.

George V (1910–36)

The first issues during this reign were the same as for the last except, of course, that they bore the effigy of the sovereign at that time with the appropriate legend.

The same plain maroon ribbon was continued until 1916 when it was altered to maroon with white edges. This change was brought about by the fact that the Long Service Ribbon was almost identical with that of the Victoria Cross which was instituted in 1856.

By a Royal Warrant dated 23rd September, 1930, the Long Service Medal was altered almost beyond recognition. The piece is now surmounted by a rectangular bar bearing the words REGULAR ARMY and the ribbon is threaded through a slit at the top.

Prior to the introduction of this medal it was the custom to award a second Long Service Medal for a subsequent qualifying period of eighteen years and it was continued in the case of all those whose first medal was of the old type. This accounts for the groups which have two Victorian Long Service Medals, or two such medals of different reigns. Such groups, as one might expect, are very rare as not many men complete thirty-six years' service.

Those whose first Long Service Medal is of the type introduced in 1930 will receive a bar thereto on completion of a further satisfactory qualifying period of eighteen years which will be indicated by a rosette on the ribbon when the medal is not worn, and by a bar attached to the ribbon when it is.

George VI (1936–52)

Except for the obvious difference in the case of the obverse, the medals are identical with those of the last reign.

Elizabeth II (1952–)

No alterations have been made except, of course, for the obverse.

COLONIAL FORCES LONG SERVICE AND GOOD CONDUCT MEDALS

These were instituted by a Royal Warrant dated 24th May, 1894, and were identical in every way with those awarded to the Home Army with the addition of the name of the colony above the wording on the reverse. The ribbons varied by means of a central stripe. The basic colour was the same crimson as for the Home medals, each colony had a distinctive central stripe as follows:

> Canada, white stripe.
> Natal, yellow stripe.
> New Zealand, light green stripe.
> South Australia, no stripe.
> Victoria, two dark green stripes.
> Cape of Good Hope, orange stripe.
> New South Wales, dark blue stripe.
> Queensland, light blue stripe.
> Tasmania, pink stripe.

The name of the colony is placed above the inscription on the reverse.

These medals remained in issue until 1909 when they were replaced by one of the same dimensions which bore the head of Edward VII, facing left, in military uniform. The reverse bore the words, FOR LONG SERVICE AND GOOD CONDUCT within a plain circle; between this circle and the edge was the wording PERMANENT FORCES OF THE EMPIRE BEYOND THE SEAS.

The ribbon was the same crimson with a central blue stripe bordered by two thin white ones.

When the new Long Service Medal was introduced for the Home Forces, in 1930, these colonial medals were discontinued. The Long Service Medals of the various forces throughout the Empire now bear their name on the bar attached to the medal except those awarded to members of the West African Frontier Force and the King's African Rifles which still carry the title of the unit on the reverse. Both these units wear the crimson ribbon with a central green stripe.

MILITIA LONG SERVICE AND GOOD CONDUCT MEDAL (1904–08)

Obverse: The effigy of King Edward VII facing left and legend EDWARDVS VII REX IMPERATOR, or that of George V and George VI with appropriate legend.

Reverse: MILITIA, at the top, and FOR LONG SERVICE AND GOOD CONDUCT.
Size: Oval, 1·5 by 1·35 ins.
Ribbon: 1·25 ins. wide. Pale blue.
Suspension: By means of a swivelling ring fitted to an ornate claw.
Naming: Impressed on the edge.

This medal was instituted in December, 1904, to be awarded to non-commissioned officers and men who, after 9th November, 1904, had completed eighteen years' service, continuous or otherwise, with a minimum of fifteen trainings.

When the Territorial and Reserve Forces Act, 1907, was passed most of the existing units of the Militia were converted to those of the Special Reserve. Those not converted were disbanded. This transference and disbandonment took place in 1908 so, naturally, as the Militia no longer existed, the medal was discontinued, in the case of home units. The Militia Medal with the George V head was, however, awarded to members of the King's other Malta Regiment of Militia, the Bermuda Artillery and the Royal Guernsey Light Infantry.

Until the formation of the Army Emergency Reserve in 1950 awards of the Efficiency Medal bearing the word "Militia" on the suspender were made to certain categories of the Supplementary Reserve. These are to be found bearing the head of King George V and King George VI. I have been informed that some were actually struck with the head of Queen Elizabeth II but that these were not issued and returned to the Royal Mint.

In the days of compulsory national service that rendered by the old Militia is either ignored or inclined to be jeered at as week-end soldiering. The irrefutable fact remains that the situation a hundred years ago, as regards the defence of these islands, was exactly the same as it is now—the duty of every citizen. The Regular Army then, as now, is little more than a glorified police force with military weapons, or the First Aid Detachment of our military strength. Now that soldiers have to be paid and the idea of them scrounging what they can in lieu of pay is no longer in official favour we have to strike a balance between our financial resources and manpower capabilities. Necessity was, therefore, the mother that produced the Militia in the first place. This nice name sounded too meek alongside those of "undeclared war", "poisoned gas", "atom bomb", etc., so it was changed to "Class 'Z' Reserve" but it is quite true to say that the ideas behind them both are identical.

Perhaps a few words about the old Militia may not be too out of place in a book which deals with the reward of those who served in it.

The Militia may be said to have owed its origin to King Alfred of Wessex who, during his reign, 872–901, made every male subject a soldier. As early as the time of the Saxons we find that the military force of the country was formed by a species of militia, and that every five hides of land, say every four hundred acres, were charged with the equipment of a man to serve the king. This is another way of saying that the owner of every approximately four hundred acres of land has to supply a fully equipped soldier. The men so raised were formed into bodies and placed under the command of an alderman who was elected by the people at the folkmotes. After the arrival of the Normans all landowners were compelled to supply men for the defence of the country under what was known as the Feudal System. The men were called out under the authority of Commissioners of Array, granted by the king, and sometimes the command was given to those who were given the commission of calling out the men of certain areas. I need hardly, I am sure, remind the reader that the term "commission" in this sense is the same as "authority". We have, therefore, arrived at the origin of the expressions such as commissioned officer, king's commission, etc. The term non-commissioned signifies that the holder of a rank said to be non-commissioned does not have the sovereign's authority but that of an officer who has himself been commissioned. For instance, a commanding officer can make a lance-corporal who then becomes a non-commissioned officer. Let me just finish the story by saying that a warrant-officer is one who has received a warrant from a body appointed by the sovereign. To recapitulate, a commissioned officer receives his commission from the sovereign (many of us old-timers received ours signed by the king himself); a warrant-officer receives a warrant from the Army Council; and, a non-commissioned officer receives his authority from a commissioned officer.

The militia as first raised was liable for service in any part of the country, but Edward III passed a law that no man should be liable for service outside the boundaries of his county of residence. In Mary's reign the responsibility for maintaining a sufficient and serviceable militia was delegated to the lords-lieutenant of counties and thus started what are now known as County Associations who are responsible to the Army Council for much that concerns the territorial units in their particular county.

Charles I, in 1641, as the result of the passing of the Petition of Right, found that he was unable to raise an army to suppress the rebellion in Ireland and was, therefore, compelled to hand that job over to Parliament. In the next year Parliament passed a bill whereby all the military forces, and the command of all forts and garrisons came into their hands. Charles refused to agree to this and sent out his commissioners and thus started that most dreadful of all wars—the Civil War.

On the accession of Charles II the national militia was re-established on its old footing and the lords-lieutenant were authorized to appoint, subject to the king's approval, officers to command local regiments which were called up for training for four consecutive days once a year.

Men who were mustered and trained by companies were called out four times a year for two consecutive days each time. These men were obliged to provide their own weapons and ammunition and I must say that if I had lived in those times I should have made certain that I always paraded in the rearmost rank.

These regulations proved unwieldly and expensive so that the easiest way of solving that particular problem was adopted and the militia disbanded. In 1756, the fear of a French invasion compelled the Government to import Hanoverian and Hessian soldiers to defend the country. This proved just a bit too much for the people to stand and they pulled themselves together and decided that even military service was preferable to having to submit to the

Herr Schmidts and Sticklegreubers parading about as the nation's sure shields.

There have been many changes in the method but the principle remains the same. *Si vis pacem, para bellum.*

IMPERIAL YEOMANRY LONG SERVICE AND GOOD CONDUCT MEDAL (1904–08)

Obverse: The effigy of King Edward VII facing left and legend EDWARDVS VII REX IMPERATOR.
Reverse: IMPERIAL YEOMANRY, at the top, and FOR LONG SERVICE AND GOOD CONDUCT.
Size: Oval, 1·5 by 1·35 ins.
Ribbon: Plain yellow.
Suspension: By means of a swivelling ring fitted to an ornate claw.
Naming: Impressed on the edge.

This medal was awarded to men who had completed ten years' service with a minimum of ten trainings. It was introduced in 1904 and discontinued in 1908.

Yeomanry Cavalry, as they were then called, were raised in almost every English county during the period of the threatened French invasion in the early years of the nineteenth century. They were mounted and equipped at their own expense and consisted of country gentlemen and farmers who, if the account in an old book of mine is accurate, did not do themselves too badly.

Their first recorded appearance in action—or perhaps it might be more accurate to say, the first time they were asked to do anything useful—was on 16th August, 1819, when some local yeomanry was sent to break up the meeting of agitators in St Peter's Field, Manchester. They performed their task with such zeal, and regrettable carnage, that the result of their efforts was styled the Peterloo Massacre. It was this massacre which, next year, caused the Cato Street Conspiracy, the ringleaders of which were first hanged then executed. It is a pity that cremation had not been introduced as this would have made trebly certain that the same individuals did not cause any further trouble.

Upon the passing of the Territorial and Reserve Forces Act, 1907, yeomanry units were transferred to the Territorial Army though they were allowed to retain their old title of "Yeomanry".

VICTORIA VOLUNTEERS LONG SERVICE MEDAL (1894–1908)

Obverse: Five stars on a cross of St George surrounded by the words AUT PACE AUT BELLO VICTORIA.
Reverse: The words FOR LONG SERVICE AND GOOD CONDUCT.
Size: 1·42 ins. diameter.
Ribbon: Dark red with even deeper red edges.

C

The specimen in my possession was very damaged and I am not sure whether it had a straight or scroll suspender originally. The naming was in indented capitals.

NEW ZEALAND TERRITORIAL SERVICE MEDAL

Obverse: His Majesty's effigy in military uniform without titles but the words NEW ZEALAND TERRITORIAL, and 12 YEARS SERVICE under the bust.
Reverse: A very mournful looking kiwi between two sprays of laurel.
Size: 1·42 ins. diameter.
Ribbon: The original colour was plain khaki but was later altered to khaki with crimson edges.
Suspension: By a scroll suspender.
Naming: In indented capitals.

This is rather an extraordinary medal in that it is a sort of interim affair which is cancelled on completion of twenty years' service by that which follows immediately.
The same remarks concerning cancellation apply if the recipient subsequently receives an imperial long service award.

NEW ZEALAND LONG AND EFFICIENT SERVICE MEDAL

Obverse: The Imperial Crown resting on the Sword and Sceptre which are crossed on a tasselled cushion. The Crown is surmounted by a five-pointed star and surrounded by a spring of oak on the left and laurel on the right.
Reverse: FOR LONG AND EFFICIENT SERVICE in three lines.
Size: 1·42 ins. diameter.
Ribbon: 1·25 ins. wide, crimson, with two central white stripes divided by a very thin one of crimson.
Suspension: By a ring.
Naming: In indented capitals.

This medal was awarded to those who had served a total period of twenty years' non-continuous service, or sixteen continuous.

VOLUNTEER LONG SERVICE MEDAL
(1894–1908)

Obverse: The crowned and veiled bust of Queen Victoria facing left, and wearing the Star of the Order of the Garter; the legend, VICTORIA REGINA. The whole surrounded by a beaded rim.
Reverse: A scroll inscribed FOR LONG SERVICE IN THE VOLUNTEER FORCE, within a wreath of laurel and palm. The whole surrounded by a beaded rim.
Size: 1·42 ins. diameter.
Ribbon: 1·25 ins. wide, plain green.
Suspension: By a straight suspender.

Naming: Usually found unnamed though some have impressed or engraved naming.

This medal was instituted in June, 1894, for award to volunteers on completion of twenty years' service. It was made obsolete in 1908.

The medal bearing the effigy of Edward VII is the same except that the rim is plain instead of beaded.

The difference between a volunteer and a militiaman is that the former volunteered to serve whereas the latter had to serve as he had been drawn by ballot to do so. There were, in addition to the individual volunteers serving with militia units, complete units of volunteers in all branches of the Army. It would take too long and perhaps serve no useful purpose to detail all the various units. Suffice it to say that many of the large firms and organizations formed their own specialized companies of volunteers who trained on their own to a great extent yet placed themselves at the disposal of the country should the need arise.

These men, and the concerns that supplied them, were true patriots as the maintenance costs of some that I could mention were very considerable indeed and the experimental work which they carried out with the designs and materials furnished by their employers were the forerunners of not a few of the inventions which played a conspicuous part first in the Boer War and then in the First World War.

By an Army Order published in November, 1906, this medal was awarded to officers of the Honourable Artillery Company who had served in the ranks but had not the necessary qualifications to earn the Volunteer Officers Decoration, providing that they were serving on the 1st January, 1906. It was also awarded to non-commissioned officers and men who were serving on the same date.

The ribbon specified was that of King Edward's racing colours, described as "dark blue and cerise longitudinal stripes with a narrow edging of yellow".

COLONIAL VOLUNTEER LONG SERVICE AND GOOD CONDUCT MEDAL (1896–1921)

The obverse and reverse of this medal are similar to that of the last except that the legend on the former reads ET IMPERATRIX or ET IMPERATOR according to the reign at the time of award.

COLONIAL AUXILIARY FORCES LONG SERVICE MEDAL (1899–1921)

Obverse: The crowned and veiled bust of Queen Victoria facing left, with legend VICTORIA REGINA ET IMPERATRIX.

Reverse: An ornamental shield, crowned, with oak leaves to the left and laurel to the right of the crown; also, FOR LONG SERVICE IN THE COLONIAL AUXILIARY FORCES.

Size: 1·42 ins. diameter.

Ribbon: 1·25 ins. wide, green.

Suspension: By a plain straight suspender.
Designer: The obverse was designed by T. Brock and engraved by G. W.
De Saulles; the reverse was designed and engraved by G. W. De Saulles.
Naming: In impressed or engraved lettering on the edge. Some are found
unnamed.

This medal, the obverse of which, naturally, bears the effigy and styles of
the reigning sovereign, was not discontinued in 1908 like the Volunteer
Medal because the auxiliary forces continued to be known as such till 1921.

TERRITORIAL FORCE
EFFICIENCY MEDAL (1908–21)

Obverse: The bust of the king in military uniform facing left.
Reverse: The words TERRITORIAL FORCE EFFICIENCY MEDAL in four lines,
or after 1921 TERRITORIAL EFFICIENCY MEDAL.
Size: Oval 1·5 by 1·25 ins.
Ribbon: The original ribbon was 1·25 ins. wide, green with a central yellow
stripe but, in 1920, it was altered to green with yellow edges.
Suspension: By a ring fitted to a swivelling ornate claw.
Naming: Impressed on the edge.

This medal was instituted by an Army Order in June, 1908, and changed
when the title of the force was altered to Territorial Army in 1921 to Territorial Efficiency Medal. A clasp is granted for each additional six years.
It was awarded to non-commissioned officers and men on completion of
twelve years' service.

EFFICIENCY MEDAL (1930–   )

Obverse: The sovereign's effigy and appropriate legend.
Reverse: The inscription FOR EFFICIENT SERVICE.
Size: Oval, 1·5 by 1·25 ins.
Ribbon: 1·25 ins. wide, green with yellow edges.
Suspension: By an ornate suspender which bears the appropriate wording to
denote for which service the award is made.
Naming: In impressed lettering on the edge.

This medal was instituted in 1930 to supersede all previous long service
awards to non-regular troops. The subsidiary title on the mount denotes
whether the service was in the Territorial Army or in any other Auxiliary
Force of the Commonwealth. It is also to be found with the clasp "Militia".
(See Militia L.S.G.C.)
Qualification for the award is twelve years' efficient service in the ranks,
service in West Africa and war service counting double and in certain circumstances officers who have served in the ranks may qualify; but see Efficiency Decoration. A clasp is given for further periods of six years providing
the service is continuous. Women of the A.T.S., now the W.R.A.C., are

eligible for this award. It is possible for a man to have qualified for both the Efficiency Medal and the previous award, the Territorial Efficiency Medal. With all these awards the Honourable Artillery Company continued to wear the special ribbon described earlier. (See Volunteer L.S.)

SPECIAL RESERVE LONG SERVICE AND GOOD CONDUCT MEDAL (1908–21)

Obverse: The sovereign's effigy with the appropriate legend.
Reverse: The inscription, FOR LONG SERVICE AND GOOD CONDUCT; above SPECIAL RESERVE.
Size: Oval, 1·5 by 1·25 ins.
Ribbon: 1·25 ins. wide; dark blue with a central light blue stripe.
Suspension: By an oval ring fitted to an ornate claw.
Naming: In impressed lettering on the edge.

This medal was awarded to non-commissioned officers and men who completed fifteen years' service and attended not less than fifteen trainings.

VOLUNTEER OFFICERS' DECORATION (1892–1908)

This decoration consists of an oval badge, consisting of a silver oak wreath tied with gold; in the centre is the appropriate Royal Cypher surmounted by a crown. The badge is suspended from a silver ring. The ribbon is plain green, 1·5 ins. wide, which was attached to the tunic by a straight brooch ornamented with oak leaves.

The object of the decoration was to "reward the long and meritorious services of officers of proved capacity". The qualifying period was twenty years.

COLONIAL OFFICERS' AUXILIARY FORCES DECORATION (1899–1921)

This decoration is in the form of an oval badge with an open-work centre consisting of the Royal Cypher. Around this is a band bearing COLONIAL AUXILIARY FORCES. The whole is surmounted by a crown and hangs from a plain wire loop suspender. The ribbon is plain green, 1·25 ins. wide.

TERRITORIAL DECORATION (1908–21)

This decoration is almost identical with the Volunteer Officers' Decoration. It has the appropriate Royal Cypher in the centre and hangs from a ribbon 1·5 ins. wide of green with a yellow central stripe.

The qualifying period was twenty years.

EFFICIENCY DECORATION (1930–)

This is now the only decoration awarded to officers of forces other than regular and supersedes all those dealt with previously.

It is in the form of an oval badge composed of a silver oak wreath tied with gold. In the centre is the Royal Cypher surmounted by a crown, both in gold. The badge is worn suspended from a green ribbon with a central yellow stripe, the whole 1·5 ins. wide. At the top of the ribbon is a bar brooch which bears the title of the force with which the recipient was serving.

The qualifying period of twenty years has now been reduced to twelve, clasp for further periods of six years. Regulations governing awards to officers who have served in the ranks are somewhat complicated but broadly speaking one-half of rank service may be counted provided it has not been counted towards the award of the Efficiency Medal. Providing that the full period of twelve years has been served both in the ranks and as an officer there is no reason why an officer should not be granted both the decoration and the medal. As with the medal war service counts double.

AIR EFFICIENCY AWARD (1942–)

Description: An oval silver medal bearing on the obverse the effigy of the sovereign, and on the reverse the words AIR EFFICIENCY AWARD.

Clasp: Of silver, bearing on the obverse an Eagle with outstretched wings surmounted by a crown.

Ribbon: 1·5 ins. wide, green, with two central stripes of pale blue, ⅛ in. wide.

I am indebted to the Air Ministry for kindly supplying me with the particulars concerning this award which was instituted by a Royal Warrant dated 17th August, 1942, which was revised by one dated 27th December, 1946, and annulled by another dated 12th April, 1951, that is now in force.

Airmen and airwomen, both officers and other ranks, of any Auxiliary or Volunteer Air Force raised in the United Kingdom, or in any of the Colonies and Dominions are eligible providing they have completed the necessary qualifying period which is ten years and shall include not less than five years' actual service. This slightly confusing qualification is brought about by the fact that certain types of service count more than their actual so that it would otherwise be possible for a person to become eligible for the award within a period of five years from joining.

The qualifying service depends on the date of enlistment as follows:

If before 3rd September, 1939:
1. Service in a flying duties category in the Royal Auxiliary Air Force, or Royal Air Force Volunteer Reserve, count as time and a half. Embodied, or mobilized service, in this category during the Second World War counts treble time. Time spent in service or training under the Reserve and Auxiliary Forces (Training) Act, 1951, counts double.
2. Other service in the above, or the Women's Auxiliary Air Force counts as single time, but embodied or mobilized service during the Second World War counts double. Periods of service, or training, under the Reserve and Auxiliary Forces (Training) Act, 1951, counts as time and a half.

If after 18th August, 1946:

1. Service in a flying duties category in the Royal Auxiliary Air Force, or the Royal Air Force Volunteer Reserve ordinarily counts as time and a half, but periods of service or training under the Reserve and Auxiliary Forces (Training) Act, 1951, count as double time.
2. Other service in the above forces ordinarily counts as single time, but periods of service or training under the Reserve and Auxiliary Forces (Training) Act, 1951, counts as time and a half.

In addition to the services already mentioned, the following are also reckonable:

1. Except for the services mentioned under those who joined before 3rd September, 1939 embodied or mobilized service in the R.A.A.F., R.A.F.V.R., or the Women's Auxiliary Air Force during the Second World War counts as single time.
2. Service in the W.A.A.F. Reserve or W.A.A.F. Volunteer Reserve counts as single time.
3. Service in a flying duties category on the Royal Auxiliary Air Force General List, in the Royal Auxiliary Air Force Reserve of Officers, or in the Royal Air Force Auxiliary Reserve of Airmen on an engagement which commenced before 3rd September, 1939, counts as three-quarter time, providing that the specified minimum amount of flying per annum has been carried out.
4. Service in units mentioned in the last paragraph which started before 3rd September, 1939, counts as half time, providing there is a liability for annual training.
5. Service in a regular force during the First World War counts as single time, and in a non-regular force double providing that the latter service counts as double for the efficiency award in the force concerned.

Service which does not entail the liability to do a certain amount of training in peace time does not qualify for the award.

A bar is awarded for the completion of every subsequent ten years of satisfactory service.

ROYAL AIR FORCE LONG SERVICE MEDAL (1918–   )

Obverse: The Royal effigy and legend.
Reverse: An Eagle surmounted by the Imperial Crown and words FOR LONG SERVICE AND GOOD CONDUCT.
Size: 1·42 ins. diameter.
Ribbon: 1·25 ins. wide, equal dark blue and crimson with white edges. The blue to the left facing the wearer.
Suspension: By a scroll suspender.
Naming: In impressed capitals.

When the Royal Air Force was formed, many of the original personnel had previous service in the Royal Navy or Army so that this service was allowed to count. This accounts for what to some of us seemed the unusual sight of a man wearing a Long Service Ribbon so soon after the formation of the service. Subsequent qualifying periods earn a bar.

ROYAL OBSERVER CORPS MEDAL (1950–)

Obverse: The Royal effigy and legend.
Reverse: A representation of an Elizabethan coast-watcher holding an upraised torch while standing by a signal fire, the whole surrounded by the words THE ROYAL OBSERVER CORPS MEDAL.
Size: 1·42 ins. diameter.
Ribbon: 1·25 ins. wide, light blue with a silver-grey central stripe bordered by narrow ones of dark blue.
Naming: In impressed capitals.
Composition: Cupro-nickel.

This medal for which the Royal Warrant of authorization is dated 31st January, 1950, is awarded to those who:

1. Have served twelve years in the Corps since 24th August, 1939, excluding the "stand-down" period, 5th May, 1945—31st December, 1946.
2. Served as a Special Constable employed in observer duties in the Observer Corps (which was the former title of the Royal Observer Corps) under Home Office administration before 24th August, 1939, excluding all service which has been reckoned towards the Special Constable's Medal, or bar thereto.
3. Performed full-time salaried or paid service between 3rd September, 1939—5th May, 1945. Only one half of such service performed at other times may be reckoned towards the qualifying period. It should be particularly noted that only continuous service will count except for that which is broken by a period of service in the Armed Forces providing that the Corps was rejoined within six months of leaving them. Those who rejoined the Corps within six months of the end of the "stand-down" period may reckon otherwise unbroken service prior to 5th May, 1945.

It is a moot point whether it would not have been better to have awarded this medal in bronze if the question of cost is in consideration. We can certainly claim to be inconsistent with our awards when a special constable gets one in bronze, an observer in cupro-nickel, yet a regular member of one of the Services need not stay long enough in a zone to even hear a suspicious noise and gets a silver medal.

One is tempted to ask whether, if voluntary service for several years is worth a medal at all, it is not worth a silver one. I wonder what is the difference in cost to the State of a silver and cupro-nickel medal. If we are to rate the service by the medal awarded then we are led to presume that some are almost valueless—why, then, all the appeals for recruits?

I contend that this Commonwealth was saved, and will be saved in the future, by the combined efforts of all the Services. I contend, too, that it is invidious and unnecessary, to make a distinction between the services rendered by special constables and observers who both performed their role to the best of their ability, as did the fire service and many other bodies that saved London and an untold number of lives.

If the Long Service Medals are the same for all the Commonwealth's regular soldiers, except for the name on the bar, then why cannot the medal for all the voluntary services be the same except for the bar? Why, I wonder, is the time factor, or whatever it is, so much easier for the Royal Observer Corps than the Special Constabulary that the former has to serve twelve years for his cupro-nickel award to the latter's nine for his bronze. Unless the Special Constable has to put in 25 per cent more time than the Observer the additional three years of qualifying period for the latter are unfair.

CADET FORCES MEDAL (1950–)

Obverse: The crowned effigy of the sovereign.
Reverse: The inscription THE CADET FORCES MEDAL, and a representation of a torch.
Size: 1·42 ins. diameter.
Ribbon: 1·25 ins. wide, green with yellow edges, and narrow stripes of dark blue, red and light blue. The dark blue stripe should be worn nearest the centre, i.e. to the left when facing the wearer.
Composition: Cupro-nickel.

This medal was instituted in 1950 for award to those granted commissions prior to 1st February, 1942, in any of the Services Cadets whether Naval, Military or Air.

The necessary service consists of twelve years' qualifying service subsequent to 3rd September, 1926, inclusive. Service during the Second World War, in the period 3rd September, 1939 to 2nd September, 1945, being reckoned as double.

A cupro-nickel clasp, to be attached to the ribbon when the medal is worn is awarded for every subsequent completed twelve years' service. A cupro-nickel rose emblem denoting the award of each clasp may be worn on the ribbon when the ribbon only is worn.

In precedence the award comes immediately after the King's (or Queen's) Medal for Champion Shots in the Military Forces.

THE ARMY EMERGENCY RESERVE DECORATION (1952–)

Description: A silver oak wreath tied with gold, having the Royal Cypher and crown in gold in the centre.
Ribbon: 1·5 ins. wide, dark blue with a central yellow stripe, suspended from a silver bar brooch bearing the inscription ARMY EMERGENCY RESERVE.
Precedence: Immediately in front of the Volunteer Officers' Decoration.

This decoration was instituted in 1952 to be conferred on officers who have completed twelve years' continuous service in the Army Emergency Reserve. Officers who completed ten years' continuous efficient service in the Supplementary or Army Emergency Reserve who were commissioned between 8th August, 1924 and 15th May, 1948, and who were transferred to the Regular Army Reserve of Officers after completion of the ten years were also eligible for the decoration.

Service in many of the other reserves is also counted providing that the same service is not also used to qualify for the Efficiency Decoration.

A clasp may be worn on the ribbon by those who complete eighteen years' efficient service with an additional clasp for each further period of six years.

Service in the ranks counts as half providing it was completed in a continuous manner in designated Reserve Forces, such as the Emergency Reserve or Auxiliary Military Forces of the Commonwealth.

Other ranks of the Army Emergency Reserve receive the Efficiency Medal suspended from a clasp inscribed ARMY EMERGENCY RESERVE and suspended from a ribbon of dark blue with three vertical yellow stripes at the centre.

CANADIAN FORCES DECORATION (1950–   )

A ten-sided silver-gilt medal. Each side represents one of the provinces of Canada.

Obverse: Head of Queen Elizabeth II (classical head), Canada in the exergue.

Reverse: Three maple leaves surmounted by a naval crown and, beneath, an Eagle with spread wings, under this again the word SERVICE on a scroll, in line with the lower part of the naval crown two fleur-de-lis.

Ribbon: Red with three narrow white stripes evenly spaced.

Suspension: Two sprays issuing from a maple leaf.

This decoration was instituted in June, 1950, with the approval of King George VI. It supersedes all long service awards previously awarded to the Canadian Armed Forces which were those commonly awarded to the forces of Great Britain and other nations of the Commonwealth. It is given for twelve years' service, under certain conditions, to the Canadian Navy, Army and Air Force both Regular and Auxiliary. Officers and men are equally eligible for this award and receive the same medal and ribbon.

COMPARISONS

It may be of interest to compare the various awards to the armed forces. Orders are conferred on the more senior officers of all three Services but in the case of gallantry and long service awards each service has its own medals. The Victoria Cross is in a class of its own. Only one consideration governs the award of the Victoria Cross—exceptional gallantry in the face of the enemy. Any man (or woman) of any rank in the Royal Navy, the Army or the Royal Air Force may win the Victoria Cross, or, indeed, in certain circumstances a civilian. Officers of all three Services are eligible for the Distinguished Service Order and in 1914 the Military Cross was instituted for award to junior officers of the Army (Captain—later Major and below).

The equivalent award to officers of the Royal Navy, the Distinguished Service Cross (formerly the Conspicuous Service Cross) was already in existence. In 1919 the Distinguished Flying Cross was instituted as an award to officers of the Royal Air Force. The Distinguished Conduct Medal for the Army and the Conspicuous Gallantry Medal for the Royal Navy have long been in existence but during the First World War the need for awards which could be more freely given was realized and for the Royal Navy the Distinguished Service Medal and for the Army the Military Medal were instituted. The special needs of the Royal Air Force were not forgotten and 1919 saw the grant of the Distinguished Flying Medal. For exceptional flying services (not in action) the Air Force Medal and the Air Force Cross were authorized. Not until 1943 was a higher gallantry award to the Royal Air Force instituted—the Conspicuous Gallantry Medal (Air). In certain circumstances all these awards may be won by a member of one of the other Services. Officers and men of the Royal Navy and Royal Air Force have been awarded the Military Cross, Distinguished Conduct Medal and Military Medal, while men of the Maritime A.A. Regiment Royal Artillery have received the Distinguished Service Medal. Recently several awards of Royal Air Force decorations have been made to the Army Air Corps. Men of the armed forces are, of course, eligble for the various civilian awards for gallantry, e.g. the George Cross, Albert Medals, George Medal, etc., also the O.B.E. and M.B.E., and the British Empire Medal. These awards have been, and indeed still are, sometimes given for actions for which one of the service awards would appear to be more appropriate.

Known to every old soldier as the "rhoot gongi" because it is said "to come up with the rations" a medal for long Service and Good Conduct has been granted to the Army since 1830. The same old soldier will tell you that the Long Service Medal is given for "eighteen years of undiscovered crime". In fact it is not lightly given. Many a man has found that a long forgotten indiscretion as a young soldier has held up this award. Similar long service medals, but, of course, with different designs, are awarded to the Royal Navy and Royal Air Force. There is, however, no long service award for officers of the regular forces. Service in the Naval Auxiliary Forces is rewarded by the Reserve Decoration for officers and a Long Service Medal for ratings, the Army counterparts being the Efficiency Decoration and the Efficiency Medal with various subsidiary clasps. The Royal Air Force strike a new note with the Air Efficiency Award which is granted to officers and men alike. The Army alone has, with the Meritorious Service Medal, a further award for which the main qualification is long service.

With the integration of the Services under the Ministry of Defence it is possible that changes in these awards may take place, perhaps on the lines of the Canadian Forces Decoration. It certainly seems that a system which permits the grant of the same award to an office cleaner for forty years' service as that awarded to a man for risking his life to save others requires some alteration.

CORONATION, DURBAR AND JUBILEE MEDALS

Though the medal awarded to commemorate the coronation of Edward VII was the first to be worn, this chapter will show that it was really the twelfth of a series which, with a gap, dates back to Edward VI.

It would be correct to say that those struck before 1902 are rare, but there must be some about as I had three of them in my collection.

The sizes of the earlier ones will be given so that the reader can see that they varied from just over 1 in. to about 2⅓ ins. All are circular except that for the coronation of Edward VII.

EDWARD VI

Obverse: The king facing right holding a sword over his right shoulder with the orb and cross in his left hand. Reading to the right around the figure, starting from the top, are a crown rose, crowned portcullis, crowned lis and crowned harp. Around the whole the legend, Edwardvs.V.I.D.G. Ang.Fr.Et.Hi.Rex.Fidei.Defns.Et.In.Terris.Ang.Et.Hib.Eccle. Capvt.Svpremvm.Coronatvs.Est.M.D.xlviixx.Febrva.Etatis.Decimo.
Reverse: The same legend in Hebrew and Greek.
Size: 2·375 ins.
Metal: Gold.

This medal is interesting quite apart from the fact that it is the first of a series. To the best of my knowledge it is the only medal which bears the age of the person in whose honour it was struck and, of British medals at any rate, to have been chased after casting.

At the time of his father's death the new king was only nine years old but Henry VIII had appointed a Council of Regency headed by the boy's uncle, the Earl of Hertford, to manage the affairs of government. One of the sixteen members of the Council was the Archbishop Cranmer who was responsible for the First Book of Common Prayer being available in English. It is impossible that the boy should be credited with the idea of striking a medal to commemorate his accession, but there do not appear to be any records to show who did.

It is difficult to understand why it should bear an inscription in two languages and doubtful whether any other medal can claim to have three languages on it altogether. This multiplicity seems particularly strange, and unnecessary, at a time when very few people could read their own language let alone three others!

71

CHARLES I. English Coronation

Obverse: The bust of the king facing right wearing the collar and badge of the Order of the Garter and legend, CAROLVS.I.D.G.MAG.BRITAN.FRAN.ET. HIB.REX.

Reverse: A mailed arm protruding from a cloud and holding a sword. Legend, DONEC.PAX.REDDITA.TERRIS. In the exergue, CORON.FEBRV. 1626.

Size: 1·19 ins.
Metal: Gold.

There is nothing of particular interest about this medal except, perhaps, the legend on the reverse which means "Until peace returns to the earth". One could infer from this that once peace was restored the king would abdicate but I expect the translation intended was to signify that he would strive for peace. We must not take some of these old legends too seriously.

CHARLES I. Scottish Coronation

Obverse: The bust of the king, facing left, crowned. Legend, CAROLVS. D.G.SCOTTAE.ANGLIAE.FR.ET.HIB.REX.

Reverse: A rose tree and thistle; in the exergue, CORON.18.IVNII 1633.

Edge: Ex.AVRO.VT.IN.SCOTIA.REPERITVR.BRIOT.FECIT.EDINBVRG 1633.

Size: 1·12 ins.
Metals: Gold and silver.

This medal, like the former, was designed and engraved by the French engraver, Nicholas Briot, who was subsequently appointed chief engraver to the Tower Mint and Master of the Scottish Mint.

The two interesting features of this medal are the inscription on the edge and the gold from which the three known specimens were made.

It is the first known British medal with wording on the edge. The gold came from the Lead Hills on the borders of Dumfriesshire and Lanarkshire.

CHARLES II

Obverse: The crowned bust of the king facing right with long hair and wearing the collar of the Order of the Garter and legend, CAROLVS.IID.G. ANG.SCO.FR.ET.HI.REX.

Reverse: The king seated, facing left, holding the Sceptre, while being crowned by peace, and legend, EVERSOMISSVS SVCCVRRERE.SECLO.XXIII. APR.1661.

Size: 1·16 ins.
Metal: Gold.

This is the first coronation medal to be distributed—in this case to spectators. An account of the event states, "The streets were gay with decorations; trumpets re-echoed throughout the highways; medals were distributed."

It was as well that the crowd could not foresee the events which were to happen during the reign of this king whose marriage to Catherine of Braganza gave us Bombay and Tangiers and him no children, though he had twelve by eight other women, six of whom were married at the time.

I wish I could find how these medals were distributed as we are left to imagine any method from them being shovelled from a cart to presentation amidst pomp. The character of the man makes either possible.

JAMES II

Obverse: The laureated bust of the king, in armour and mantle facing right. Legend, JACOBVS.II.D.G.ANG.SCO.FR.ET.HI.REX.

Reverse: A hand holding a crown over a laurel wreath on a cushion. Legend, A.MILITARI.AD.REGIAM. In the exergue, INAURGRAT. 23.A.P.1685.

Size: 1·36 ins.

Metal: Gold.

This medal was also distributed to spectators but, again, I have been unable to trace the method of distribution.

WILLIAM III and MARY

Obverse: Conjoint busts, facing right. Legend, GVLIELMVS.ET.MARIA.REX. ET.REGINA.

Reverse: A representation of Phaeton falling from his chariot on to burning ground. Legend, NE TOTVS ABSVMATVR. In the exergue, INAVGRAT.II A.P.1689.

Metal: Gold.

Two hundred of these medals were distributed and caused considerable dissatisfaction in the Jacobite ranks as the representation of Phaeton was taken to be James II who fled the country four months before. The inference is of course, correct, but one might doubt the wisdom of calling attention to the fact on his successor's coronation medal.

ANNE

Obverse: Her draped bust facing left and legend, ANNA.D.G.MAG.BR.FR. ET.HIB.REGINA.

Reverse: Athene, the goddess of wisdom, hurling thunder against a double headed monster with four arms and a long tail. Legend, VICEM GERIT. ILLA . TONANTIS. In the exergue, INAVGRAT.XXIII.AP.MDCCII.

Size: 1·39 ins.

Metal: Gold and silver.

The chief interest in this medal lies in the fact that two strikings were made. A specially thick one was presented to foreign representatives in addition to the 800 gold and 1,200 silver ones for home distribution.

A month or so after the coronation a further striking was made so that every member of the House of Commons could receive a medal but these are included in the number quoted.

GEORGE I

Obverse: A bust of the king in armour facing right. Legend, GEORGIVS.D.G. MAG.BR.FR.ET.HIB.REX.
Reverse: The king, seated, being crowned by Britannia. Legend, INAVGRAT. XX.OST.MDCCXIIII.
Size: 1·35 ins.
Metal: Gold and silver.

This medal, of which 300 gold and 1,200 silver were struck, is unusual in that it depicts the sovereign on both sides.

GEORGE II

Obverse: A bust of the king in armour and mantle facing left. Legend, GEORGIVS.II.D:G.MAG.BR.FR.ET.HIB.REX.
Reverse: The king, seated, being crowned by Concord who carries a cornucopia. In the exergue, CORON.XI.OCTOB.MDCCXXVII.
Size: 1·35 ins.
Metal: Gold and silver.

Two hundred gold and eight hundred silver medals were struck.

GEORGE III

Obverse: The king in armour facing right. Legend, GEORGIVS.III.D.G.M. BRI.FRA.ET.HIB.REX.F.D.
Reverse: The king, seated, being crowned by Britannia. Legend, PATRIAE. OVANTI. In the exergue, CORON.XXII.SEPT.MDCCLXI.
Size: 1·33 ins.
Metal: Gold and silver.

In addition to this medal, of which the same number as the last were struck, there was one with the effigy of his consort, Queen Charlotte. The reverse of this shows her being crowned by an angel while standing before the altar. It is a minute fraction larger than the king's and was struck in both gold and silver for distribution among the royal ladies.

GEORGE IV

Obverse: The laureated head of the king facing left. Legend, GEORGIVS IIII D . G BRITANNIARUM REX F . D.
Reverse: Figures representative of England, Scotland and Ireland advancing towards the king who is seated on a dais on the left in the act of being crowned by a winged figure. Legend, PROPRIO JAM JURE ANIMO PATERNO. In the exergue, INAVGVRATVS DIE JUL II.XIX.ANNO. MDCCCXXI.

Size: 1·38 ins.
Metal: Gold and silver.

This medal, of which the same numbers as the last were so I infer, awarded, recalls the unique scenes which took place prior to the coronation.

Queen Caroline, disgusted with George's behaviour when Prince Regent, had gone to the Continent. One of his first acts on accession was to present to Parliament accusations against his wife's conduct while she was abroad. Owing to an insufficient majority having been obtained the bill for allowing a divorce was not passed. On the day of the coronation the queen, with obviously every right to be crowned as the king's consort, was repulsed when trying to gain admittance to both Westminster Hall and the Abbey.

I smiled when I read of the disappointment of many of those who could not get into the Abbey for the coronation of our present queen, Elizabeth II, and wondered how many realized that there was an occasion when even the queen herself could not get in.

WILLIAM IV

Obverse: The king's head facing right. Legend, WILLIAM THE FOURTH CROWNED SEP : 8 1831.
Reverse: Queen Adelaide facing right. Legend, ADELAIDE QUEEN CONSORT . CROWNED SEP : 8 1831.
Size: 1·32 ins.
Metal: Gold and silver.

I particularly like this medal because I do not have to strain my limited knowledge of Latin to translate the legends. It has always struck me as a little strange that at a time when only a few people could read their own language practically all the legends on medals were in Latin.

It is noteworthy that the number of gold medals struck outnumbered those in silver and copper combined; the figures being, gold 1,067, silver 727 and 100 of bronzed copper.

VICTORIA

Obverse: Head of queen facing left. Legend, VICTORIA D G . BRITANNIARUM REGINA F . D .
Reverse: The queen seated on the right holding the Orb and Sceptre. The three figures of Britannia, Scotia, and Hibernia are depicted advancing towards her while jointly holding the Imperial Crown. A lion holding four thunderbolts is immediately behind the queen. Legend, ERIMUS TIBI NOBILE REGNUM. (We will be a noble kingdom to thee.) In the exergue, INAUGURATA DIE JUN II XXVIII MDCCCXXXVIII.
Size: 1·44 ins.
Metal: Gold, silver gilt and silver.

This medal was designed by B. Pistrucci who also designed that of George IV. The similarity of the obverses should be noted. The detail is superb and may be equalled but never surpassed by any medal struck in this country. The relief on the obverse is considerably deeper than on the reverse. How true was the legend to prove as I think it is generally agreed that the Empire was at the height of its glory during her reign. When the British lion growled people took notice and we did not have to take our orders from upstarts who climb on to the international bandwaggon by murder, blackmail or bloody (but sometimes bloodless) revolution and then, pistol in hand, pretend that they got there by popular vote.

EDWARD VII

Obverse: Crowned bust of the king facing right wearing the collar of the Garter. Legend, EDWARD VII CROWNED 9 . AVGVST 1902.

Reverse: The crowned and veiled bust of the queen facing right. Legend, ALEXANDRA QUEEN CONSORT. Below the bust is a wreath of roses and the date 9 . AUG . 1902 on a scroll.

Sizes: Gold and silver 2·18 ins. and 1·22 ins. Bronze 2·16 ins.

Metal: Gold, silver and bronze.

This medal is interesting in that it is the only one struck to commemorate this coronation which bears the correct date. The date fixed for the coronation was 26th June but the king developed appendicitis so that the ceremony had to be postponed to the date 9th August. I believe that specimens with the June date were distributed but I have not seen any.

These medals cannot be considered awards as known today. They appear, in many cases, to have been distributed indiscriminately and apparently were not intended to be worn as they have no means of suspension; rather they should be considered as purely commemoration medals although they seem to have been official.

DELHI IMPERIAL ASSEMBLAGE COMMEMORATION MEDAL, 1877
(Commonly known as the Empress of India Medal)

Obverse: Crowned and veiled bust of the queen facing left. On the left is the word VICTORIA; on the right 1st JANUARY; under the bust the date, 1877. The whole is surrounded by a dotted border.

Reverse: Across the centre is EMPRESS OF INDIA; above this the same in Persian and below the same in Hindi. Around the circumference is an indented border.

Size: 2·3 ins. diameter.

Ribbon: 1·75 ins. wide. Dark red with ⅛ in. wide yellow stripe at each edge.

Suspension: A plain flat suspender, with a curved depression in the centre where attached to the post.

Designer: C. G. Adams.

Metal: Gold and silver.

Although not strictly a Coronation or Jubilee medal this medal was awarded to commemorate a significant event affecting the status of the sovereign and should be included here.

Queen Victoria was proclaimed Empress of India on 1st January, 1877, and this medal was awarded to a few British officials and native princes in gold. Silver specimens were similarly awarded to lesser dignatories and a specially selected private of every European and native regiment in India.

Although the medal had a straight suspender it was intended to be worn suspended from the neck. In 1882 it was ordered that military recipients were not allowed to wear this medal in uniform.

QUEEN VICTORIA GOLDEN JUBILEE MEDAL, 1887

Obverse: Crowned and veiled bust of the queen with the legend: VICTORIA D.G. REGINA ET IMPERATRIX F.D.

Reverse: In eight lines the words IN COMMEMORATION OF THE 50TH YEAR OF THE REIGN OF QUEEN VICTORIA 21 JUNE 1887, inclosed in a wreath of roses, thistles and shamrocks tied at the base by a ribbon and surmounted by a crown.

Size: 1·25 ins.

Ribbon: 1·25 ins. wide. Pale blue with centre stripe of Garter blue and Garter blue edges.

Suspension: Ring.

Metal: Gold, silver and bronze.

Designer: C. Emptmeyer.

By an order dated 10th October, the Queen commanded that this medal took precedence over all other medals which means that it was to be worn immediately after decorations and before all campaign medals. This regulation, however, no longer applies and all Coronation and Jubilee medals are now worn immediately before awards for long service. Gold medals were awarded to members of the Royal household and foreign nobility, silver to military officers and officials and the bronze to Imperial and Dominion troops, native orderlies, etc., who took part in the ceremonies.

QUEEN VICTORIA DIAMOND JUBILEE MEDAL, 1897

This medal is the same in all respects as the last medal, except that "60th" replaces "50th", and the date "20th, June, 1897" replaces "21st June, 1887" A clasp dated 1897 surmounted by a crown was given to recipients who had already received the 1887 medal.

A unique medal was awarded to Lord Mayors in gold (14) and to Mayors in silver (512) which is included here as a matter of interest. The obverse bears the diademed and veiled bust of Queen Victoria (as on the India 1895 Medal) surrounded by the legend, VICTORIA ANNVM REGNI SEXAGESIMVM FELICITER CLAVDIT XX IVN MDCCCXCVII. On the reverse is the famous "Young Head" as used on medals and coins from 1837 to 1887. To the left of the head is the legend, LONGITVDO DIERVM IN DEXTERA EVIS and

on the right ET IN SINISTRA GLORIA. The head is set above a spray of laurel
and the date, 1837. These designs are in a circle on the medal which is
diamond shaped (each side 1½ ins. in length) and the remainder of the
medal is filled with a conventional scroll-like design.

EDWARD VII CORONATION MEDAL, 1902

Obverse: The conjoint busts of the king and queen crowned and facing left
surrounded by a laurel wreath which forms the edge of the medal.
Reverse: The Royal Cypher surmounted by a crown underneath the date,
26 JUNE 1902. A raised border of laurel which with that on the obverse
makes a wreath.
Size: The medal is ovoid 1·325 by 1·225 ins.
Metal: Silver and bronze.
Ribbon: 1·25 ins. wide. Dark blue with central red stripe and white edges.
Suspension: A ring attached to the medal by a crown.

This medal was awarded in a similar manner to Queen Victoria's Jubilee
medals. It was made by Messrs Elkington & Co. and designed by E. Fuchs
whose name appears on the obverse.

A somewhat similar medal was awarded to mayors and civic dignataries.
This medal was round instead of ovoid, and the raised and ornamental
border was comprised of roses, thistles and laurel and there was no crown
between the ring and the medal. It was worn from a ribbon with scarlet
edges with a wide blue stripe divided by a white stripe.

Although the date on the medal is 26th June, 1902, the ceremony did not
take place until 9th August as King Edward developed appendicitis and the
coronation had to be postponed.

EDWARD VII DELHI DURBAR MEDAL, 1903

Obverse: The crowned head of the king facing right with the legend,
EDWARD VII DELHI DURBAR 1903. Below the bust is a sprig of laurel.
Reverse: A Persian inscription reading: BY THE FAVOUR OF THE LORD OF THE
REALM EDWARD, KING, EMPEROR OF INDIA, 1901.
Size: 1·51 ins.
Ribbon: 1·26 ins. Pale blue with dark blue edges and a narrow centre stripe
of dark blue.
Suspension: By a ring.
Metal: Gold and silver.
Designer: G. W. De Saulles.

This medal, larger than the normal was awarded in silver to 140 senior
British officials and native princes and to 2,100 other officials who attended
the Durbar. It was given also to selected N.C.O.s and men of the Army,
Indian Army, State forces and Police forces.

Both silver and gold medals were awarded to women. It is interesting to
note that the inscription on the reverse forms a chronogram, that is that the

numerical value of the letters of the inscription when added together amount
to 1901 which is the date of His Majesty's accession.

GEORGE V CORONATION MEDAL, 1911

Obverse: The conjoint busts of King George V and Queen Mary crowned
and robed facing left; a spray of laurels to the right and a spray of roses
to the left.

Reverse: The Royal Cypher surmounted by the Imperial Crown beneath the
date, 22 JUNE 1911, the whole within a narrow ornamental border.

Size: 1·2 ins.

Metal: Silver.

Ribbon: 1·25 ins. wide. Dark blue with two narrow central stripes of
crimson.

Suspension: By a ring attached to a plain stud.

This medal was awarded in a similar manner to the previous Coronation
and Jubilee medals, perhaps rather more freely.

GEORGE V DELHI DURBAR MEDAL, 1911

Obverse: The busts of King George V and Queen Mary crowned and robed
facing left: a spray of laurels to the right and a spray of roses to the left.

Reverse: An inscription in Persian, reading: DELHI 1911, surrounded by an
inscription which literally translated reads: DURBAR OF GEORGE THE
FIFTH EMPEROR OF INDIA AND KING AND LORD OF THE COUNTRIES OF THE
ENGLISH.

Size: 1·51 ins.

Ribbon: Dark blue with two narrow central stripes of crimson.

Suspension: By a ring.

Metal: Gold and silver.

Awards were made in a similar manner to the Durbar of 1903. Some 150
native officers and men who had attended the Coronation and had received
the medal were awarded a clasp inscribed DELHI to their Coronation Medal.

GEORGE V SILVER JUBILEE MEDAL, 1935

Obverse: Crowned and robed busts of King George V and Queen Mary
facing left surrounded by the legend: GEORGE V AND QUEEN MARY, MAY
VI MCMXXXV.

Reverse: The Imperial Cypher surmounted by a crown, to the left in two
lines MAY 6, 1910, and to the right MAY 6, 1935, the whole surrounded
with a thin raised border.

Size: 1·2 ins.

Ribbon: Red with stripes of blue, white, blue at each edge.

Suspension: By a ring.

Designer: Sir W. G. John, R.A.
Metal: Silver.

Awarded in similar manner to previous Coronation and Jubilee medals.

GEORGE VI CORONATION MEDAL, 1937

Obverse: The conjoint busts of George VI and Queen Elizabeth, crowned and robed facing left.

Reverse: The Royal Cypher surmounted by the Imperial Crown. Underneath the inscription: CROWNED 12 MAY 1937, the whole surrounded by the inscription: GEORGE VI QUEEN ELIZABETH, the two being separated by the cross of the crown.

Size: 1·2 ins.

Metal: Silver.

Ribbon: 1·25 ins. wide. Garter blue with stripes of white, red, white at each edge.

Suspension: By a ring.

Awarded in similar manner to other Coronation medals.

ELIZABETHAN II CORONATION MEDAL

Obverse: Crowned and robed bust of Her Majesty Elizabeth II facing right.

Reverse: Royal Cypher surmounted by a crown with the legend: QUEEN ELIZABETH II, CROWNED 2ND JUNE 1953.

Size: 1·2 ins.

Metal: Silver.

Ribbon: Crimson with narrow white edges and two narrow central stripes of blue.

Suspension: By a ring.

Fourteen Queen Elizabeth II Coronation medals inscribed MOUNT EVEREST EXPEDITION were presented to Sir John Hunt and his companions of that expedition.

Special medals suitably inscribed were struck and awarded to police and certain other public services who were on duty at either of Queen Victoria's Jubilees or King Edward VII or King George V Coronations. This practice has now been dropped and only selected officers and men are awarded the ordinary medal. The organizations so rewarded have varied with the different events and, among others, medals are to be found for the City of London, Metropolitan, Country and Scottish Police, St John's Ambulance Brigade, Royal Parks, London Fire Brigade, etc.

INDIAN MEDALS

Before dealing with the medals instituted by the Honourable East India Company, and others awarded after the dissolution of the Company in 1858, it might be as well to say a few words about it.

The Company originated in a few London merchants who subscribed a small amount each for the purpose of fostering trade with the East. In the course of time it became a tremendous undertaking which, due to unforeseen circumstances, assumed sovereign power while its directors remained private individuals with no political power whatever. The situation thus created is unique in British, and I can well imagine all, history.

In the early part of 1599 these merchants had subscribed a total of £30,000 which represented 101 shares. On 31st December of the same year they obtained a charter from the Crown and formed a corporation under the title of "The Governor and Company of Merchants of London trading to the East Indies" with a trading licence for fifteen years. By 1617 the capital had increased to nearly two million pounds. During the first years of its existence it contented itself with trade, but in 1624 it received Royal Assent to use the full powers of both civil and martial law, including the carrying out of the sentence of death.

During those extraordinary years 1629–40, when Charles I ruled without Parliament and granted various monopolies he also played a major part in the formation of another company to work in opposition to, and competition with, the East India Company. However, by this time the original company had become too strong to be affected and all the chicanery of the Monarch seemed childish to these men who were not altogether devoid of it themselves and had, in addition, learnt a few tips in this line from their years of trading. However, after Charles I had lost his head, literally, an amalgamation was formed between all the companies trading with the East and although various competitors came into the field from time to time, with whom we are not concerned, it about sums it up to say that the power of the Company was never really in danger because it had the backing of the Government. Queen Anne gave the Company exclusive trading rights to the East which precluded any competition until 1813. In this year trade was thrown open but it is not difficult to see that the many years of monopoly and complete government protection had given it such a start on all new competitors that its position was never seriously assailed.

While on the subject of competition from other companies in the Kingdom, it might be original news to the reader to know that there were also foreign companies trading under similar titles.

The Dutch had an East India Company before we did, it was founded in

1602 and was later to own the principal trading areas and ports in the East such as, Ceylon, Java, Borneo and, of course, other possessions in Africa which were on the route to India. All its property was transferred to the State in 1795.

The Danish East India Company was formed in 1618 and lasted with one dissolution and reformation till 1729 when its sole Indian possession of Tranquebar, south of Madras, was ceded to the Danish Government. It was purchased by the British East India Company in 1845.

The French East India Company was formed in 1664 and lasted till 1769 when its property was transferred to the State.

I was surprised to learn on one of my travels that there had been a Swedish East India Company, formed in 1741, but I have been unable to trace anything about its subsequent history or date of demise.

The first occasion in which the Company had to take warlike action was in 1664 when the Mahrattas, under Sevajee, attacked the Bombay district of Surat. The inhabitants fled but the few British traders on shore, helped by men from the merchant ships, defended stoutly and eventually forced Sevajee to retire. The Mogul was so impressed by this display that he promptly gave the Company further trading concessions. The point is that the British had shown their metal at the start and the natives of India started to show respect, which we like to think even now, in spite of partition, has not been lost.

The chief competitor to the British East India Company was the French East India Company that had received its charter in 1664 and, some seventy or so years later, had founded the colony of Pondicherry, south of Madras.

These two companies eventually occupied the stage and the power of the Mogul declined. Not only did Anglo-French competition take place in India, but there started a general grab of outposts. Our company bagged St Helena and the French the Mascarene Islands (better known by their individual names of Mauritius, Réunion, Rodrigues, etc., for the capture of which, in 1810, medals were awarded which I deal with elsewhere).

Whereas the advantages of trade with India were fully realized by our Government it was not by the French with the result that their East India Company alternated between going bankrupt and reforming. We are not here concerned with the wars between the two in which names like Clive, Eyre Coote, Dupleix and Lally took the leading roles but we are with Major Stringer Lawrence who went out to India to take command of the Company's forces and immediately proceeded to train the Sepoy in the ways of a soldier which earned for him the title of "Father of the Indian Army".

In about 1758 the Madras Government formed a military force from natives recruited in the Carnatic; the Bengal Army, founded by Clive, was recruited from Rajputs, Afghans and Hindus while that of Bombay was probably the most cosmopolitan of them all with an admixture of African natives who had found their way to India but not out of it.

The forces of the Presidencies were joined to form the Indian Army in 1796 at which time the number of native troops was about 57,000 with a further strength of 13,000 Europeans in the regiments of each Presidency.

Most histories, when dealing with the rise of India, harp on the land campaigns and forget that the original landing could never have become a final occupation without sea power. In 1758 the French sent out a fleet and an army under Admiral d'Ache and Count Lally respectively. Lally endeavoured to capture Madras but without help from the sea his task was hopeless and he eventually retired to Pondicherry where he surrendered in 1761. What had happened to the French fleet? It had been sent for six by Admiral Pocock. It returned next year and was again beaten and what was left departed never to return.

In 1762 the East India Company decided to enlarge its territory still more and embarked on an expedition to the Phillippines and captured Manilla from the Spaniards. This, as one might expect, was an act which led to complications that were settled at the Second Treaty of Paris by returning it to Spain and, incidentally, Pondicherry to the French.

The prestige of the British Raj was greatly enhanced by the expedition which was the first occasion in which Indian natives had left their shores in our service. It spoke well that the native would go as he has an overwhelming dislike of the sea.

As the Company's territory extended so did its commitments which had to be paid for by its trade which in this case was not sufficient to maintain an army, police, and all the other expensive items that go towards the cost of running an empire—as that is what the original company's small beginnings had now become.

When the Company's charter was renewed in 1833 its powers were considerably restricted to the territorial and political management of its empire. The executive government of the Company's territories was, in each of the presidencies administered by a governor and three councillors. The governor of Bengal was also governor-general of India, and had control over the other governors.

In 1858 a bill was introduced to remodel the government of India which, when it was passed in August had the effect of doing away with the East India Company and transferring everything to do with it, including the Indian Army, to the Crown. This is why the obverses of the first Indian medals bore the Arms of the East India Company and those awarded after this year (except for the hundred Long Service Medals of faulty design issued in 1859) referred to the Queen as Kaisar-I-Hind (Empress of India).

We will deal with the long service awards to the Indian Army officers and other ranks first; then the Meritorious Service Medals; finally the various medals for good shooting—the first two classes in their order of institution.

LONG SERVICE DECORATIONS AND MEDALS

1848

Obverse: A military trophy and the Arms of the East India Company in the centre.

Reverse: A plain circular centre on which the particulars of the recipient are engraved, surrounded by the words FOR LONG SERVICE AND GOOD CONDUCT.

Size: 1·42 ins. diameter.

Ribbon: 1·25 ins. wide, crimson.

Suspension: By a scroll bar suspender.

Designer: It is said to have been designed by W. Wyon, but I think that the most that can be said is that it is an adaptation from the obverse of the Long Service Medal awarded to the Home Army.

Naming: See above against *Reverse.*

The origin of the award of these medals lies in an order of the Board of Directors of the East India Company dated 19th December, 1845, but it was not until the 20th May, 1848, that the Governor-General, the Earl of Dalhousie, published his authority for their issue.

These medals, awarded to European soldiers only, did not agree with their description given on the Warrant as, on that, it stated that the recipients particulars would be on the same side as the Company's Arms.

There appear to be no regulations concerning the ribbon so that the same as for the Home Army was adopted.

1873

The preceding medal was discontinued and the non-commissioned officers and men (Europeans) received the same medals as those of the Home Army.

1859

Obverse: The diademed head of Queen Victoria and legend, VICTORIA REGINA.

Reverse: The inscription FOR LONG SERVICE AND GOOD CONDUCT between two oak branches, with a crown above and anchor below.

This is a most extraordinary medal for which there does not appear to be any official explanation. About a hundred of them were sent out in 1859 and duly awarded and it was not until the next year that they called for any comment.

I have seen it stated that they were for award to the Indian Marine but were given to the Army instead. This must be wrong because even if there is no explanation for the design there would have been a record of the order from the Court of Directors and, surely, some order somewhere in India that referred to the award of a medal to the Indian Marine. It seems, to me at any rate, far easier to believe that an error had been made in the design than that all papers, both at home and in India, on the subject of a proposed Long Service Medal to the Indian Marine had been lost without trace.

If it is suggested that the medal was for the Indian Marine I should like some explanation as to why the only issues made were all to soldiers. Surely somebody could have spared one or two for the rightful recipients. I cannot believe, even after the mistake had been noted and explanations asked for, that if the intention really was that the medal should go to the Indian Marine that one would not have been started as soon as possible to, so to speak, try and make up for the lost year.

1888

Obverse: The diademed and veiled head of Queen Victoria, and legend, VICTORIA KAISAR-I-HIND.

Reverse: A wreath of lotus flowers and leaves with an inner one of palm. Between these two are the words FOR LONG SERVICE AND GOOD CONDUCT. Inside the inner one is the word INDIA.

Size: 1·42 ins. diameter.

Ribbon: 1·25 ins. wide, crimson.

Suspension: A scroll suspender.

Designer: L. C. Wyon.

Naming: Engraved on the edge.

These medals were sanctioned for award with effect from 1st April, 1888, to native soldiers in the armies of the three presidencies, Bengal, Bombay and Madras. The native gunners of the Nizam of Hyderabad's contingent were also included.

VOLUNTEER OFFICER'S DECORATION (INDIA) 1894

By a Royal Warrant dated 24th May, 1894, the decoration awarded to officers of the Volunteers at home was extended to those in India. The decorations were identical except for the central Imperial Cypher which, in this case, was V.R.I. The two decorations remained the same, except for the additional "I", until discontinued in 1930.

LONG SERVICE AND GOOD CONDUCT (INDIAN VOLUNTEERS)

1896

This medal was identical with the one introduced in 1894 for the Volunteers at home except that the legend on the obverse reads VICTORIA REGINA ET IMPERATRIX. It, with the necessary alteration to the obverse on the accessions of Edward VII and George V, remained in issue till 1930. The king's titles varied with different issues.

1902

This and subsequent issues showed the sovereign in the uniform of a field-marshal on the obverse. His titles varied with the different issues.

ROYAL INDIAN NAVAL RESERVE OFFICERS' DECORATION

ROYAL INDIAN NAVAL VOLUNTEER RESERVE OFFICERS' DECORATION 1908

These, with the added "I" in the monogram were awarded to the above services in India in the same way as to those at home.

INDIAN MERITORIOUS SERVICE MEDALS (1848–1947)

The only difference between these and the Long Service Medals is in the wording on the reverse which reads, FOR MERITORIOUS SERVICE instead of FOR LONG SERVICE. There was no corresponding Meritorious Medal to the faulty Long Service one issued in 1859.

GOOD SHOOTING MEDALS

BEST SHOT NATIVE ARMIES (1817–83)

Obverse: The diademed head of Queen Victoria, and the unique wording, VICTORIA QUEEN.

Reverse: The laureated figure of Victory holding a wreath in her outstretched right hand and a Union Jack in the other; massed troops and a mountain behind her. Beside her is an oval shield bearing THE BEST SHOT OF THE NATIVE ARMIES IN INDIA.

Size: 1·58 ins. diameter.

Ribbon: 1·15 ins. wide, red with black borders, down the centre of which is a white stripe.

Suspension: By a scroll bar above which is a plain bar on which is put the year of award.

Designer: The obverse bears the same held as the India General Service Medal, 1854, designed by W. Wyon but there does not appear to be a record as to who designed the reverse.

Naming: In script on the edge.

This medal, instituted in 1871, was given in bronze in the case of the first two and in silver from 1873 till its discontinuance in, I believe 1883, the same year as the Queen's Best Shot Medal was discontinued at home.

LORD NAPIER'S BEST SHOT MEDAL, INDIAN NATIVE TROOPS (1873–80)

Obverse: The central design is the same as for the last medal except that the centre of the oval shield is blank. Around the design is, PRIZE PRESENTED BY THE RIGHT HON'BLE LORD NAPIER OF MAGDALA G.C.B., G.C.S.I.

Reverse: The centre is plain and takes the recipient's name. Around the central circle is, BEST SHOT AMONGST THE NATIVE TROOPS IN INDIA.

Size: 1·85 ins. diameter.

These medals were of gold and presented by Lord Napier at his own expense. The first seventeen awarded were worn from a ribbon but I have been unable to trace its colour or the type of suspender used. Permission to wear the medal was withdrawn in 1890, after which date the subsequent issues of the commander-in-chief's personal awards were simply circular medallions without means of suspension.

BEST SHOT, NATIVE TROOPS, BENGAL

Obverse: Similar to last medal.
Reverse: Legend, BEST SHOT NATIVE TROOPS BENGAL PRESIDENCY.
Size: 1·85 ins. diameter.
Suspension: There is no means of suspension.
Metal: Gold.

BEST SHOT, NATIVE TROOPS, BENGAL

Obverse: THE MAGDALA MEDAL, within a wreath of laurel: around this, PRESENTED BY GENERAL SIR F. P. HAINES K.C.B. COMMANDER-IN-CHIEF IN INDIA.
Reverse: The centre plain to take recipient's name, etc; around the circumference, BEST SHOT NATIVE TROOPS BENGAL PRESIDENCY.
Size: 1·85 ins. diameter.
Suspension: There is no means of suspension.
Metal: Gold.

BEST SHOT, NATIVE INFANTRY, BENGAL

Obverse: A view of Magdala; above, CAPTURED 13 APL 1868. Under the view is the word MAGDALA. Around the circumference, PRESENTED BY H. E. GENL. SIR DONALD STEWART BART. G.C.B. 1881–82.
Size: 1·515 ins. diameter.
Suspension: The piece is surmounted by a baron's coronet affixed to which is a rectangular ring.
Ribbon: 1·25 ins, wide, dark red with a vertical wavy stripe and two straight ones near the edges, all of yellow.
Metal: Gold.

The only specimen of this medal of which I know had on the reverse the title, THE MAGDALA MEDAL, in the centre surrounded by wreaths of laurel with BEST SHOT above. Around the bottom half of the circumference was NATIVE INFANTRY IN BENGAL in engraving.

I also know of this medal in silver with a plain back except for the central wording.

BEST SHOT, INDIAN VOLUNTEERS

Obverse: A pointed-helmeted rifleman, waist high over cover, loading his rifle. In the background, two palm trees and a high hill. Around the whole, PRESENTED BY THE GOVERNMENT OF INDIA.
Reverse: A central circular space for the recipient's name enclosed by a wreath of laurel and ornamental scroll. Around the whole, BEST SHOT OF THE VOLUNTEERS.
Size: 1·85 ins. diameter.
Ribbon: 2 ins. wide, plain green.

Suspension: A horn-shaped suspender with a high swivelling claw of the same pattern as the Indian Mutiny Medal.

This medal was only awarded in the Bengal Presidency and was worn by the winner on the right breast.

BEST SHOT, INDIAN PROVINCIAL VOLUNTEERS

Obverse: A shield, surmounted by a crown, with words, THE PROVINCIAL MEDAL AWARDED TO THE BEST SHOT AMONG THE VOLUNTEERS IN THE PROVINCES.
Reverse: A space for the recipient's name surrounded by a wreath.
Size: 1·36 ins. diameter.
Ribbon: 1 in. wide, plain green.
Suspension: By a small ring.

This medal was competed for annually in the provinces and the winner in each wore a rectangular bar on the ribbon bearing the name of the province for which it was awarded.

It was worn on the right breast.

MEDALS COMMEMORATING NAVAL AND MILITARY ACTIONS

This chapter concerns medals which were struck to commemorate certain military events that took place before the awarding of medals to all participants became general after every campaign.

I must make it clear that not all commemorative medals are included and that in some cases I have not described every one struck for the particular event. What I have tried to do is to give the particulars and historical detail of those which are the more common, though "common" is hardly the word to use to describe any of them.

All are circular unless otherwise stated.

ARMADA MEDALS (1588–9)

Obverses: A bust of Queen Elizabeth either to the left or full-face.
Reverses: (1) A closed ark with smoke coming from its chimney.
    (2) A bay tree on an island with three ships on the horizon.
    (3) A fleet in full sale with legend, VENIT . VIDIT . FUGIT. (It came, it saw, it fled.)
    (4) Fire ships and a fleet in confusion with legend, DUX . FŒMINA . FACTI . (A woman was in charge of the exploit.)

The above medals are all oval with approximate dimensions of 2 by 1·75 ins. They were struck in gold, silver and copper.

Obverse: (5) The Pope and kings in council with their eyes bandaged.
Reverse: A fleet being driven on the rocks.
Size: 2 ins.

Obverse: (6) A full-face bust of Queen Elizabeth.
Reverse: A bay tree on an island.
Size: 2·35 ins.
    No. 6 is a circular version of No. 2. No. 5 is of silver, No. 6 of gold.

Several medals were struck at about this time which are said to have been awarded for service against the Armada, but definite proof to this effect is lacking.

I hardly think that there is room for doubt that some were awarded. Where, however, there is genuine doubt is in regard to whom.

Camden in his *History of Elizabeth*, written soon after the event, when referring to them says, "The medals and jettons, however, which were struck on this occasion were entirely Dutch. None were struck in England." The most remarkable, and of considerable size, is that which represents the Spanish fleet upon the obverse, with the words FLAVIT JEHOVAH ET DISSI-PATI, 1588 (Jehovah blew and they were swallowed). Reverse, a church on a rock beaten by waves, ALLIDOR NON LOEDOR.

He seems to be very definite as to where the medals were struck and, until we can find a mention of them in the writings of an author equally reliable, we have no evidence on which to doubt his statement.

The defeat of the Spanish Armada (derived from the Spanish word "armata", meaning fleet) was not completed in a day or even a year. The general conception is that it was a devil of a battle which took place somewhere in the Channel, whereas the true facts are that the debris of the Spanish fleet littered the shores of Holland, the west coast of Ireland, the Hebrides and Orkneys.

Mary Queen of Scots had spent the latter part of her life in fomenting trouble aimed at obtaining the throne for herself and the advancement of the Roman Catholic religion in England. Philip of Spain claimed to be the leading Roman Catholic so naturally backed Mary in all her schemes. She also promised him the succession to her throne—that is the throne of England as she had assumed the title of Queen of England in 1559.

When Mary was beheaded in 1587, Philip decided that, what with the riots against Roman Catholics in Holland and the continual plundering of his possessions in the New World, the time had come to crush Elizabeth and all Protestants in general. He had a certain pecuniary interest in the matter as well because, after excommunicating Elizabeth, the Pope had promised him a million crowns when his army landed in England.

He collected an armada of some 130 ships and an army of 27,000 men, while the Duke of Parma assembled another of 30,000 at Nieuport and Dunkirk together with a large number of flat-bottomed landing craft manned by specially chosen seamen from the Baltic. Most of these vessels had been built at Antwerp and, to prevent them being destroyed by the Dutch during the short sea voyage, they were sent by river and canal to Bruges from whence a special canal was dug to Nieuport. I mention this solely to show the similarity of these preparations with those of the Germans in 1940.

Elizabeth raised two armies; one an anti-invasion force under the Earl of Leicester some 18,000 strong, and another under Lord Hunsdon 45,000 strong to guard the Queen's person.

In 1587 Drake, with four naval vessels, two of the queen's yachts and thirty-four converted merchantmen, entered Cadiz harbour and destroyed nearly a hundred ships preparing to take part in the coming invasion.

In the beginning of May, 1588, the Spanish commander, the Marquis of Santa Cruz, and his second-in-command, the Duke de Paliano both died, so the command was given to the Duke de Medina Sidonia who sailed from

D

Lisbon on 28th May. Having taken on troops and stores at Corunna he set sail and ran into a heavy gale which caused considerable delay. He eventually arrived in the Channel where Lord Howard, instead of attacking him immediately, watched the course taken so as to ascertain the destination. It was found to be the Straits of Dover up every mile of which he was harried.

The Spanish ships were very much larger than the English and consequently what they gained in size they more than lost in the power to manoeuvre and, what was even a greater disadvantage, their guns were mounted too high above the water line to be brought to bear on their low opponents.

They suffered many casualties before arriving off Calais where Medina ordered Parma to embark his force. The latter declined to allow his unarmed barges to leave the shore until the Dutch fleet blockading Nieuport and Dunkirk had been driven off. With no alternative, Medina set sail for Dunkirk with the Dutch fleet in front and the English behind. Shortly after sailing he ran into a dead calm. On 7th August a breeze sprang up which Lord Howard used to great advantage as he had been making fire-ships which he now released, in pitch darkness, to drift down wind towards the Spaniards. They were completely disorganized and indulged in a *sauve qui peut*. The next morning, having been reinforced by all the ships that could be sent him, Lord Howard attacked the disordered rabble which had once been the allegedly Invincible Armada.

Medina, realizing that his chances of success had gone, decided to call the whole thing off and return to Spain. To do so via the Straits of Dover was out of the question so he set sail to the northward to go round Scotland. Lord Seymour was detached to follow him but, finding that his powder was defective, was unable to continue the attack, which, in all probability, would have forced Medina to surrender.

A dreadful storm arose after the remnants had rounded the Orkneys and the whole fleet was again dispersed. Some ships were driven ashore on the Norwegian coast; some sank in the North Sea; some were dashed on the rocks on the east coast of Scotland, and others on the Western Isles. One of these latter ships occasionally appears in the news as the object of a treasure hunt at Tobermoray in the Isle of Mull. Fifteen ships are said to have been wrecked on the Irish coast and there are many awesome accounts of the savagery with which the survivors were treated.

The Duke of Medina eventually arrived at Santander with the remnants of his fleet and, judging by the somewhat harrowing time he must have had during his circuit of Scotland—in fact the British Isles—he deserves considerable credit for still having sixty ships with him.

There are two facts concerning the defeat of the Armada which, though unrelated, always strike me as strange. The first is that the only English vessel sunk during the whole period during which the Armada was near our shores was a pinnace. The second is that the Queen conferred no honours on those who saved her throne, her country, her religion—in fact prevented what might well have been a complete alteration in the course of English history.

EDGE HILL (23rd October, 1642).

(i) *Obverse:* Half-length figure of Charles I standing by a table on which his right hand is resting. On the left is a hanging curtain, on the right, in indented lettering, CAR . D . G . MAG . BRI . FRAN . ET . HIB . REX .
Reverse: The king on horseback facing right with a baton in his hand.
Size: Oval, 1·65 by 1·25 ins.
Metal: Silver.

(ii) *Obverse:* Crowned bust of Charles I facing right.
Reverse: The king in armour riding a prancing horse with the letters "C" and "P" stamped in the field at the top.
Size: Oval, 1·5 by 1·2 ins.
Metal: Silver.

These oval medals remind us of the struggles between King and Parliament. The king's finances and power had been waning for some time. By the Treaty of Ripon he had agreed to pay the Scots a daily indemnity until peace was restored but he had no money to pay unless Parliament gave him a grant.

He summoned his fifth (or Long Parliament) but it voted against him. The last stumbling block to a peaceful solution was the refusal of the king to give his assent to the Militia Bill the object of which was to transfer all military power to Parliament.

The country took sides—the Scotch almost entirely with Parliament. The king, who had mustered his forces at Oxford for an attack on London, was met on a Sunday at Edge Hill, near Banbury. The battle was indecisive with the result that the country became more involved than ever till, at last, Civil War broke out. The battles of Newbury 1643, Marston Moor 1644 and Naseby 1645 followed. The king finally surrendered to the Scotch army encamped before Newark.

DUNBAR MEDAL (3rd September, 1650)

Obverse: Bust of Oliver Cromwell facing left and legend, THE LORD OF HOSTS WORD AT DUNBAR SEPTEM Y 1650.
Reverse: A scene in the House of Commons.
Size: 1·35 by 1·15 ins. in silver and copper .
　　　1 by 0.85 ins. in gold, silver and copper.

In addition to the above medal to commemorate this battle, which took place during the time that England was a republic, and a year after the House of Lords and government by a single person had been declared by Parliament to be useless, burdensome, dangerous and unnecessary, there was another medal 1 by 0·85 ins. with a plain reverse.

Charles II, son of the beheaded Charles I, landed in Scotland in June, 1650, whereupon the people rose to support him—especially as he promised to uphold Presbyterianism.

Cromwell went north to defeat him. Crossing the Tweed, he besieged Edinburgh Castle but the shortage of food compelled him to withdraw to Dunbar. He was surrounded by the Scots who were too impetuous to wait to starve him out. They attacked and were outmanoeuvred and subsequently chased off the field by Cromwell's Ironsides with he himself proclaiming, if the records are correct, "Let God arise and his enemies be scattered". They certainly were and he received the surrender of Edinburgh Castle in December, much to the mortification of the citizens who, I am proud to record, had shortly before instituted at the university a Professorship of Humanity carrying a salary of £87 . 2 . 2 per annum. It is with profound regret that I must also record that there were no students in the records of 1839 and no trace of any previously. I should be interested to know whether it has since been decided that the teaching of this subject to Scotsmen has proved impossible or unnecessary and the professorship abolished!

VICTORIES OVER THE DUTCH (1653)

Obverses: An anchor from the stock of which is suspended either two or three shields bearing the St George's Cross, the St Andrew's Cross and the Harp.

Reverses: A naval action or, in the case of the medal with only two shields on the obverse, the House of Commons with the Speaker in the Chair.

Size: All oval varying between 2·2 by 2 ins, to 0·95 by 0·85 ins.

Metal: Gold.

The above medals commemorate the battles with the Dutch which resulted in the passing of the Navigation Act. This Act, passed on 9th October, 1651, forbade the Dutch to bring to England any goods except those made, or grown, in their own country. In other words, they were forbidden to act as seaborne carriers as far as these islands were concerned.

The year 1653 is memorable for the victories of Blake, the soldier-turned-sailor, and of Deane, Monk and Popham who ranked as generals at the time.

In November, 1652, Blake's impetuosity had drawn him into an engagement off the Goodwin Sands in which he suffered such a defeat that Van Tromp sailed up and down the Channel with a broom at his masthead to signify that he had swept the English from the seas.

Blake, stung by this insult, bided his time. He collected as large a fleet as he could and then sailed up the Channel to attack Tromp while escorting several merchantmen. Both sides, with some eighty ships each, were well matched and a running fight which lasted three days ensued. The Dutch lost eleven men-of-war and thirty merchant ships.

On 3rd and 4th June another action took place between Tromp and generals Deane and Monk. It was another slogging match between two equally matched sides. In the evening of the second day Blake arrived with eighteen ships so the Dutch withdrew.

Blake was not present, owing to illness, during another action fought on 29th July in which Tromp was killed but, in view of his previous service against him, he was awarded one of the gold chains as given to the admirals present.

The Dutch struck what have been called Martin Tromp Medals which portray him on their obverse and a naval action on the reverse.

Blake and Tromp were an equally matched pair who deserved, and received, the honour of their respective countries.

The dual notes played by the generals is easy to understand when one remembers that at that time the military and naval services were not separate as now. Perhaps this is well exemplified in the Dutch admiral de Ruyter's title which was Lieutenant-Admiral-General of the United Provinces.

LOWESTOFT (3rd June, 1665)

Obverse: The Duke of York (later James II) facing right.
Reverse: The Royal Charles in action with the legend, NEC MINOR IN TERRIS, 3 JVN, 1665.
Size: Oval, 1·6 by 1·5 ins.
Metal: Gold, silver and copper.

The Duke of York returned with the king (Charles II) at the Restoration (May, 1660) and was made Lord High Admiral and Lord Warden of the Cinque Ports. He took a keen interest in the naval side of the war with the Dutch.

This medal commemorates a battle with their fleet, under Admiral Opdam, off Harwich. The admiral was killed and nineteen of his ships either captured or sunk with a loss of only one of our's.

BATTLE OF THE BOYNE (1st July, 1690)

Obverse: Bust of William II facing right.
Reverse: The king on horseback charging through the river at the head of his troops. In the exergue, ELECIT IACOBVM RESTIVT HIBERNIAM MDCXC.
Size: 2·25 ins.
Metal: Silver.

After the flight of James II the invitation to William to succeed was far from popular to many in Scotland and Ireland. The Scots were made to swear allegiance to the new regime which antagonized them more than ever. They delayed as long as possible and in so doing prompted the foul massacre of the Macdonalds at Glencoe.

In the meanwhile the Irish were in their element with several excuses for causing trouble. They could carry on the age-old struggle between the Catholics and the Protestants; they could show resentment at the arrival of so many settlers, or take part in the struggle between James and the new king. They did not stop to choose but did all three. The Catholics, led by Tyrconnel, obtained arms and formed themselves into bands to harry the

Protestants. Many Protestants fled to England while others shut themselves up in Derry and Enniskillen.

James landed at Kinsale in March, 1689, with a small force with which he had been supplied by Louis XIV. On failing to capture Derry he proceeded to Dublin whereupon the Irish Parliament declared the complete independence of Ireland from England.

In the spring of 1690 William went over with an army, mostly composed of Dutchmen, which had been raised for the occasion under the command of General Ginckel. James was encountered on the banks of the River Boyne outside Drogheda. Owing to the brave stand put up by the French, under Marshal Lauzan, James was able to escape and return to France.

The international flavour of the armies engaged in the Jacobite troubles was well maintained by James's son, the Old Pretender, who sent his followers a small army of Spaniards. This army was short-lived as it was defeated by the Hanoverians in George I's army in the Ross-shire valley of Glenshiel soon after it landed.

One can only suppose that the inter-religious fervour was such that the Catholics and Protestants would go anywhere for a chance of fighting each other. If this assumption is not correct, the only alternative suggestion is that there were armies on the Continent waiting to be hired by the week, month or year, as the case may be, on exactly the same lines as jazz bands today. The arrival of one of the latter has the same effect on some of us as, probably, did the phlegmatic Dutch on the volatile Irish. The trouble is, though, that we must give them a chance to kill us before we are allowed to retaliate.

LA HOGUE (19th May, 1692)

Obverse: The conjoint busts of William and Mary facing right.

Reverse: The stern view of three ships one of which, the French *Soleil Royal*, is on fire. Above, Nox . Nvlla . Secvta . Est . In the exergue, Pvgn : Nav : Int : Ang : Et : Fr : 21 : May : 1692.

Size: 1·95 ins.

Metal:: Gold and silver.

This was one of the battles in the Nine Years War during which William III and Louis XIV were continually trying to get the better of each other. For a while the war went in favour of Louis whose fleet had decisively defeated Lord Torrington off Beachy Head in 1690. The Earl of Marlborough and Admiral Russell were involved in about the basest treachery known in our history. While ostensibly serving William they were fostering the cause of the exiled James by telling him the naval and military plans which he, in turn, passed on to Louis. He, taking advantage of this state of affairs, sent Marshal de Tourville to invade England. Mary, during William's absence acted promptly in a way which must have surprised Louis as much as it did Marlborough. She ordered Russell to go out and meet the invaders, cancelled the embarkation orders of regiments ordered to the Continent, and put Marlborough in the Tower.

Russell, with the help of Sir Cloudesley Shovel, Rear-Admiral of the Red, went off to do as he was told and with eighty-eight ships he met the French with fourty-four off La Hogue. The engagement lasted two days and in the end the French lost fifteen ships together with any hope of the command of the sea.

Three other medals were struck, presumably to commemorate this victory. They are recognizable because on one side or the other they bear the date 19 May 1692; 29 May 1692; or 19–29 May 1692.

WAR OF SPANISH SUCCESSION (1701–14)

Blenheim Medal (13th August, 1704)

Obverse: Bust of Marlborough and Prince Eugene facing other.
Reserve: A scene of the battle and surrender of Marshal Tallard and legend,
     PIACULA TEMERITATIS GALLICAE. In the exergue, the date and inscription.
Size: 2·2 ins.
Metal: Silver.

Ramillies Medal (23rd May, 1706)

Obverse: Bust of Queen Anne facing left.
Reverse: The map of the Low Countries being held by two Fames.
Size: 1·3 ins.
Metal: Silver.

Oudenarde Medal (11th July, 1708)

Obverse: Castor and Pollux (representing Eugene and Marlborough) mounted, facing right.
Reverse: A battle scene with spires in the background. In the exergue, a legend and date.
Size: 1·6 ins.
Metal: Silver.

Malplaquet Medal (11th September, 1709)

Obverse: Bust of Queen Anne facing left, crowned and draped.
Reverse: A battle scene surmounted by a flying figure of Victory.
Size: 1·85 ins.
Metal: Silver.

This war arose out of the disputes about who should succeed Charles II to the Spanish throne. England, Holland, Austria and Portugal sided against France and Spain.

The medals commemorate Marlborough's four famous victories.

SHERIFFMUIR (13th November, 1715)

Obverse: The laureated bust of George I facing right.

Reverse: The running figure of Victory chasing cavalry. In the exergue, in
three lines, AD DUNBLANE 13 NOV 1715.
Size: 1·75 ins.
Metal: Silver.

This medal commemorates one of the battles of the Jacobite Rising
usually referred to as "The Fifteen".

The leader of the Jacobites was the Earl of Mar who raised forces in
Scotland while the Earl of Derwentwater and a Mr. Thomas Forster did the
same in the northern counties of England. The latter surrendered without a
fight to the English at Preston. On the same day Mar met Argyll on the
lovely banks of Allan Water at Sheriffmuir, near Dunblane. Here the right
wing of each army chased the other round a central pivot till Mar finally
retired to Perth.

He who leaves the field cannot claim a victory, but I deplore the fact that
Argyll's army was almost entirely composed of Dutchmen.

DETTINGEN (27th June, 1743)

Obverse: George II in cloak and armour facing left.
Reverse: The king on horseback in the foreground of a battle scene.
Size: 2·6 ins.
Metal: Gold.

On the death of the Emperor Charles VI of Austria both his daughter
Maria Theresa and the Elector of Bavaria claimed succession which resulted
in the war known as the War of Austrian Succession, 1741–8.

France, Spain and Prussia supported the Elector; Maria had Britain as
her sole supporter.

A combined British and Hanoverian army under Lord Stair, animated
by the presence of George II in person, while marching southward from the
Netherlands was practically surrounded by the French under de Noailles at
Dettingen. Prompted by hunger, still animated by the king and encouraged
by bad tactics on the part of de Noailles, we, as we had done before and were
to do so often again, extricated ourselves by a superb combination of all the
military movements not found in textbooks on the subject.

Dettingen was the last battle in which an English sovereign was present
throughout. The reverse of the medal depicts the king withstanding the
cavalry charge, led by the Duc de Grammont, which took place during one
of the less clearly definable periods of the action.

CULLODEN (16th April, 1746)

Obverse: Bust of duke facing right; above, CUMBERLAND.
Reverse: Hercules raising Britannia while trampling on Discord.
Size: 2 ins.
Metal: Gold.

This medal, designed by R. Yeo, must not be confused with the Cumberland Society's private one designed by T. Pingo.

This battle recalls the second Jacobite Rising known as "The Forty Five". The Young Pretender, Charles Edward, had landed on the west coast of Scotland and immediately gathered an army of adherents to his cause. He defeated the English under Cope, at Prestonpans, and then besieged Stirling. After defeating Hawley at Falkirk, Nemesis came in the form of the Duke of Cumberland with his Hessian levies who routed him at Culloden Moor and perpetrated terrible atrocities on the wounded.

PLASSEY (23rd June 1757)

Obverse: Victory, seated on an elephant, with palm and trophy.
Reverse: A Roman warrior, (representative of Clive) with standard in left hand, presenting sceptre to Meer Jaffier.
Size: 1·5 ins.
Metal: Silver.

This medal commemorates the battle which led to the foundation of what became our Indian Empire.

The news that the Surajah Dowlah had captured Calcutta and imprisoned 123 prisoners in what was known as the awful Black Hole reached Clive in Madras. With one British regiment (the Dorsetshire Regiment) and some 2,000 Madras sepoys he sailed in two transports in a fleet commanded by Admiral Watson which suffered many vicissitudes on the way up the Hooghly. After the capture of Budge-Budge and Fort William, Clive landed at the latter and proceeded on foot towards Calcutta. The battle of Chandernagore preceded that of Plassey where the Nabob fled the field. He adopted the disguise of a beggar but was recognized by one whose ears he had ordered to be cut off when in power. He was handed over to Meer Jaffier whose son put him to death.

The British losses at Plassey were twenty-two killed and fifty wounded which was a small price to pay for an empire and brought home the fact that it does not pay to cut off people's ears.

LOUISBOURG (27th JULY, 1758)

Obverse: A globe with the words CANADA and AMERICA thereon resting on a prone figure representing France. The globe is supported by a soldier on the left and sailor on the right. Above, a scroll inscribed PARITER IN BELLA; over this is a Union Jack and the flying figure of Victory blowing a trumpet and carrying a wreath.
Reverse: A view taken from the fort of the attacking ships and their small boats cutting out the *La Prudente* and *La Bienfaisante*. Around the top is the inscription LOUISBOURG · TAKEN · MDCCLVII.
Size: 1·7 ins.
Ribbon: Bi-coloured deep orange and purple.

Suspension: By a circular ring rivetted at right-angles to the piece.
Designer: Thomas Pingo.
Naming: Unnamed.

This medal was awarded in gold or silver to certain officers who took part in the capture of the town. It is also found in bronze but, as these specimens have no means of suspension, I should doubt whether they are more than replicas.

One of the clauses of the Treaty of Utrecht, 1713, was that the French had to relinquish Newfoundland. They decided, therefore, to occupy the Isle Royale (now called Cape Breton Island) and spent a great deal of labour and money in making Louisbourg on the east coast, into a fortified town with additional batteries to guard the adjoining bay.

Though our two countries were theoretically at peace there was continual fighting for the lucrative Ohio Valley in which the French, with the help of the local Indians, were getting somewhat the better. Failing to get help from home, Sir William Pepperell, with the help of the Governor of Massachusetts, raised a private army and set off to attack Louisbourg. By a stroke of good fortune it met a British squadron on the way which joined forces and between them they captured the fortress on 17th June, 1745.

By the Treaty of Aix-la-Chapelle, 1748, which ended the War of Austrian Succession, all recent conquests were returned so that Louisbourg became French again.

In 1757 Parliament decided to send a strong expeditionary force to North America to assist the provincials in their struggles with the French. General James Abercromby commanded the land forces with a strong fleet under Admiral Edward Boscawen in support. A part of this force under General Amherst was directed to capture Louisbourg, off which it arrived on 3rd June, 1758. In addition to the strong fortifications and beach defences there was a fleet of five line-of-battle ships and seven frigates lying in the bay.

Beachheads were established under protection of the guns of our fleet and then, in conjunction with a landward attack on the town, the small boats of the ships entered the harbour and attacked the *La Prudente* and *La Bienfaisante*. The former was set alight by her crew and the latter captured and added to the Royal Navy.

After heavy fighting, in which Colonel Wolfe played a distinguished part, the town was surrounded and forced to capitulate. General Drucour and 5,600 prisoners were taken.

Louisbourg, spelt Louisburg on the Colours, has a particularly interesting place in regimental histories in that it forms the first Battle Honour of seven regiments of the twelve that received it.

MINDEN (1st August, 1759)

Obverse: A Roman soldier with a lighted touch-stick in his right hand and a shield over his left shoulder. To his right are two guns; to his left, a shield and five flags. Around the top, VIRTVTI CEDIT NVMERIS; in the exergue, in two lines, PRŒ LVM MINDENSE I AUG MDCCLIX.

Reverse: A tall tree with a grape vine entwined around the trunk. At the foot is a rock on which lies two coronets each with a key passing through its centre. In the background to the left is a precipitous tree-covered cliff; to the right, two high hills. Legend, POST TOT DISCRIMINA RERUM. In the exergue, in two lines, FERD PR BRVNSV EXERC FOED DVX.
Size: 1·95 ins.
Metal: Silver.

This medal commemorates the defeat of the French, under Marshal de Contades, by the English, Hanoverians and Hessians under Prince Ferdinand of Brunswick. It was one of the many battles in the Seven Years War which established our colonial empire. It was during this war that France lost to us both her India and American possessions.

The battle is probably best remembered by the celebrations which take place on its anniversary by the six British regiments present who, through a mistaken order, performed one of those brilliant *faux pas*, that stud and enlighten our military history. In this case infantry marched with drums beating to attack cavalry—and succeeded.

CAPTURE OF QUEBEC (13th September, 1759)

Obverse: Head of Britannia facing left.
Reverse: The figure of Victory with a seated captive and the prow of a ship.
Size: 1·5 ins.
Metal: Silver.

The captures of Louisbourg, Fort Dusquesne and Niagara left Quebec as the last fortress of the French in Canada.

Pitt decided that it should be taken as well so an army of 7,000 under Wolfe, who had returned to England after the taking of Louisbourg, and a fleet under Admiral Saunders was despatched. It arrived at the island of Orleans on 26th June; the fort of Niagara surrendered to Amherst the day before. The French, under Montcalm, had concentrated all their forces in the province of Quebec. July and August were spent in trying to drive them from their strongly fortified position at the mouth of the Montmorenci.

Quebec was found to be strongly fortified and the garrison disinclined to venture out. While debating what should be done, a severe storm arose which grounded many ships. The necessity for prompt action was further encouraged by the approach of winter. The ruse eventually adopted was to take the ships' small boats up the river and embark the soldiers who would then drift down with the current so as to land on the opposite shore. A landing was made at the foot of the Heights of Abraham up which the troops crawled. Severe fighting took place at the top during which both Wolfe and Montcalm were killed and their respective seconds-in-command severely wounded.

A large share of the successful navigation of the St Lawrence was due to the skill of the master of the sloop *Mercury*, James Cook, whose later voyages to the Pacific in the *Resolution* made him famous.

QUIBERON BAY (20th November, 1759)

Obverse: Britannia seated side-saddle on a sea-horse. Legend, BRITAIN TRIUMPHED HAWKE COMMANDED. In the exergue, OFF BELLE ISLE NOV XX MDCCLIX.
Reverse: A somewhat inept caricature of Britain, France and Night. In the exergue, FRANCE RELINQUISHES THE SEA.
Size: 1·6 ins.
Metal: Silver.

This victory was one of those that took place during what Walpole described as "The Year of Victories" in the Seven Years War.

The French, in spite of their many defeats, had accumulated ships for an invasion of England, Ireland and Scotland. A fleet to counter these intentions was sent to patrol off Brest; another off Dunkirk; and a third, under Rodney, to bombard Havre. A violent storm got up on 12th October which necessitated the withdrawal of the blockading squadrons. As soon as it subsided Admiral Conflans put to sea and, as it turned out, so did Hawke from Tor Bay. They met off Belle Isle and a running fight ensued which ended with the total destruction of the French fleet at a cost of only 250 casualties to the English in the actual fighting though the *Resolution* and *Essex* were driven ashore by a gale and became total losses.

CAPTURE OF ST EUSTATIUS (3rd February, 1781)

Obverse: Bust of Admiral Rodney facing right.
Reverse: An inscription concerning the event surrounded by a wreath.
Size: 1·35 ins.
Metal: Silver.

This small island, a dependency of Curaçoa, has had a chequered career. Its history as regards changes of ownership is: settled by Dutch, 1632; captured by French, 1689; by British, 1690; changed hands eight times between 1690–1810; and was eventually restored to Holland in 1814.

The medal commemorates its capture by Admiral Rodney who, in conjunction with General Vaughan, originally intended to capture St Vincent. On their arrival there they found the reception too warm for comfort so they moved on and took St Eustatius instead. They were well rewarded for they captured an enormous treasure, six warships and 150 merchant ships.

GLORIOUS FIRST OF JUNE (1794)

Obverse: Bust of Admiral Howe.
Reverse: Britannia, seated on a rock, receiving a trident from Neptune.
Size: 2·2 ins.
Metal: Silver.

Soon after the overthrow of the monarchy in France the revolutionary government declared war on Britain. This lasted, with two short intervals, till after the battle of Waterloo, in 1815.

The history of France at this period is rather similar to that of certain countries at present in that anyone who had been in authority was now considered a spy or traitor. Admiral Kerguelen and many captains had either been imprisoned or beheaded. A junior officer, Villaret-Joyeuse, was made commander-in-chief and deputies were appointed to every ship to preach revolutionary doctrines and stamp out any attempt to show common sense or decency. La Fayette's invention, the Tricolor, was hoisted and death promised for so many actions that it must have been difficult for the wretched sailors to know what they could do without punishment.

Lord Howe collected a huge fleet at Spithead to watch the French and guard convoys arriving from America. Joyeuse sailed from Brest on 16th May and was joined by French squadrons under Nielly and Vanstabel. The combined fleets of both sides first met on the 28th after which a sporadic engagement continued for three days, due to fog and rank disobedience on the part of certain senior French officers.

The fight was as severe as any in our history. At the end both sides claimed a victory. The French, like the Germans after the battle of Jutland, in 1916, though vociferous in their claims were far too frightened to come out.

This medal is a commemorative one and must not be confused with the gold one which was awarded to admirals and ship's captains.

CAMPERDOWN (3rd October, 1797)

Obverse: Bust of Admiral Duncan facing right.
Reverse: A sailor nailing a flag to the mast.
Size: 1·9 ins.
Metal: Silver.

This medal commemorates the defeat of the Dutch fleet off Texel by Admiral Duncan. The defeat was overwhelming and thoroughly deserved as the Dutch and Spaniards had changed sides.

Coming soon after the Mutinies at Spithead and the Nore in April of the same year it acted as a tonic to the Navy as a whole.

A sailor at the Nore by the name of Parker promoted himself rear-admiral and styled himself "President of the Floating Republic". He was hanged at the yard-arm of his ship as a deterrent to others with ideas about floating or any other kind of republic.

MEDALS MISCELLANEA

In this chapter I have included medals which have been awarded to our soldiers and sailors for the various acts which are described.

Many foreign decorations have been given to members of our Services since the outbreak of the First World War which, if all were included, would necessitate a separate book to deal with them.

Some of the obvious omissions in this chapter will be found in their chronological order in *British Battles and Medals* by Major Laurence L. Gordon, while others have been omitted because I do not feel that their inclusion would be of interest to more than one or two collectors at the most.

CALLIS MEDAL (5th July, 1742)

Obverse: George II dressed as a Roman Emperor holding a medal towards a kneeling officer but looking in another direction at the time. Legend, PRO TALIBUS AUSIS (For such enterprises). The exergue is plain.

Reverse: A squadron of four ships and a fireship attacking five galleys anchored in line. In the exergue, OB. V. TRIREM. HISPAN. A. S. CALLIS. COMBUST. V. JUL II. MDCCXLII. (On account of five Spanish galleys burnt by A. S. Callis, 5th July, 1742.)

This gold medal was awarded to Captain Callis, R.N., of the fireship *Duke* which entered the harbour of St Tropez, in Provence, and set alight five Spanish galleys.

This award is particularly interesting in that it appears to be the first given to a captain of a fireship though such an award had been sanctioned in 1665 by the Duke of York, Charles II's Lord High Admiral.

Fireships were first used by the Prince of Parma, a Spanish general, during the seige of Antwerp, in 1585, when they were sent in to destroy the bridge of boats stretched across the Scheldt.

They were first used by the Royal Navy in 1588 when Lord Howard sent eight of them into Calais where they caused destruction and panic among a portion of the Spanish Armada which had taken refuge there against the violent storm which played such a part in its defeat.

They, like the one-man submarines, were an Italian invention. Their inventor, Frederigo Giambelli, then serving with the Spaniards, came to England and showed us how to use them against his employers! It seems that, even in those days, "beezness vas beezness" and the Italian looked upon war as a means of lining his own nest providing someone else did all the fighting.

These fireships must not be confused with those employed as floating batteries by the Spaniards in 1782 during their attack on Gibraltar. The Giambelli fireships were little more than floating layers of powder barrels covered with shavings and other combustibles which were set off by a fuse left trailing over the stern. At the last moment the crew got into their boat, lit the fuse, and, if I am not mistaken, rowed like they had never rowed before!

In addition to an amazing assortment of combustibles, these ships were also filled with carcasses (metal cylinders filled, as an account of the period says, "with a composition which burns with violence during eight or ten minutes"). As many of these ships were of several hundreds of tons, there must have been a lovely bang when they went off.

The fireships used at Gibraltar were invented by a French engineer, Claude D'Arcon, whose ships were supposed to be exactly the opposite to combustible being provided with all the latest ideas on fireproofing. Nevertheless those that were not set on fire by the red-hot shot used by the garrison were set alight by their crews and burnt splendidly.

CIVITA VECCHIA MEDAL (1793)

Obverse: The bust of Pope Pius VI and legend, PIUS SEXTUS PONT. MAX. XVII.

Reverse: The seated figure of Ceres holding a cornucopia. Above, the legend, AGRO POMPTIN COLONIS REST. In the exergue the date MDCCXCI.

Civita Vecchia—Michelangelo, where is the connection? Surely he was a painter. Yes, but hardly less distinguished as a sculptor and architect. It was he who is responsible for the glory of St Peter's in Rome, and he who designed the marble piers, lighthouse and citadel in Civita Vecchia, the port of the Papal State.

Twelve of these medals, all of gold, 1·5 ins. diameter, were given by the Pope to officers of the 12th Light Dragoons, who were in Civita Vecchia while the rest of the regiment was with Lord Dundas capturing the island of Corsica. Lieutenant R. Sainthill, R.N., also received one of these medals which appears to have been given to the officers as a mark of appreciation by the Pope of the good behaviour of the men.

Pope Pius VI reclaimed some 200 square miles of the Pontine Marshes, restored the Via Appia, restored the ports of Terracina (approximately fifty miles south-east of Rome), and Civita Vecchia which is about forty-five miles north-west.

The medal in question was struck to celebrate the restoration of the latter port and given to officials and those who took part in the work. I expect our fellows attended the celebrations and got in the way because it signifies absolutely nothing as do so many foreign awards. This statement will, I am sure, be borne out by others who attended some of the distributions of foreign awards during the First World War and took part in some of the lively competitions which preceded the presentations.

VILLIERS-EN-CROUCHÉE MEDAL (1794)

Obverse: Bust of Emperor Francis II of Germany facing right and legend IMP. CAES. FRANCISCVS. II P. F. AUG.

Reverse: The legend, FORTI BRITANNO IN EXERCITV FOED. AD CAMERACVM. XXIV. APR. MDCCXCIV. In the exergue, two sprigs of laurel.

This large gold medal, 2·375 ins. diameter, was suspended from a heavy gold chain worn round the neck. It was awarded by the Emperor, together with the Order of Maria Theresa, to eight officers of the 15th Light Dragoons whose bravery prevented his capture.

Crouchée is also found spelt Couchée and Couché but I prefer another title which the medal has, i.e. the Cambrai Gold Medal.

There must be many of us who remember this place with mixed feelings— especially those who recall the bloodbath which was given the high-sounding title of the battle of the Somme where we lost over 60,000 men on the day the attack opened. In the end we gained a sea of mud in which those who slipped off the path were drowned. This 1916 attack was followed by another in 1918 with results that led all the way to Cologne.

The 15th Light Dragoons, later the 15th Hussars, now amalgamated with the 19th Hussars to form the 15th/19th The King's Royal Hussars, are a unit of the Royal Armoured Corps. The actions for which this medal was given is on the Regimental Colours as Villiers-en-Cauchies and so, incidentally, is "Cambrai, 1917/18" for service in the same area during the First World War.

WOOLDRIDGE MEDAL (11th April, 1809)

Obverse: A three-masted fireship, alight, breaking through a boom behind which three ships are moored. Below, on an arc-shaped panel, XI APRIL MDCCCIX; the whole surrounded by a cable border.

Reverse: The inscription, CAPTAIN JAMES WOOLDRIDGE LED THE BRITISH FIRE SHIPS WHEN FOUR FRENCH SAIL OF THE LINE WERE BURNT UNDER THEIR OWN BATTERIES IN AIX ROADS. Around the inscription is a wreath of oak and laurel with a shell at the bottom.

This gold medal, which was suspended from a gold chain, appears to be last of the special awards to the captains of fireships. The action referred to was that for which the bar "Basque Roads, 1809" to the Naval General Service Medal was awarded.

Fireships and bomb vessels played an important part in this action against nine line-of-battle ships and four frigates lying in the Roads.

Lord Cochrane was in command of the attack while Lord Gambier waited in the offing. Eight transports and the storeship *Mediator* were converted to fireships and another three into explosive vessels. While these alterations were being made a further twelve fireships arrived from England.

Led by the *Mediator*, commanded by Captain Wooldridge, the fireships and bomb vessels entered the Roads. The French panicked and in the end their whole fleet was either destroyed or badly damaged.

There were three bomb vessels present and each contained 1,500 barrels of powder, 350 shot, and several thousands of hand grenades. The effect when one of them blew up must have been well worth watching. The interesting items in their contents are the hand grenades. These, for the moment are, I believe, obsolete in modern naval warfare, but it would be a rash person who said that they would never return. I remember catapults and darts in the First World War and the Home Guard in the Second were, by all accounts, about to be issued with, or actually were issued with, pikes.

WINDSOR CASTLE MEDAL (1824)

Obverse: The head of King John VI in relief, facing right, on an oval gold centre, surrounded by a band of blue enamel bearing the words WINDSOR CASTLE in gold capital lettering; the whole resting on two crossed anchors, to each of which is attached a small length of rope.

Reverse: Plain gold with no enamelling. The oval centre bears the recipient's name in engraved capitals and, in the case of the specimen I know, a numeral underneath. The centrepiece is surrounded by a mottle-faced band bearing in embossed lettering the words WINDSOR CASTLE.

Suspension: The badge is suspended from a gold, and hinged double-sided and hollow, representation of the Portugese crown surmounted by a ring.

The history concerning the cause of the award of this pretty badge belongs to Portugal, which, in 1824, had recently lost the colony of Brazil and was in the throes of a revolution. On 30th April, 1824, the king retired for safety on board H.M.S. *Windsor Castle*, 74 guns, which was anchored in the Tagus. He remained on board till 14th May.

As a mark of appreciation for the sanctuary and hospitality that he had received on board, he presented every officer with one of these badges.

SAINT SEBASTIAN MEDAL (1836)

Obverse: A lion surrounded by the Collar of the Golden Fleece with the word ESPANA above, and AGRA DECIDA below.

Reverse: A cross patté with crowns between the arms. In the centre, ST SEBASTIAN 5 DE MAYO, 1836.

Ribbon: A deep purple with two yellow stripes at each edge.

This medal which was awarded, in silver to officers and pewter to the other ranks, by the Spanish government to Englishmen only for their share in a campaign which cannot by any possible stretch of imagination be considered anything to do with us.

We need not be concerned with Spanish history or their laws of succession but suffice to say that there was a pretender to the throne by name Don Carlos whose followers were known as Carlists. He refused to agree to the repeal of the Salic Law passed by his brother Ferdinand VII and later started a Civil War which lasted from 1873 to 1876. Things got so out of hand that foreign legions were enlisted, one of which, 8,000 strong, was raised in

England under the command of General Sir George De Lacy Evans. On 1st October, 1836, the legion defeated the Carlists at St Sebastian and again in the following May at Irun. They did not leave the country till 1840. Evans, an Irishman, born in County Limerick, who had already served in the Peninsular War and in America, was probably rather loath to leave but he saw service again as a divisional commander in the Crimea.

THE ORDER OF MEDJIDIE (Turkey, 1852)

Obverse: A silver seven-pointed star each point of which is formed of four cut silver leaves. Between each point is a small star and crescent. The circular centre is of gold or silver according to class, and is surrounded by a red enamelled band bearing thereon the Turkish for zeal, devotion, fidelity and what would be the English date of 1852.
Reverse: Plain.
Ribbon: Crimson with green edges.
Suspension: A gold and red enamelled crescent and star connect the badge to a ring through which the ribbon is threaded.

The Order, which is now obsolete, consisted of five classes. The sizes of the various classes vary slightly and the centres of the first four are of gold while the fifth is of silver. The first, second and third classes were worn suspended round the neck. In addition to the badge, there was a star for those of the first and second classes which the former wore on the left breast and the latter on the right.
The Order was somewhat freely distributed to senior officers. It was not—even in the fifth class—awarded to more than two or three other ranks.

FRENCH LEGION OF HONOUR (1802)

Obverse: A white enamelled gold badge consisting of a ten-pointed star with gold balls on the tips of each point mounted on a wreath of oak leaves. In the centre is the effigy of Napoleon I on a silver-gilt circlet, surrounded by a band of blue enamel on which are the words NAPOLEON EMP. DES FRANÇAIS in gold.
Reverse: Similar, but with the Imperial Eagle in the centre and the words HONNEUR ET PATRIE on the surrounding blue band.
Ribbon: Red.
Suspension: The badge is surmounted by a crown at the top of which is a ring.

The Order was instituted by Napoleon Bonaparte, when first consul, in lieu of the orders of knighthood which had been suppressed. It was confirmed by Louis XVIII and remained in force till the deposition of the Imperial Dynasty at the hectic meeting of the French Assembly on 4th September, 1870—the day the news of McMahon's surrender to the Germans at Sedan.
There is still a Legion of Honour but the central designs, suspension and ribbon are all different so that the only thing that remains the same is the

name. Anyhow, we are not concerned with it here and it is only mentioned to avoid confusion with the Order of the same name which was awarded by Napoleon Bonaparte's nephew, Napoleon III, to many officers and men who distinguished themselves in the Crimea.

VALEUR ET DISCIPLINE (1856)

Obverse: The bust of Napoleon III, facing left, on a silver-gilt circle surrounded by a blue enamelled circlet bearing the words LOUIS NAPOLEON in gold. A silver laurel wreath, surmounted by the French Imperial Eagle in gold, surrounds the whole.

Reverse: A circular silver-gilt centre bearing the words VALEUR ET DISCIPLINE surrounded by a narrow blue circle. The whole is surrounded by a wreath of laurel and surmounted by the rear view of the Imperial Eagle in silver-gilt.

Ribbon: 1·6 ins. wide, orange watered silk with green edges.

Suspension: By two rings interlocked at right-angles: a small one attached to the piece and a larger one through which the ribbon is threaded.

Naming: They were issued unnamed.

This silver-gilt medal was given by Louis Napoleon, after the Crimean War, to 497 N.C.Os. and men of the British Army and a few members of the Royal Navy who held corresponding ranks. It was also, at the personal request of Marshal Jacques Pelissier, the French Commander-in-Chief, awarded to his British opposite number, General Sir William Codrington and H.R.H. The Duke of Cambridge.

The medal is often confused with the early examples of the French Medaille Militaire which was instituted on 29th February 1852. The quickest way to distinguish the two is to look at the reverses for in the case of the Medailles Militaire the blue band surrounding the central silver-gilt circle is omitted. The ribbon of the Medaille Militaire is of the same colourings but not of watered silk. Incidentally, the first Medailles Militaire bore the head of Napoleon III, which was replaced in 1870 by that of the female figure representing the French Republic. A blue band bearing the legend REPUBLIQUE FRANCAISE and the date "1870" surrounds the head. The whole is surmounted by a somewhat mixed arrangement of naval and military trophies which is itself surmounted by a loop for suspension from a yellow and green-edged ribbon.

SARDINIAN WAR MEDAL (1833)

Obverse: The Arms of Savoy surmounted by a crown and flanked by a branch of laurel on the right and one of palms on the left, both of which are tied together at the bottom with a silk ribbon. The legend AL VALORE MILITAIRE surrounds the whole.

Reverse: Two laurel branches tied at the bottom; the legend SPEDIZIONE D'ORIENT around the top half, and the dates "1855" and "1856" at the bottom.

Size: 1·3 ins. diameter.

Ribbon: 1 in. wide, watered dark blue.

Suspension: By a partial ring attached to the piece.

Naming: The recipient's name and unit are engraved in the centre of the reverse.

This silver medal was awarded to 400 officers and men of the Army and fifty of the Navy by the King of Sardinia for services of special distinction during the Crimean War.

PART II

HISTORY OF MEDALS

The study of medals is the smaller part of the science of numismatics though, in itself, so vast that I seriously doubt whether any one person could lay claim to be an expert in all its branches. Speaking for myself, I can say that I have collected British campaign medals for nearly forty years and have written over four hundred pages about them and am still learning. Every country in the world has its own medals, and the history of some of them dates back hundreds of years. I contend, therefore, that it is absolutely impossible for any one person to be an expert in them all.

I propose to try and interest the laymen in the subject of British medals only, though it will be necessary to poach on the preserves of coin enthusiasts and historians so as to get a more complete picture.

A few general remarks concerning the subject as a whole must be given before we start.

The word "medal" is taken from the Italian "medaglia", which in turn one suspects is derived from the Greek for metal, of which all medals are made.

There is not, as far as I know, any mention of medals in early Greek history. The first writer who mentions them was, I believe, the Roman biographer and historian Caius Suetonius, who lived during the first part of the second century. In his *Lives of the Caesars*, an anecdotal account of the first twelve, he mentions that Augustus presented medals to his friends as marks of favour.

There are very few Greek medallions, or medals, in existence prior to the establishment of the Roman domination of that country. There are, however, examples of early Sicilian medals portraying the head or person of Ceres, the goddess of grain and harvest, and on the reverse the figure of Victory in the act of crowning a figure.

Before proceeding further I must define what is meant by a medallion. A common definition is that it is a large medal, which I consider to be incorrect as it is only half a truth. Medallions were larger than their contemporary medals, but it would be nonsense to say that the smallest medallion is larger than the largest medal. They were what we would now call a medal in that they were given to mark an especial occasion or service and were never in circulation as coins. Medals, on the other hand, were also awarded for special occasions, or shall we say produced for special occasions, and did, occasionally, get into circulation as money.

A common feature of some of the earliest medallions is that they were composed of two metals; the centre being of copper surrounded by a ring of another metal, or vice versa, the design covering the piece as a whole.

The interesting thing about these early medallions and medals is that the designs on them always depicted a mythical character. Though the ancients left us many statues and carvings of famous contemporaries, it is rather extraordinary that history and biography were not combined with medals till about the middle of the fourteenth century.

The originator of the idea of portraying living individuals on medals was Francesco Petrarch, the celebrated Italian poet and biographer, who was commissioned by Charles IV, Emperor of the Holy Roman Empire, 1347–78 to write the lives of eminent men. On their completion he presented Charles with gold and silver medals bearing the portraits of those about whom he had written. Shortly after this came the period of the Renaissance, the period of the fifteenth and sixteenth centuries which saw the revival of the arts, during which many beautiful medals were produced. The outstanding name of this period was that of Vittore Pisano, surnamed Pisanello who was born in Verona in 1380, and died 1451. His medals all bear, strange to say, the words OPUS PISANI PICTORIS. He was the most famed portrait painter of his time and did not turn his hand to making medals till 1440. Seldom, indeed, has a man won such renown in two entirely different professions.

The longest and most complete series of medals in the world are those of the Popes which runs continuously from 1464 as originals, and those of prior pontiffs have been added.

Now let us return to English medals of which there are seven different kinds. They are, together with the dates of their introduction, as follows: Commemoration, 1480; Coronation, 1547; Bravery 1642; Campaign, 1650; Medalets, 1661; Miniature, 1816; Long Service, 1830.

Commemoration medals are of three kinds. They either commemorate a person, an event, or both.

The first of the series is of bronze and was found in Knaresborough Forest. On the obverse it bears the bust of John Kendal in armour wearing the Cross of the Order of St John of Jerusalem. On the reverse is a shield bearing the Arms of Kendal and the inscription TEMPORE OBSIDIONIS TURCHORUM. MCCCCLXXX. The medal is of foreign origin, probably Italian, and was either given to him or ordered by him to commemorate his work in the defence of the island of Rhodes against the attacks by the Turks. From that date onwards commemorative medals have been cast or struck for a variety of reasons almost equal to their number. The great mistake made by many people, and daily papers, is that they fall into the trap of saying "the" without stopping to find out whether it should be "one". There were, for instance, to my certain knowledge five medals commemorating the Peace of Breda, five for the battle of La Hogue, 1692, and, if we go back a bit, ten or more for the Armada. There was not then, and is not now, any restriction against anyone designing a medal said to commemorate anything, providing royalty is not illustrated thereon.

Two interesting names occur in the history of commemoration medals—those of Alexander Davison and Matthew Boulton.

The reader will have heard of prize money which was the sum obtained from the sale of captured goods and ships as far as naval prize money was concerned. During the period about 1750–1840 this involved large sums which had to be collected and distributed in certain proportions to all officers and men who took part in the capture. It can be readily understood that a senior naval officer could hardly look after all this complicated business himself so he appointed what was known as a prize agent to manage his affairs. Alexander Davison was a friend of Nelson who appointed him to be his agent after the battle of the Nile, 1st August, 1798.

At that time there were no such things as campaign medals or, in fact, a general award of medals of any kind. Davison thought that the men who took part in such a decisive victory should receive some award and so, at a personal cost of something like £2,000 agreed to present a medal to every officer and man who took part. He went, therefore, to his friend Matthew Boulton, who owned the Soho Mint, in Birmingham. He in turn set his designer, C. H. Küchler, a native of Flanders (whom coin collectors will recall designed the 1798 Isle of Man coinage), to work with the result that a medal slightly smaller than two inches diameter was produced. It was given in gold to admirals and the captains of ships; in silver to lieutenants and warrant-officers; in bronze gilt to petty officers; and in bronze to seamen and marines. Around the edge is indented, A TRIBUTE OF REGARD FROM ALEXR DAVISON ESQ. ST. JAMES'S SQUARE.

Here, then, is the first medal to be awarded to all officers and men the result, be it noted, of private enterprise. The fact is commemorated for all time, and for all to see, in Westminster Abbey on the bust of the great admiral. The medal was entirely unofficial so there was no particular ribbon worn with it; some wore it from a plain dark blue, and others from one of dark blue with white edges but we need not worry ourselves over this detail here.

Küchler and the army, in the person of an ex-soldier, James Hadfield, crossed the numismatic firmament for a strange reason in 1800. A medal was struck to commemorate the attempted assassination of George III as he entered the Royal Box at Drury Lane Theatre. It was of silver, about 2 ins. diameter, and bore the bust of the king in armour on the obverse, with an altar surmounted by a large eye on the reverse. The idea being, I suppose, that Divine Providence was watching over the king. The design of the obverse is stupid as he would hardly go to the theatre in full armour.

In 1801 Küchler designed another silver medal of about the same size as the last to commemorate the Act of Union, 1st January, 1801, by which the parliaments of England and Ireland were united. I believe the Irish issued another in 1921 when the opposite took place.

The battle of Trafalgar was commemorated by two private medals, one given by Mr Davison and the other by Mr Boulton. The former is interesting in that the name of the recipient's ship was engraved round the rim and therefore constitutes the first medal on which the recipient's unit is mentioned.

Commemorative medals, in copper, were struck in 1820 to commemorate the battles of the Peninsular War and the generals that took leading parts. They have been made for many events since then and, as far as those which I have owned and seen, have gradually deteriorated in workmanship so that it is more of a kindness not to mention them.

The first coronation medal was that of Edward VI and then there was a gap till that of Charles I. The first to be worn with campaign medals was that of Edward VII, and the practice of awarding them to certain selected personnel has continued ever since. They are not very interesting as it is really only luck that gets them. Luck that is in that one happened to be holding a particular job at the time.

The first medal awarded for bravery, or an act of special merit, was that given by Charles I to Sir Robert Welch for the recapture of the standards of the King's Own Regiment, which had been captured by the Parliamentary Forces (which Charles referred to as "the rebels") at the battle of Edgehill, the first battle of the Civil War, fought on 23rd October, 1642. The medal was of gold and worn, according to old accounts, suspended from a green ribbon over the shoulder.

As a matter of fact Charles also awarded a gold oval medal somewhat similar to this to Captain John Smith who recovered the Royal Standard by stealth in that he mingled with the so-called rebels after the battle and grabbed it from the hands of Cromwell's secretary, a Mr Chambers. That he should have done this and got away seems a tall story for us to believe. The fact remains that both medals depict the Royal Standard on the reverse.

A certain amount of confusion exists as to what is a medal and what a decoration. The correct answer is that if a medal, as for instance the Distinguished Conduct Medal, is awarded for bravery it is a decoration though it may be in the shape of a medal. A man is decorated with the Victoria Cross and decorated with the Military Medal, George Medal, and other decorations which include the word medal in their titles. I propose, therefore, to use the term decoration in its general sense whatever be the actual shape of the article awarded.

The first medals awarded to officers and men for battle service were the Dunbar Medals which were struck in 1650, by order of Parliament, to be given to members of the Parliamentary Forces that took part on 3rd September, 1650. Those given to officers were of gold, oval in shape, about an inch high and slightly less in width. There was a ring at the top from which they were suspended from a ribbon worn round the neck. The men received the same medal made of silver. I have never seen it stated that all the officers and all the men received their appropriate medal. As a matter of fact there was a third medal which was of silver which had the same obverse, a bust of Oliver Cromwell, but the reverse was plain instead of the illustration of the House in Session.

The first medal to be awarded to all officers and men was the silver one for the battle of Waterloo, 1815. As a matter of strict accuracy I should say that it was also given to those present at Ligny, 16th June, and Quatre Bras, 16th June, whether they were subsequently present at Waterloo or not.

In my humble, and quite unimportant opinion, the granting of medals has now gone completely off the rails. The wretched fellow who served in the Peninsular War and fought in fourteen historic actions from Talavera, 1809, to Toulouse, 1814, got one medal. Those five years must have been pure hell from the physical point of view alone. His great grandson may have landed in France in the beginning of 1916 and been present during some of the greatest human slaughters war (except for the two atom bombs on

Japan) has ever known, and endured physical discomfort in the way of mud and cold which I have not yet seen a pen sufficiently describe. What did he get? A silver and a bronze medal. His son could have stayed at home during the last war and got as many; whereas, if he went abroad he got more.

Campaign medals today can signify so very little as regards service that I cannot understand why so many are awarded. The naval man who served on H.M.S. *Valiant*, a battleship, within two miles of the shores of Palestine got a medal; so did the airman who made one sortie; so did the soldier who was ambushed and sniped every time he went out. I believe that concert parties get them now but, the greatest condemnation of all lies in the fact that something like two and a half million medals were not even claimed for the last war and, I believe, over a million for the first. They cannot be worth much when people cannot be bothered to fill up a form to get them.

Would it not be better to have one genuine silver medal and use discretion as regards the number of bars, so that it really signified service, rather than a plethora of them which *may* signify nothing more than travel?

I have no fault to find with the individuals who wear the medals to which they are entitled, but I do think that the system which makes so many available is wrong.

It used to be possible—and may still be now for all I know—to buy packets of labels of various colours and sizes to stick on to handbags to give the impression that one was much-travelled. The fellow who printed these must have had a certain sense of humour for each packet contained the name and place of an hotel which those of us who really have travelled knew to be best left unmentioned. I well remember travelling in the same compartment with two young ladies who were so proudly advertising themselves in a way which I hardly think they meant!

I must mention some medals which are very rare indeed and not even mentioned in most books on the subject. I am quite prepared to be told that they are not medals at all, and equally prepared to disagree.

The items to which I refer were called medalets (which must not be confused with miniature medals with which I will deal later), or touch-pieces for the following reason.

There was a disease known as scrofula, or king's evil—but please don't ask me its present name—which it was believed could be cured by a touch from the sovereign. I think it had something to do with glands, or boils on the neck, but it doesn't really matter what it was as far as we are concerned. The practice of scrofulous persons being touched by the sovereign dates back to the time of William the Conqueror though I believe I am correct in saying that the first medalets were given by Henry VII—at any rate they are the first of which I am aware. The last were those given by Queen Anne, as George I would have nothing to do with the practice. The piece given was the small gold coin known as an angel which was suspended from a white ribbon (signifying purity) and hung round the sufferer's neck by the sovereign. The obverse depicted a ship; the reverse Michael overcoming the dragon. The designs on the two sides varied from reign to reign as do coins of the same value so that a full description of them comes more under the study of coins than medals.

The first miniature medals are those for Waterloo. The extraordinary thing about miniatures is that nothing official about them was published till 1873, though they appear to have been worn on the same occasions as they are today for the previous fifty-eight years.

A miniature medal is, naturally, presumed to be a small replica of the original but such is often far from the case. The reason is that there is no standard size, or necessary degree of quality, so that as long as there is some resemblance to the originals they get by. Speaking generally, I would say that more attention to detail is given to miniature orders than to miniature medals, though it is hard to understand why this distinction should be made.

The first Long Service Medal was authorized by a Royal Warrant dated 30th July, 1830, which stated that soldiers discharged after meritorious conduct should be entitled to wear a silver medal. The Royal Navy did not take the Army's water for long for an Order in Council dated 24th August, 1831, authorized, the award of a Long Service Medal to all non-commissioned ranks who had served twenty-one years without crime. The Royal Air Force corresponding medal was introduced in 1918 and has the strange distinction of having been awarded to those who had not completed the qualifying eighteen years in the service. Men who had previous army, or naval service were allowed to count it towards the qualifying period. I am rather surprised at the number of airmen I see wearing the ribbon who have it on the wrong way round. The ribbon is a combination of the dark blue of the Naval Long Service ribbon and the maroon of the Army one. As medals are worn in the order of seniority from the centre towards the shoulder, and the Navy is senior to the Army it should not be difficult for recipients to remember to wear the dark blue towards the centre, i.e. on the left when facing the wearer. Incidentally, wearers of the ribbon of the Africa Star might remember this too as it is almost as common to note this worn incorrectly as correctly.

I receive many questions of a general nature concerning medals, the most common of which concerns the replacement of those that have been lost. Medals of serving personnel will be replaced free if their loss is a result of circumstances beyond the recipient's control, such as fire, shipwreck, etc. Retired personnel can get theirs replaced after fulfilling certain necessary conditions. They must be paid for and will not be reissued till after the lapse of two months from the date of application. Relatives of the recipient cannot claim another issue whether he be dead or alive. Exceptions to this regulation have been made when the medals have been lost through enemy action. Replacements of the Victoria Cross, Distinguished Service Order and the medals for the First World War were given to the brother of Major George Lance Hawker, Royal Engineers and Royal Flying Corps who won the Victoria Cross in May, 1915, and was killed in action in November, 1915. The medals were lost when the Germans overran France in 1940.

No person except the recipient is allowed to wear medals though courtesy sometimes permits widows to wear their late husband's medals on certain occasions.

There are no age limits concerning the awarding of decorations for bravery and, may I add, women of the various services are eligible for the Victoria Cross though none have gained it. The cross can only be won in face of the enemy so the chances are that extreme heroism on the part of a woman would gain the George Cross, as some have. Several women, however, have been awarded Military Medals in both World Wars, two at least being civilians (during the Irish troubles).

KNIGHTHOOD AND CHIVALRY

The present word knight originally signified a servant, being derived from the Saxon "cniht" who was a member of the king's bodyguard and pledged to be at his service at all times. The power of a sovereign was, therefore, dependent on the number of his knights. This in turn led to the truism that the strength of a nation depended on the number and efficiency of the knights whom its sovereign could summon to war.

There was undoubtedly a number of men of good social standing and wealth who had nothing special to do so served voluntarily, but the number of such would have been too small to maintain an army so that a system of compulsory service linked with the tenure of land was introduced. This was known as the Feudal System, and the amount of land considered sufficient to support the dignity of a knight was known as a knight's fee. This fee varied according to the quality of the land and other factors, but was normally somewhere between 680 and 800 acres. The tenure of land in connection with military service was known as Tenure by Knight's Service, or Tenure in Chivalry, from the time of its institution by William the Conqueror till its abolition by Charles II in 1672.

The senior nobles were, of course, given vast tracts of land which were subdivided into so many knight's fees so that they were responsible for being ready for war service with the requisite number of followers. The holder of a complete fee—that is the full acreage—was liable to serve for forty days in any one year; the holder of half a fee was liable for twenty days, and that of a quarter for ten days. In certain cases a knight was allowed to supply a deputy. Though it would seem that the system made a large army always available I should doubt whether its number ever exceeded 10,000 at any one time.

War, as we are all too well aware, requires money as well as men so that the financial side was looked after by certain aids, reliefs and wardships. A full description of these is outside our scope so suffice it to say that they included the profits from an estate until the heir became of age, and a lump sum on his becoming so prior to taking over his inheritance. There was also a law known as Primer Seisin which gave the Crown the right to demand a cash payment equal to the profit made in the last year should the heir be of age on succeeding.

It soon became obvious that if all the farmers and their employees were called off the land there would be no food in the country so that knights were allowed to return home with their followers on payment of a sum. I have rather harped on the connection between the farmer and the knight so as to rub in the fact that the farmer and the knight (or, if you prefer it put differently, the landowner and the knight), were one and the same person.

From this remark it is obvious that not all could become knights, and such was the case. If, so to speak, you were detailed to be a knight you were, *ipso facto*, also detailed to own land. The converse was equally true.

There were certain exceptions made as regards those who had to perform military service, but none for those who had to pay. The exceptions as regards service were those who were over a certain age, or had some physical disability, or had some incurable disease, or (as it was put) an impediment of children. Those who claimed to have an excuse for not serving had to appear before two commissioners appointed by the king who fined them according to their several means.

The right of compelling those who could not, or would not, serve was soon perverted into a form of extortion which was used as late as the reigns of Edward VI and Elizabeth I. It was, the reader will no doubt remember, also used by Charles I.

The Romance of Chivalry—a branch of fiction writing—gradually influenced the state of knighthood by weaving tales of great bravery and splendid behaviour round imaginary knights. The church gradually laid hold on chivalry and used it as a means of instilling religion and some form of moral behaviour into the young men of the period. It became the fashion for a knight to take a vow to perform some special act which might mean that he would protect all pilgrims, help to recover the Holy Sepulchre or to be a knight-errant which meant that he would be delighted to join in any fight.

It is more romantic to call work service and easier to make a good yarn from that term. Had the period of romance extended to the early Victorian age, when railways came into being, we should have had tales about the wonderful knights of the footplate and their squires who stoked the shining steeds. The fact that most people at the time considered that the railway engine with its smoke and sparks should be disallowed would not have been mentioned in these stories and we should have been so surfeited with the wonderful accounts of the glamour attached to being an engine driver or stoker that it would be almost impossible to believe that they could be anything else but heroes. Having got so used to believing this sort of thing a story about a charming engine driver who, having found a dead cockerel on the front of his engine, walked back ten miles in the pouring rain to find the owner would seem more like truth than fiction.

The period between the eleventh and fourteenth centuries, which was that during which chivalry flourished, was probably the most barbarous in our history. Corruption, fiendish tortures, treachery and all the basest aspects of human nature were commonplace. Those with power descended to a plane of violence on a par with Hitler and his foul minions. This sort of thing was general throughout Europe so that it was impossible for any particular knight to take the stage as did Hitler and Mussolini who, with education available, will no doubt go down in history as two of the worst specimens of mankind the world, including fictional history, has ever known.

At the time of feudalism and chivalry there were two powers in the land—the Sovereign and the Church. The former had few, if any, scruples so that it was up to the latter to try and introduce a code of decency which it did, as

I have said, by inducing people generally, and the knights in particular, that there was more to chivalry than glamorous feats of arms. It gradually taught that the killing of fellow humans was not the sole reason for our existence but, should men become involved in war there should be some sort of mutual understanding that the maimed and innocent should be spared as much as possible.

The introduction of religion to chivalry had, at first, rather the opposite effect to that intended. The young knight, having received the Church's blessing thought that he had a divine right to do what he liked and that having attended church all his actions were above criticism.

I am reminded of an African native who was soliciting employment on the quayside at Mombasa while a liner was disembarking its passengers. The usual form was for the natives to submit the references which they had been given by their last employer and then leave it to the reader to decide just how bad he was. One fellow considered himself far superior to all the others and was shouting, "Me bloody fine nigger; me God-palaver". This was his way of saying that he had attended a missionary school. On reading the chit he produced it was obvious that he was about the biggest scoundrel on the quayside, and that in itself was no mean distinction!

In the early history of knighthood there were two kinds of knights and two distinct ceremonies at which the honour was conferred. A knight who was only given the accolade was known as a knight of the sword; one who had gone through a religious ceremony prior to the accolade was referred to as a knight of the bath. The reason for the latter title will be obvious when I deal with the ceremony. Before dealing with it, however, a few words must be said about the early training that a young man had to undergo before he was considered eligible for knighthood.

In the period of knighthood and chivalry with which we are dealing the youngster who aspired to become a knight had to serve his youth as a page to a prince, or some high nobleman. There are in the Royal Household today a number of youthful attendants, selected from noble families known as state pages, pages of the presence, pages of honour and pages of the back stairs.

The second rank in the dignity of knighthood was the esquire (from the French éscurier, a shield bearer). He was responsible for carrying the shield of the knight, whose apprentice-in-arms he was. The esquire was considered a gentleman, and had the right to bear arms on his shield; he also had the right to carry a sword, which denoted nobility or chivalry, though in his case it was not worn from what was known as the knightly belt. He also wore a distinguishing kind of defensive armour which was easily distinguishable from that of a knight. In addition to the esquires of chivalry there were others who might be termed feudal esquires who were tenants by knight's service who had a right to claim knighthood but, not wishing to take up what we would now call a military career, had done no more that serve their obligatory service.

In accounts concerning precedence mention is made of esquires by creation, with the investiture of a silver collar and silver spurs; but these would appear to be only the insignia of the esquires of the king's person, which descended with the title of esquire to the eldest sons in succession. The sons of younger sons of dukes and marquesses, the younger sons of earls, viscounts and barons, and their eldest sons, with the eldest sons of baronets, and of knights of all the orders, are correctly esquires at birth, though their precedence is determined by the rank of their fathers. Officers of the Royal Household, and of the fighting services down to the rank of captain in the Army and its equivalent in the other two services, doctors of law, barristers and medical practitioners, are entitled to the style of esquire. A justice of the peace is only an esquire during the time he holds the appointment, but a county sheriff is an esquire for life.

The general assumption of the title by those who are not entitled to it has virtually robbed it of any distinction whatever. Those who were quite content to be called charwomen must now be addressed as charladies. Everyone has decided to upgrade him—or her-self so that the charprincess of the future will, in every respect except, perhaps, her output of work be the same as the charwoman of the past.

After showing the necessary zeal and aptitude the esquire was eligible for knighthood so we will now deal with the more spectacular and romantic ceremony of his initiation as a Knight of the Bath. The actual ceremonies varied slightly in the different centuries, and at various courts, and, of course, in their descriptions given by the writers of the times. Let us, therefore, take as our example a ceremony that might have taken place at about the middle of the Age of Chivalry, say about the end of the twelfth century.

The esquire was first of all undressed and put into a bath, the symbol of purification. When he came out he was made to wear a white tunic, the symbol of purity; a red robe, emblematic of the blood which he must be prepared to shed in the cause of faith; a black doublet, as a token of the death which awaited him and all mankind. Finally a white belt, as a sign of chastity. Thus clothed he was made to fast for twenty-four hours. The next evening he was taken to church where he was made to spend the night in prayer, sometimes alone, sometimes in company with the priest and his sponsors. The next morning he made his confession followed by the administration of the Holy Communion. The priest then gave him a sermon on the duties and mode of conduct expected of a knight. After the sermon the aspirant walked slowly up to the altar with his sword suspended from his belt worn round the neck the priest removed it, blessed it, and returned it to the same position. He then knelt before the king, or nobleman who was to invest him. "To what end," he was asked, "do you desire to enter this order? If it is that you may be rich, repose yourself, and be honoured without doing honour to knighthood, then you are unworthy of it, and would be to the knighthood you should receive, what the simoniacal clergyman is to the prelacy." If the esquire answered that he would do all in his power to uphold the ideals the service continued.

The knights in attendance then advanced towards him carrying his accoutrements. They first put on his spurs then his hauberk or coat of mail, then his breastplate, then the brassarts or arm-pieces, then the gauntlets, and finally girded on his sword.

The final act was the receipt of the accolade, that is three strokes with the

E

flat of the sword on his shoulder, and sometimes an additional blow with the palm of the hand on the cheek. While doing this the lord would say, "In the name of God, Saint Michael, and Saint George, I make thee a knight. Be thou brave, bold, and loyal."

On leaving the church the new knight mounted his horse and showed himself to the crowd which always assembled for such occasions.

In this account it is easy to see the origin of the expression "to win one's spurs" which signified being suitable for high acclaim. It is also easy to note the influence that the Church had throughout the initiation ceremony, which was the most important in the young man's life. Not only did the novice receive the sacrament, but his sword was blessed and the whole procedure from the time he first knelt in prayer till he left the church a knight, took place under clerical supervision. Much the same may be said of the regimental colours of today because they are blessed before presentation and then, when replaced by new ones, end their lives hanging in the regimental chapel. If we study the various oaths which were required of the knights during the period of chivalry we find that there is a religious significance in them all, though it would be hard to define exactly what it is. If a knight misbehaved himself he was considered to have committed a crime against both God and his fellow knights; if, on the other hand, he had performed some particularly meritorious feat he was praised for having championed the dual cause of God and man. It seems incredible that there co-existed knights who, if they carried out all their vows and behaved as they were told, were just too good to be true; while on the other side of the picture were those whose acts of fiendish cruelty, and arrogance, were a blot on our history for several centuries. In this connection the Church itself has something to explain. Why was it so keen on instilling the virtues of courtesy and brotherly love while at the same period it was promoting crusades against what it termed the infidels. What was the Church doing in taking upon itself the right to proclaim that one section of humanity should be spared, and another exterminated. It is no good the historians trying to throw bouquets or bricks at knighthood and chivalry as practised in the Middle Ages unless he is prepared to do the same at the church which either controlled them or was doing its level best to do so. The fairest thing one can say about that period is, I suggest, that it was like the curate's egg—good and bad.

In my opinion only extremely wise men or utter fools would try to draw definite divisions between heraldry, chivalry and knighthood—especially in the case of the latter two. There are terms which concern two or more of them so that the critic has the grand opportunity of accusing the author of either repetition or omission, or both. If he cannot criticize under these headings he can accuse him of including items in the wrong chapter—no groundsman could ever hope to produce such a perfect wicket! Let us further tempt him by including one or two things which may, for all I know, be outside the scope of all three of these headings.

I would say that it is impossible to give the exact date of origin of the following terms. There is a vast difference between knowing the date of the first known example and the first example ever. If I say that I first met Mr

Smith in 1950 it is a vastly different thing from saying that he was just born in that year; the poor old gentleman may just be going round the last bend before his finishing straight. The dates that I shall mention must not, therefore, be taken otherwise than to mean that they are the first of which I have trace.

I have already mentioned that there were two kinds of knights which were known as knights of the sword and knights of the bath. The distinction arose owing to the different ceremonies at the time of their initiation. In both the giving of the accolade formed part. The word is derived from two Latin ones, "ad", to, and "collum" the neck, so that the combination would signify an embrace rather than a tap on the shoulder. Some authors have supposed, and I think correctly, that when the term accolade is used in reference to the ceremony of conferring knighthood, the particular act to which it referred was the embrace, which was frequently accompanied by a kiss and a light smack on the cheek. It is, however, more generally accepted that the accolade signifies the dubbing, which is the slight blow given on the cheek or shoulder of the new knight. Gibbon describes this as the last affront which was lawful for the knight to endure, but I should gravely doubt this remark as it seems to me unlikely that any part of such an important ceremony would signify an affront. The custom of giving the accolade, whatever form it took, is extremely old, for Gregory of Tours who wrote during the sixth century, mentions it in an account he gives of a ceremony at which the king of France bestowed a knighthood.

The next term we come to in alphabetical order is a coat of arms which many people confuse with a crest, and almost all know nothing about its origin; yet, when explained it is all so clear and obvious.

The forerunner of a coat of arms was a surcoat which was a plain, probably white, garment like a sleeveless nightgown which was worn over the armour to protect it against the heat of the sun. It must be remembered that many knights blazoned their armour so that they could be recognized when their visors (facepieces) were closed. If many knights wore surcoats the question of recognition cropped up again so that the surcoats were blazoned. This meant that they then bore the arms of the knight and thus became coats of arms. To prevent the somewhat voluminous effect which the garment would otherwise have a belt was worn round the waist. A plain blue surcoat is known to have been worn in about 1200. The colour was probably adopted as a means of recognition so that the plain white ones must have been of an earlier date.

We next come to the collar which is of very old origin indeed as an indication of rank, office or achievement. It was the custom of earliest man to show that he had killed some dangerous animal by wearing some part of it hung from his body. The part easiest worn was a tooth which, either singly or with others from a similar animal, was threaded and worn round the neck. The custom still maintains among some of the tribes of Africa and South America who wear such necklaces together with, or without, additional adornment of the same sort. Torquis, or torques of gold or silver were worn as indications of rank by the Persians. Did not Torquatus take his name from the collar which he took off a Gaul in somewhere about 360 B.C.?

To return to comparatively modern times, we find that collars as articles of distinction were awarded by Richard II. They were known as "Collars of the King's Livery". They were given in token of loyalty, and very often a badge was suspended from them. These badges were the personal marks of the donor, so that the two articles combined signified loyalty by the wearer to the person represented by the badge.

One of the most famous collars was that known as the Collar of SS, but there is doubt as to what these letters stood for. There are two theories. One that they stand for "souvereigne" as representing the claim of Henry IV to the throne; the other that they stood for Saint Simplicius. I find both rather difficult to follow. Collars, as we shall see later, from part of the insignia of orders of knighthood.

The next item is a crest, from the Latin "crista", signifying the ornament on top of the helmet. The early helmets consisted of a metal framework, covered with leather, with a flat top on which was placed the crest. The composition of them varied, some were made of wood, others of leather, to represent a real or fictitious animal. They were fastened to the helmet by a silken cord. Before the adoption of animal crests, plumes were used. The same sort of plume as adorned the helmet was often worn on the head of the knight's horse. Though often worn in addition to carrying the shield, they were intended to act as marks of recognition at jousts and such occasions when the shield was not carried.

In the first instance of them being worn, a knight had to obtain royal permission but, with the process of time the wearing of them became general. Strictly speaking, they are not hereditable though this, too, has become common practice. In this connection it is interesting to note that as they were orginally granted as special royal favours to certain noblemen, and never to women, none are allowed to bear one. Hence, therefore, there is no such thing as a widow's crest, which is a term I have heard used.

An interesting example of the place and use of the old crests is to be found in the church, at Cobham, Kent, where it will be noted that the warrior's head is resting on his helmet, at the top of which is his crest. The original crest was, I believe, granted to William Montacute by Edward III in 1333. In this case it was called a tymbre and consisted of an eagle. Feathers by themselves, as opposed to an image, were, as I have said, of a much earlier date and were worn during the reign of Edward I. The fact that the wearing of small replicas was introduced some time after that of wearing feathers must not be taken to mean that they replaced the latter for there are recorded illustrations of knights wearing both types of crests during the reign of Richard II.

We now come to a garment of which I have seen very little mention indeed—the cyclas. I have seen it described as a short surcoat, which is on a par with calling a revolver a short rifle. If you are going to call it a short anything then it must be a short coat of arms. This is not comprehensively accurate for it could be short in front and long behind or short all round. A cyclas was, therefore, a coat of arms, either cut away in front or all round, whose purpose was to display the wearer's arms on its front while enabling him to walk. They were sleeveless and their low edges were scalloped, or engrailed to use the correct heraldic term. The cyclas superseded the coat of arms in about 1300.

The cyclas was in turn superseded by the jupon which was similar to the former except that it fitted tightly. It came into vogue about 1320 and lasted for approximately a hundred years.

One of the insignias of orders of knighthood is the mantle, a long trailing cloak-like garment, which was worn by knights during the Age of Chivalry. Now known as robes of estate they are still worn by Peers of the Realm on ceremonial occasions. Those worn on such occasions are of crimson velvet; their parliamentary robes are of scarlet. The rank of the wearer is denoted by what are called doublets of ermine. A duke wears four; a marquess three and a half; an earl three; a viscount two and a half; a baron two. The mantles of the different orders of knighthood each have their own colouring as I shall describe presently.

Fictional stories about the days of chivalry often make mention of the hero carrying an article belonging to his sweetheart. When this was a glove, or handkerchief, I have no idea where the fellow wore it. If, however, it consisted of a scarf he tied it round his helmet immediately under his crest and it was then known as a contoise. He wore a ribbon round his waist and it was then known as a cointoise. The difference between these two is, therefore, determined by the position in which it was worn. The contoise was replaced by a lambrequin, or mantling, a short mantle which covered the shoulders. This was an ornate garment, made of silk or velvet, and lined with ermine, which was attached to the helmet by a cord ended with silk tassels.

No mention of chivalry would be complete without a reference to a motto which, incidentally, I find very difficult to explain. The word is of Italian origin and originally signified a war-cry. For instance, "Saint George for England", and many of the other war-cries one reads about in early history are the forerunners of our present motto. By their war-cries tribes were known so that in the course of time families became known by their mottoes. This interconnection between the motto and the family, or a particular noble, was "adopted" (I cannot think of a better expression) by the Army, so that regiments, being in essence one family naturally adopted mottoes too. Heraldry has done much to unite the military with the civilian. It is common practice for the latter to deride the Services but I used to note that there were very few members of the local councils who did not attend our functions, or were extremely hurt if they were not asked to do so. I doubt whether there is any community of human beings where seniority plays such an important part as in any Urban District Council. We had to be most careful to ensure that dignity was not slighted. If an error was unwittingly made the stags took it well, but not so the hinds! I never quite mastered their ascending and descending order of merit as so many factors appeared to be involved. Mrs Sanitary Inspector sat on the left of the Road Safety Officer if the Harbour Master was present, but on the right of the Deputy Surveyor on all other occasions—and God help you if you got that wrong! The saying that Hell knows no fury like a woman scorned must have originated from a

Mess Secretary's office after he had tried to organize what was called on the invitation card, a "Social".

This is rather by the way so I will return to the subject by saying that some regiments had as their badge something which was a direct connection with their depot, town or county. The Devonshire Regiment, for instance, had Exeter Castle; the King's Own Scottish Borderers that of Edinburgh; the East Surrey Regiment's badge included an escutcheon of the Arms of Guildford; the Queen's Own Royal West Kent Regiment wore the White Horse of Kent.

Now for some historical details concerning the four senior orders of knighthood the first of which is the Most Noble Order of the Garter.

The actual date of its institution is unknown. It was founded by Edward III either in, or between, the years 1344 and 1350. We are all allowed to conjecture so for my part I would say that the Order was instituted sometime between 1347 and 1350. It is rather fun trying to fix a date when things might have happened and, providing one can find reasonable evidence, there is no reason why one's final deduction need be too wide of the mark.

Let us examine that most interesting period in our history that played such an important part in the subjects of knighthood and chivalry.

In 1338 Edward landed in Flanders and in doing so began what was subsequently known as the Hundred Years War. Not only did he have no success on land but after a while found that the French had collected a fleet and was threatening his lines of communication and perhaps England itself. He hurried home and appealed to the merchants of London and the Cinque Ports to lend him ships, as there was no regular navy at that time. A strange battle, known as the battle of Sluys, 1340, followed during which English merchant ships sailed by merchant seamen and armed with bowmen routed the French —nay, captured the lot of them. This is ranked as the first English naval action. There is a story of how the defeat was announced to Philip VI which, in various forms, has formed the subject of music-hall jokes ever since. The story goes that nobody dared tell the king what had happened so finally the court jester was prevailed upon to break the news. "The English are cowards your majesty." "Why", the king is said to have asked. "Because they were frightened to jump into the sea as our braves did" replied the jester.

The events in Flanders during the period 1338–41 demonstrate in a most remarkable manner the complexities of war. The area of France most affected by the war was that in which the sheep were reared, so that townsfolk were unable to obtain the raw supplies for their industry without obtaining it from England. Edward III was no fool for he realized that a great part of the money which he wanted for fighting came from what was known as the maltolt on wool. This maltolt (derived from the French "mal", meaning bad, and "toll" tax) had to be paid by the English merchants prior to export as Edward was taking no risks. Providing the wool districts in France were kept unproductive so the demand for English imports was maintained. As the money to pay the Army that ravished the country came from the wool the whole business was as near to perpetual motion as we shall ever get. In the end, however, Edward, not content with just enough money wanted more and angered Parliament by his demands. Incidentally, it was during this reign that the Houses of Parliament adopted the principle of sitting in two chambers. The Commons was composed of the knights of the shires and merchants who gradually put a brake on the attitude of the divine right of the king and his powerful nobles to do as they pleased.

In spite of opposition Edward raised money but not quite the amount that he wanted and in this deficiency lies the main reason for the decline of chivalry. The first battle that was fought after the king landed in France is one of which all Englishmen should for ever be proud. If, as Sir Winston Churchill said, 1940 was our finest hour, then the duration of the battle of Crecy on 26th August, 1346, must have been one of our finest minutes.

Edward, disgusted with the performances of his hired German and Flemish soldiers decided that he would raise an army of Englishmen. Being short of cash he could not afford cavalry so all, knights and yeoman alike, fought on foot. Landing on the Cherbourg peninsula Edward wreaked his vengeance on the villages of Normandy for the damage done by marauding seamen along our south coast and then, having driven the French back over the Somme and Seine he found that they had taken up positions near the village of Crecy within a few hundred yards of the site from which the German long-range gun was to shell Paris at a range of seventy-six miles in 1918. Against the 20,000 Englishmen there were 12,000 French cavalry, nearly 40,000 foot soldiers, augmented by 10,000 Genoese mercenary bowmen. The Englishmen were drawn up in three divisions with those commanded by the Black Prince and the Earls of Arundel and Northampton in front, with the king commanding the other in reserve. While so arranged it was attacked by the French. How many little items of future historical interest then occurred! During the French advance, led by the Genoese bowmen, a heavy rain storm developed and their bowstrings, which were not protected against such an event as were those of the English, became wet. The English archers shot arrows as if it had snowed and thus proved the value of rapid shooting 358 years before the retreat from Mons when the Germans imagined that our infantrymen were armed with automatic weapons owing to the rate of rapid fire which they produced. The Genoese could not stand this hail of arrows and fell back only to be killed by the French and thus proved that allies who are not allies at heart are better out of it. The Germans had the same opinions as these about their Italian allies in North Africa, and then in Sicily and Italy afterwards. The sheer weight of numbers gradually forced the Black Prince back and he sent a message to his father asking for help. "Is my son, dead, wounded, or unhorsed?" asked the king of the messenger. "Neither," replied the man. "Go back to them that sent you, and tell them to send no more as long as my son is alive. Let the boy win his spurs."

The French mass poured on but the English bowmen and the lightly armed infantrymen stood their ground and matched fire-power and agility against armour and eventually won. The result proved that the days of the knights in armour had gone. The humble yeoman with his bow was a better man than the blazoned knight when it came to a fight. As the machine gun was called the queen of the battlefield during my time in France during the

First World War, so did the arrow rule till it had to give way to the shot and bullet.

In the next year, that is 1347, Edward surrounded Calais and forced it to surrender. This surrender was granted on condition that twelve of the citizens came out and placed themselves at the king's mercy. His idea of mercy was that they should be put to death, in spite of many requests from his army that they should be spared. Finally Queen Phillipa, his wife, intervened on their behalf and so, "for his dear wife's sake he spared the twelve hostages". There is more hidden in these two sentences than one would at first think. If Crecy marked the end of chivalry what do we find had happened since its inception? First of all we find a revulsion on the part of the Army that the inhabitants of a captured fortress should be murdered in cold blood after their surrender; secondly, we note that the wishes of a woman were granted.

After he had turned the people of Calais out and replaced them with Englishmen and women, Edward returned home.

The reader is probably wondering what the wool tax, Crecy, Calais, and so on, has to do with the Order of the Garter. There are two possible answers—nothing whatever, or quite a lot. It is the latter that we are dissecting as it were. The king had returned triumphant on both land and sea and had proved for himself that it was better to have a small homogeneous force than just mere numbers. He must have been very pleased with himself and those who had helped in his victories. He gave a party at Windsor—he called a round table as it was then styled—at which he reminded his guests of their knightly vows. "Let us," one might almost imagine him saying, "form a brotherhood of the elite in which we will include members of the Church." He must, I contend, have had some reason in mind for instituting the Order. I find some suggestion like this much easier to believe than that he woke up one morning with a hell of a liver and commanded a number of nobles and clergy to present themselves and then said to them, in so many words, "You you, you, etc., are in future to consider yourselves Knights of the Garter, dismiss."

However, whatever the reason, the fact remains that Edward III instituted the Order whose membership is now limited to twenty-six knights, excluding the Sovereign and Royalty. The original statutes have been lost and the numbers quoted are taken from one dated 17th January, 1805. Each knight has a stall in the Chapel of the Order, which is the Chapel of St George, Windsor. He has also what is known as a stallplate on which his arms are emblazoned. His banner hangs over his stall.

The ceremony of installing a new knight is most impressive and probably bears more resemblance to those carried out in the Middle Ages than any that still remain. It starts in the Throne Room of Windsor Castle where the sovereign summons the Garter King-of-Arms and Black Rod to conduct the new knight to the Presence. The Garter is then buckled round the left knee, while the Prelate admonishes the new knight to be courageous and stand firm in any undertaking. The Ribbon, Star, Mantle and Collar are then bestowed on him. He then takes the Oath of the Order that "wittingly or willingly he shall not break any statute of the Order".

It is then the traditional custom that the new knight has lunch with the sovereign, after which the knights go in procession from St. George's Hall to the Chapel. This procession is headed by the Governor of Windsor Castle and the Military Knights of Windsor, followed by the sovereign's bodyguard of the Yeoman of the Guard, followed by the Kings-of-Arms, the Pursuivants and Heralds. Then come the Knights of the Order headed by the new member, the sovereign walking last. A fanfare is blown as the procession enters the Chapel. After the National Anthem, the sovereign commands that, "It is our pleasure that the Knight Companion be installed". His name is called and he is then conducted to his stall by Garter King-of-Arms. The service, which lasts about half an hour, concludes with a prayer of thanks for the founding of the Order, and the Te Deum.

The Military Knights of Windsor, whom I mentioned as taking part in the procession, are an adjunct to the Order of the Garter. The charity, for such it is, was originally known as the Poor Knights of Windsor, or Alms Knights, was founded by Edward III soon after the institution of the Order of the Garter. Its object was to maintain twenty-four (afterwards raised to twenty-six) poor individuals who had rendered distinguished military service. The change in title was made by William IV in 1833.

Ladies have been admitted to the Order since its institution. Froissart describes the fine appearance of Queen Philippa at the first feast held by the Order. "The Queen and some of the knights companions wives, and other great ladies" he says, "had robes and hoods of the gift of the sovereign, the former garnished with little embroidered garters." The ensign of the Garter was also delivered to them, and they were expressly termed "Dames de la Fraternité de St George". Effigies of ladies wearing the Garter are to be found. For instance, there is one of the Duchess of Suffolk, of the time of Henry VI, wearing the Garter round her wrist. This is to be seen at the village of Ewelme, about thirteen miles south-east of Oxford. There is another of the next reign depicting Lady Harcourt wearing the Garter on her left arm. This can be seen at Stanton Harcourt, about seven miles almost due west of Oxford.

Elias Ashmole in his *Insitutions, Law and Ceremonies of the Order of the Garter*, published in 1672, says:

"After a long disuse of these robes by the queens of England and knights-companions' ladies, there was at the feast of St. George, celebrated in 1638, endeavour used to have them restored; for the then deputy-chancellor moved the sovereign in chapter (held the 22nd May), that the ladies of the knights-companions might have the privilege to wear a garter of the Order about their arms, and an upper robe, at festival times, according to ancient usage. Upon which motion the sovereign gave order that the queen should be acquainted therewith and her pleasure known, and the affair left to the ladies' particular suit. On the 10th October of the following year, the feast of St George being then also kept at Windsor, the deputy-chancellor reported to the sovereign in chapter the answer which the queen was pleased to give him to the aforesaid order, whereupon it was then left to a chapter to be called by the knights-companions to

consider of every circumstance, how it were fittest to be done for the
honour of the Order, which was appointed to be held at London about
Alhollandtide after; but what was then or after done doth not appear;
and the unhappy war coming on, this matter wholly slept."

It is recorded that when Queen Anne attended a thanksgiving service in
St Paul's in 1702, and again in 1704, she wore the Garter set with diamonds,
as sovereign of the Order round her left arm.

The second senior Order is that of the Most Ancient and Most Noble
Order of the Thistle whose date of origin is uncertain.

Attempts have been made to give it great antiquity but the reasons for this
belief do not stand the test of investigation. One, for instance, attributes its
foundation to the Scottish king Achaius to commemorate his defeat of
Athelstan. As Achaius died a hundred years before Athelstan was born, I
think that we might be justified in dismissing this claim. As a matter of fact,
the thistle was not adopted as the badge of Scotland till towards the end of
the fifteenth century.

Sir Nicholas Nicolas in his *History of the Orders of Knighthood of the British
Empire*, published in 1841, says that it is difficult to believe in the existence
of the Order until the reign of James VII of Scotland and II of England. Be
this as it may, the orders of knighthood were considered relics of popery by
the Scottish nobles so, as Sir Nicolas says, "it is not pretended that there
were any Knights of St Andrew, or of the Thistle, after the accession of
James VI, in 1567".

A Warrant for the reinstitution of the Order, signed by James II bears
place and date, Windsor, 29th May, 1687; but, though statutes were issued,
and eight knights nominated, the patent never received the Great Seal. James
II abdicated in the next year and, incidentally, chucked the Great Seal into
the Thames so that no public business could be transacted till a new one was
made. Nothing further was done about the Order till it was finally revived
by Queen Anne in 1703.

The Warrant of 1687 stated that the Order consisted of the king and
twelve brethren (symbolical of Our Lord and the Twelve Apostles), Queen
Anne decreed the same number, though the full complement was not completed for several years.

This number continued to be the same till 1821, when, George IV ordered
that it should be increased to the sovereign and sixteen knights. In 1827 this
number was made permanent and vacancies filled as they occur. As originally intended, the Order was for Scottish noblemen only, but since the reign
of George I it has been conferred on English peers as well. Foreigners are
admitted as Honorary members.

The third senior Order is that of the Most Illustrious Order of St Patrick
which was instituted by George III on 5th February, 1783, and, as it was
intended to be the national knighthood for Ireland, was named after the
appropriate saint.

The original number of brethren was fifteen but it was subsequently
increased to twenty-two; there are, however, now less than ten, and the
Order is moribund.

The fourth senior Order is the Most Honourable Order of the Bath which derives its name from the custom of bathing prior to the installation of a new knight. Due to the fact that bathing has been associated with the granting of knighthood since the earliest days, I think that some authors have presumed that this Order dates from the same period.

The facts are that it was instituted on 11th October, 1399, by the Duke of Lancaster two days before he was crowned as Henry IV. Historians will recall that it was he who landed at Ravenspur, in Yorkshire, while Richard II was in Ireland endeavouring to quell a rebellion against his tyranny. After being delayed by a storm, he landed in Wales and was betrayed at Flint Castle subsequently flung into the Tower. He was then taken to Pontefract Castle, and then, in 1400, his corpse was publicly displayed in St Paul's. Such were methods of succession used in those days!

One might be right in assuming that, in order to curry favour, the new king, who in any case was not the rightful heir, considered it a good plan to make a few knighthoods.

Froissart, writing of this period, says:

"The Saturday before his coronation (which took place on the following Monday) he departed from Westminster, and rode to the Tower of London with a great number; and that night all such esquires as should be made knights the next day, watched, who were to the number of forty-six. Every esquire had his own bayne (bath) by himself; and the next day the Duke of Lancaster made them all knights at the Mass-time. Then had they long coats with strait [sic] sleeves, furred with mynever like prelates, with white laces hanging on their shoulders."

It became the practice for the sovereign to create Knights of the Bath prior to their coronation, and on other occasions connected with the Royal Family, such as births and weddings.

Robert Fabian in his *Chronicles*, which were collated by Sir Henry Ellis and published in 1811, recalls in the one that he wrote somewhere about 1516, that Henry V dubbed sixteen Knights of the Bath after the taking of Caen in 1416—I do not recall a similar ceremony at the capture of the same town 528 years later.

In Guillim's *Heraldry*, published somewhere about 1679, there is a list of the sixty-eight knights of this Order who were made by Charles II on the occasion of his coronation. The Order from that time, as far as I can ascertain, remained in complete abeyance till revived under writ of Privy Seal, dated 23rd May, 1725, by George I. There is a story that its revival was due to the efforts of the Prime Minister, Robert Walpole, who thought that he might look nice all togged up in the appropriate robes. Be this as it may, the fact remains that he was made a Knight of the Bath in the same year which leaves us to draw whatever inference we care to. Incidentally, he was made a Knight of the Garter in the next year, which must have annoyed his many enemies in the House.

The statues and ordinances of the Order, dated 23rd May, 1725, directed that membership should consist of thirty-six companions [sic], which number should be maintained. The officers appointed were, in addition to the

Grand Master, a Dean, Registrar, King-of-Arms, Genealogist, Secretary, Usher and Messenger. The officers at present are known as, Great Master and Principal Knight Grand Cross, Dean (who is the Dean of Westminster), Bath King-of-Arms, Registrar and Secretary, Genealogist, Gentleman Usher of the Scarlet Rod and a Deputy Secretary.

The statues and ordinances just mentioned further directed that the badge should be composed of a rose, thistle and shamrock, issuing from a sceptre between three Imperial Crowns, surrounded by the motto *Tria Juncta in Uno*, and to be of pure gold, chased and pierced, and to be worn from a red riband worn obliquely over the right shoulder. The collar was to be of thirty ounces troy weight, and composed of nine Imperial Crowns, and eight roses, thistles and shamrocks, issuing from a sceptre, enamelled in their proper colours, and joined together by seventeen gold knots of white enamel, and having the badge of the Order pendant from it. The Star was to consist of three gold Imperial Crowns, surrounded by the motto of the Order upon a circle gules (that is red), with a glory (issuing rays) from the centre, to be embroidered on the left side of the upper garment.

The apparel was to consist of a surcoat of a white satin, a crimson mantle of the same material lined with white silk, tied at the neck with a cord of crimson and gold, with gold tassels, and the Star of the Order embroidered on the left shoulder; a white silk hat, with a standing plume of white ostrich feathers; white leather boots, edged and heeled; crimson and gold spurs; a sword in a white scabbard, with cross hilts of gold.

The date 2nd January, 1815, is a most important one in the history of this Order, and I shall have to make a considerable digression to show why this is so. Much of what I shall have to say during this digression concerns the story of medals so that I must ask the indulgence of experienced collectors while I deal with a subject that must be well known to them.

It will make the reason for the important steps which were taken on this date clearer if I deal with the situations prevailing at this time in the Navy and Army separately. In both cases I shall have to antedate my remarks so as to get continuity.

Prior to 1849 there had been no general award of medals to the Royal Navy. In that year one known as the Naval General Service Medal was introduced to be given to all survivors of some 231 actions which were specifically named by a Board of Officers convened by the Admiralty. It was also decided that they should be given to the surviving relatives of those who had applied for them but died prior to the general issue. Admirals and ships' captains were, however, catered for by what were known as Naval Gold Medals. They were only awarded for eighteen actions, but the fact remains that there were medals which could have been given had superior authority decreed. These medals were of two sizes; the larger were given to admirals, the smaller to captains of the ships engaged. It will be seen how few of the officers were rewarded with one of these medals when I say that between the period 1796–1815, during which they were, so to speak, available only 22 of the larger, and 117 of the smaller, were given.

The way these medals were awarded caused a great deal of irritation among senior officers and, if I may say so, quite rightly. It is, for instance, difficult to understand why one large and fourteen small gold medals were awarded for the battle of the Nile and none for service off Copenhagen.

Admiral Lord Collingwood was one who had every reason to grouse. He was present at the battle of the Glorious First of June, 1794, in command of H.M.S. *Barfleur*, which was one of thirty-seven ships present. Seventeen captains were selected to receive small gold medals for this action, but not he. He was subsequently recommended to receive one for the battle of St Vincent but declined to receive it till he had got one for the First of June, which he subsequently received, but not that for St Vincent!

On 7th October, 1813, the Prince Regent, commanded that gold crosses, and large and small gold medals should be awarded to certain officers who had distinguished themselves in actions for which the Military General Service Medal was subsequently awarded in 1848. Though these were made retrospective to service in Egypt, in 1801, nothing would influence the Lord High Admiral, the Duke of Clarence, to forward the requests of the naval officers who served at Copenhagen for recognition. It is difficult to say, without knowing the actual numbers involved, whether the Army was better served by its gold crosses and medals than the Navy, the total awards were, 163 gold crosses, 85 large gold medals and 599 small.

I think I have now said enough to show that only a chosen few senior officers of both services received any awards at all; there was nothing for the others.

Now let us return to the Order of the Bath and see what happened on 2nd January, 1815. Before opening the account with a bit of official jargon let me say that, owing to the debility of George III, the Prince of Wales was made Regent in 1811.

In order to make the Royal Warrant easier to understand I will leave out the twiddly bits and "officialese" and use the past tense.

In 1815, the Prince Regent, in order to show his appreciation of the services rendered by senior officers of both Services in the recent campaigns decided to extend the limits of the Order of the Bath and so ordained that in the future it should be composed of three classes, which were to differ in their ranks and degrees of dignity.

The first class to consist of Knights Grand Crosses, a designation which was to be substituted for that of Companions previously in use. These knights, exclusive of princes of the blood-royal, were not to exceed seventy-two in number which was to include existing K.B.s; of which twelve might be nominated for distinguished services in a civil or diplomatic capacity. In order that recipients of a class should be distinguishable, it was ordained that naval and military officers should bear upon both the badge and star a wreath of laurel encircling the motto, and issuing from an escroll inscribed *Ich Dien* (I Serve). This class was not conferred upon officers below the rank of rear-admiral in the Navy, or major-general in the Army.

The second class was to consist of Knights Commanders, whose number was not to exceed one hundred and eighty exclusive of foreign officers. This number could, however, be extended "in the event of future wars". A *sine qua non* to membership was that the nominee must hold a commission not below the rank of lieutenant-colonel in the Army, or post-captain in the

Navy. These ranks have now been raised to major-general and rear-admiral respectively. It was also laid down that the dignity of Knight Grand Cross could only be conferred on those who previously held that of Knight Commander of the Order.

The third class was to be composed of regular officers of the two services, not below field rank (major) or the equipalent rank in the Navy, who were to be styled Companions. The essential qualification in their case was that they must have been mentioned in despatches published in the *London Gazette*.

This ruling fell heavily on officers serving with the Honourable East India Company so that four days later another decree was issued to the effect that fifteen of its officers not below the rank of lieutenant-colonel, might be raised to the dignity of Knights Commanders. It went on to say that in the event of future wars this number would be increased and, in addition, a certain number of appointments to Companions would be made. It will be noted that the officers serving with the Company's ships were entirely ignored.

On 25th May, 1847, another important change was made in the constitution of the Order in that all classes were made open to civilians. The limitations as regards the numbers of each were decreed to be as follows: Knights Grand Cross: military, 50; civil, 25. Knights Commanders : military, 102; civil, 50. Companions : military, 525; civil, 200.

This Order has been remodelled twice, and enlarged thirteen times since its inception so that the figures just given have been considerably increased.

When the Order was divided into military and civil divisions it was decided that the badge and star of the latter should be different from the former.

A great many questions arise concerning orders of knighthood, and others whose proper category is difficult to define, which, judging by the number of times I am asked them, might interest the reader. It seemed to me that here, as a sort of postscript to this chapter, was as good a place as any to include them.

Let me start by answering the most common query of all, by saying that not all Orders confer knighthood or precedence. The senior of such is the Order of Merit, the next the Order of the Companions of Honour. The first ranks, as an Order, immediately after that of Knight Grand Cross of the Order of the Bath; the latter, immediately after that of Knight Grand Cross of the British Empire. There are two kinds of members to the former, military (which, of course, includes all three Services) and civil. The badge of the former has an additional cross swords. Both are open to men and women. There is a distinction which is not called an Order, it is known as the Royal Victorian Chain. Strange as it may seem, it was instituted by Edward VII, in 1902, and between sixty and seventy awarded.

There are Orders which are only open to ladies, the senior of which is the Imperial Order of the Crown of India. The Royal Red Cross, instituted in 1883, is the first and only military Order open to ladies. It is divided into two classes whose recipients are known as members or associates respectively.

It is awarded for distinguished service in the care of the sick and wounded of any, or all, of the three Services.

The Distinguished Service Order, instituted in 1886, also carries no precedence. It is an award to members of the military forces, for, as its name applies, distinguished service. Members of the Merchant Navy were made eligible to receive it in 1942.

Having digressed so far, I think it will be necessary for me to go even further and say a few words about what is known as precedence. Omitting royalty, the order is, Dukes, Marquesses, Earls, Viscounts, Barons, Knights of the Garter, Baronets, Knights of the Thistle, Knights of St Patrick, then Knights Grand Crosses according to the seniority of their Orders, and lastly Knights Bachelor. Baronetages and knightages are conferred without an order of knighthood. This means to put it bluntly, that a person can be Sir Somebody without having G.C. or K.C. anything after his name. The Knights Bachelor do not constitute a Royal Order and the title does not descend at death, and neither does it in the case of the Orders of Chivalry.

The rules regarding the precedence of women are somewhat complicated. The daugher of a peer retains her title if she marries a commoner, otherwise she ranks with her husband. She may, therefore, go up or down, so to speak. An elder sister who marries someone lower in the order of precedence to the husband of her younger sister will change places with her in precedence.

I am occasionally asked the maximum number of initials signifying Orders that a person can have after his name. I am not aware that there is any limit. I know of one person, excluding royalty, who has seven.

NAVAL AND MILITARY NOTES

During the period 1848–51 two medals were instituted known as the Military General Service Medal, 1793–1814, and the Naval General Service Medal, 1793–1840.

The former was issued in 1848, the latter in 1849. We are not here concerned with the medals or the actions for which they were awarded, but it is worth calling attention to the lapse of time between the issue of the medal and the last action. This period could well be sixty-six years after the action!

In the case of medals for the Peninsular War it is said that some men could not remember in which actions they had fought so were unable to claim several bars for which they might have been eligible!

When these medals come up for sale the particulars as regards the recipients' ranks are given, but many of these are now extinct. This chapter is intended to interest those who see these old military and naval ranks and classifications mentioned but would like to know more.

At the outbreak of the war with France in 1793 the rates and classifications of naval vessels were as follows:

Class I	Rated ships.
First	All three-decked ships.
Second	One of Her Majesty's yachts, and all two-decked ships whose war complements consisted of 700 men or more.
Third	Her Majesty's other yachts and all ships with a complement between 600 and 700 men.
Fourth	Ships with complements between 400 and 600 men.
Fifth	Ships with complements between 250 and 400 men.
Sixth	Ships with complements under 250 men.
Class II	Sloops and bomb vessels and others commanded by a commander.
Class III	All smaller vessels and those commanded by a lieutenant or junior.

There is rather an interesting point here in that ships of the line really had four decks known as the lower, middle, main and upper. Frigates and corvettes had main and upper decks; sloops and brigantines had only main decks.

The classifications as regards guns were: line-of-battle ships 120, 110, 92, 84, 80, 78, 72, 70 guns; frigates 50, 44, 42, 38, 36, 26 guns; corvettes 26, 24 guns; sloops 18 guns; brigs 16, 10 or 3 guns.

The particulars of the guns are as follows:

Description of gun	Weight of shot	Bore
Cannon	42 lbs. and over	8 ins.
Demi-cannon	32 lbs.	7 ins.
Culverin	18 lbs.	$5\frac{1}{2}$ ins.
Demi-culverin	12 lbs.	4 ins.
Saker	6 lbs.	$3\frac{1}{2}$ ins.
Three-pounder	3 lbs.	2 ins.

It is worth noting that the use of the term demi did not mean half as will be seen by a reference to the weights of the shots fired by the cannon and demi-cannons, also culverins and demi-culverins. The three pounder was a naval term for the weapon known as a falcon.

Though the Navy and the Army used the same weapons as regards bore and weight of shot the naval guns were much larger. This was caused by the fact that the naval weapons used heavier charges so as to obtain longer range and greater power of penetration. There was then, as there is now, limits beyond which it is not practicable to build a weapon. After a certain size it became unwieldy, used too much powder, required too large a crew and so on. We now come to the personnel.

In many cases their roles are self-evident but it should be remembered that in the days of sailing ships it was the object to get alongside the enemy so that the crew had to be allotted duties either in the case of boarding, or being boarded, in addition to manning the sails and guns. The ranks were:

Admiral of the Fleet
Admiral
Vice-Admiral
Rear-Admiral
Captain
Commander
First Lieutenant, of 7 years' standing
All other Lieutenants
Master
Chaplain
Surgeon
Purser
Naval Instructor
Mate
Second Master
Assistant-Surgeon
Gunner
Boatswain
Carpenter
Engineers

Midshipman
Master's Assistant
Volunteer 1st Class
Clerk
Master-at-Arms
Seamen's Schoolmaster
Captain's Coxswain
Gunner's Mate
Boatswain's Mate
Quartermaster
Captain of Forecastle
Ship's Corporal
Coxwain of Launch
Captain of Hold
Sailmaker
Carpenter's Mate
Caulker
Ropemaker
Blacksmith
Ship's Cook

Captain of Main-top
Captain of Fore-top
Captain of Mast
Captain of Afterguard
Yeoman of Signals
Coxswain of Pinnace
Sailmaker's Mate
Cooper
Armourer
Caulker's Mate
Captain of Mizen-top
Carpenter's Crew
Sailmaker's Crew
Cooper's Crew
Purser's Steward
Painter
Able Seaman
Yeoman of Storeroom

Sick-berth Attendant
Trumpeter
Captain's Steward
Captain's Cook
Ward-room, or Gun-room
    Steward and Cook
Midshipmen's Steward
    and Cook
Ordinary Seaman
Purser's Steward's Mate
Cook's Mate
Barber
Landsman
Seaman Gunner
Boy 1st Class
Boy 2nd Class
Engineer Boy

The word admiral is said to have been derived from the Arabic Emir-al-bahr, Lord of the Sea. Gibbon, in his *Decline and Fall*, states that the Emir of the Fleet was the third Officer of State; the first being the Great Duke, and the second the Great Drungaire. The first reference that I can find of the rank of admiral, omitting the question of orthography, refers to the year 1284 when William de Seybourne was styled Admiral de la Mer du Roy [sic] Angleterre. This is interesting because at that time England had no fleet but relied on a sufficient number of merchant vessels being available for conversion when, or as, required. The King's Admiral of the Sea was not a commander of a fleet; he was the Great Officer of State responsible for maritime affairs. As often as not he had no qualifications whatever. The title was bestowed as a great honour, but knowledge of the subject, as is so often the case with the granting of honorary degrees today, was quite unnecessary. In 1673, for instance, Charles II appointed his infant son, Charles Lennox, afterwards Duke of Richmond, to the title.

The duties which the office entailed were performed by persons acting in the holder's name and consisted of supervising the Navy and administering justice therein. The former later became the function of the Admiralty, the latter that of the High Court of Admiralty.

In the early part of the fourteenth century we find that admirals were appointed to certain areas, for mention is made of such titles as Admiral of the King's Fleet from the Mouth of the Thames Northward, Admiral of the King's Fleet from the Mouth of the Thames Westward and; of course, Admiral of the Cinque Ports.

The rank of Admiral of All England appears to have been instituted in 1837 but, even this high-sounding individual had a superior in the person of the King's Lieutenant of the Sea who was referred to in Latin by the very mediocre-sounding name of Locum Tenens super Mare.

Before the term Admiral was used at all, there had been an officer called the Custos Maris, or Guardian of the Sea.

The style of Lord High Admiral was in use between 1405 and 1709 in which latter year it was abolished.

Much of what I shall now say about the naval ranks applies today, sometimes almost exactly and others with slight variations. There will also be occasions when my remarks appear absurd so I would remind the reader that I am dealing with a period of well over a hundred years ago. To make this point clear I shall use the past tense.

The Navy was composed of two bodies of men—seamen and marines. There were commissioned, warrant and petty officers. The commissioned officers consisted of flag-officers (i.e. admirals), captains, commanders and lieutenants.

The flag-officers were classified as follows:

Admirals of the Fleet.
Admirals of the Red, White and Blue Squadrons.
Vice-Admirals of the White, Red and Blue Squadrons.
Rear-Admirals of the White, Red and Blue Squadrons.

The Admiral of the Fleet, when in command, wore the Union Flag at the main-top-gallant-mast. The other flag-officers wore a square flag of the colour of their squadron at the main, fore, or mizen top-gallant-mast, according to their rank.

Modern inventions brought many additions to naval ranks, too numerous to mention. Medals are to be found to stoker, telegraphist, torpedoman, mechanican, wireless operator, writer, and many other specialists. Occupational ratings also have their different ranks; ordinary, able, leading, 1st or 2nd class, petty officer, etc. These may not be named similarly, for example, on a pair of medals to a man of the Fleet Air Arm on one is the inscription, P.O. Air and on the other A/P.O. Tel.

The flag-officer in command of a fleet or squadron employed within certain geographical limits, known as a station, was designated a commander-in-chief. All vacancies however caused, which occurred in any of the ships under his command were his gift. This means that he had the authority to make promotions to fill gaps caused by casualties in action, sentence of court-martial, death, etc.

A temporary rank was given to certain captains who were placed in command of two or more ships, detached from the main fleet or squadron, known as commodore. They were of two classes; the first received the pay and allowances of a rear-admiral, with a captain or more under him. Both classes wore a broad pendant which had to be struck in the presence of a senior captain.

Captains and commanders were appointed to the command of ships by Her Majesty's consent under a regulation that was instituted by William IV when Lord High Admiral.

The rank of post-captain was that at which when the commander of a ship had arrived, his subsequent promotion to a flag rank took place only by seniority. The captain was then said to be "posted" which had quite a different meaning to "appointed", the latter having a meaning similar to being ordered to command.

A commander had to serve one year as such on full pay before he became eligible for promotion.

A senior lieutenant was appointed by the captain and no lieutenant was eligible for promotion to the rank of commander until, or unless, he had completed two years' service at sea. He was responsible for the internal arrangements of the ship, its cleanliness, discipline and general efficiency of the crew.

No mate was eligible for promotion to lieutenant until he had served six years in the Navy, was over nineteen years of age and had passed the necessary examinations in seamanship and navigation.

Masters, secretaries, physicians, chaplains, surgeons, assistant-surgeons and pursers had no executive powers of command. They ranked with, but subordinate to, lieutenants.

The master was responsible for the stowage of the holds and in general charge of all the stores on board as well as for the navigation of the ship under the captain. Later, the rank of staff-commander was introduced to denote a senior master. To distinguish the junior rank of master from the second (there were no third masters), those who joined the service as masters were known as masters' assistants.

Secretaries were appointed by the flag-officers for whom they served and, as already stated, had no executive power but only an honorary rank.

I cannot trace the original introduction of clergymen into the Navy, but I suspect that captains of noble birth originally took them to sea with them until some time in the reign of Elizabeth I when authority woke up to the fact that nothing had been done to look after the spiritual needs of seamen. Clergymen were, in the first place, signed on as seamen, though not expected to carry out the latter's duties. They were granted commissioned status in 1843.

I cannot refrain from a slight digression before dealing with the naval surgeon.

The present Royal College of Surgeons originated in the company of Barber-Surgeons which was incorporated by a Royal Charter given by Edward IV. The connection between the two callings originated in the practice of the latter to employ the former to give baths and to apply the ointments which they had prescribed, and also to assist in surgical operations. The surgeons, since the tenth century, were almost all monks, but an edict of the Council of Tours which sat in 1163 prohibited the clergy from having anything more to do with surgery. The result was that the barbers and believe it or not, the smiths took over the roles vacated by the clergy. The barbers were, however, considered the better. Now, you see, when you get slashed in the barber's chair, you must not be too hard on the fellow as it may only be his hereditary instincts coming out.

The barbers practicing surgery in London were given a charter by Edward IV and they formed the Company of the Barbers in London whose members were given the monopoly of plying their trade within the metropolis.

This charter was varied from time to time until 1512 when Henry VIII decreed that "no person within the City of London, or within seven miles of same, should exercise as a physician or surgeon, except that he be first examined and approved by the Bishop of London or the Dean of St Paul's". Those who passed this test, which must have been as big a strain on the bishop, or dean, as the candidates, were enrolled as members of the Mystery and Commonality of Barbers and Surgeons of London.

In 1778 the union between barbers and surgeons was dissolved, and surgeons were constituted a separate company and in 1800 the present Royal College of Surgeons received its charter.

This brings us back on to the naval rails as students at this college were, after three years attendance, allowed to apply for jobs as assistant-surgeons in the two Services.

The first record that I can find mentioning barbers or surgeons relates to the time of Charles I (1625-49). He, so my research leads me to believe, was the first monarch to realize that a naval man might require medical attention but, being a bit hard up for cash himself, he was not inclined to pay the barber's or surgeon's wages, so hit upon the idea of deducting 2d. a month off the pay of every seaman. As the money-making idea it was brilliant but such riches, even on the biggest ship, were not particularly attractive for a man who had satisfied a bishop that he could be let loose with a scalpel. Noting that the cream of the profession were not being attracted to the Navy, Charles agreed that they should receive a basic wage of a pound a month in addition.

By 1839 the conditions of the surgeon had been so improved that one with six years' service got six shillings a day while those newly joined got two. The latter, probably not quite so handy with figures as with knives, no doubt thought this a form of generosity, as some of us did a century later when we received more pay but had our allowance taxed.

The medical branch of the Navy, in the form that we know it today, dates from 1843 when surgeons were given commissioned rank and could gain promotion from Surgeon-Lieutenant to Surgeon-Vice-Admiral. The wearing of the red between the gold rings denoting rank dates from 1864.

The purser had charge of all provisions and of the "slop chest", as the place from which such articles as clothing, soap, tobacco, etc., were issued. His assistants were known as stewards. The roguery that went on—the modern term is fiddling—reached such proportions that in the end pursers had to deposit a cash bond. Even this did not deter the more avaricious so sureties were introduced as well. This had the strange effect of producing a sort of professional surety who took the risk, for a substantial commission that his "horse" would run straight.

The rank of naval instructor dates from 1702 when it was thought advisable that the theoretical side of naval training should be disseminated. They —that is those capable of doing so—were also requested to teach the noble arts of reading and writing as it was found most inconvenient to have illiterate signallers. I have found their early career in the Navy hard to follow beyond the fact that they were there. In 1843 they were given the status of warrant-officers, and in 1861 raised to commissioned rank by which time they mostly served in training establishments ashore. Their place at sea was taken by naval schoolmasters with warrant rank. Members of this branch wear a light blue band between the stripes, or in addition to the stripe, of their rank.

Mates were midshipmen who, having passed the examination qualifying them for the rank of lieutenant, received a warrant from the captain; their rank and command ceased on their discharge, or when the ship was paid off. They were eligible for promotion providing they had six years' service in the Navy, were more than nineteen years old, and had passed the necessary examinations in seamanship and navigation.

The gunner was responsible for all ordnance stores such as guns, muskets, powder, etc., and for the discipline in the gun-room which was situated in the after part of the lower deck. It was in this that the volunteers and younger midshipmen lived. The rank of chief gunner was introduced in 1864.

The boatswain came under the direct orders of the master. He detailed the crew to their various duties. He was the ship's provost marshal and responsible for the custody of the prisoners and for seeing that the punishments awarded by the captain were carried out. His calls were made on a silver whistle which was, and still is, known as a pipe.

The carpenter, in addition to the duties which his name implies, was responsible for seeing that all the ports were water-tight. He also had to sound the bilges and ensure that all the pumps were efficient.

The introduction of steam brought the rank of engineer with it. Engineers were graded into three classes—not ranks. There were four classes of engineer boys, the last being the lowest form of human life in the Navy.

The modes of addressing engineers must have varied considerably as I have found them referred to as Engineer First Class, Chief Engineer and First Engineer, while correspondence from the Admiralty uses the word Mister and Chief Engineer 1 in the same letter.

The title of paymaster was really an offshoot of that of purser. In the times that we are dealing with the men did not receive their pay on board but were given "pay checks" at the end of the ship's commission. These were cashable at what was known as the Port Navy Office. The fact that men might require money during the commission was not appreciated till 1825 when pursers were authorized to issue small advancements. The title of paymaster was not introduced till 1852 when that of purser was abolished. The rank was commissioned in 1842, and in 1864 the wearing of the white band on the sleeve was introduced. Naval pay-mastering, if I may be forgiven for using such an expression, was made a separate profession in 1918 when paymaster cadets were introduced who can now rise to the rank of Paymaster-Rear-Admiral (S). The prefix "Paymaster" was discontinued in 1944 when the branch was renamed Supply and Secretariat—hence the initial "S" after the rank.

There were, as my reader will have noticed, several ranks which started with the word captain. There was, for instance, the Captain of the Hold, Captain of the Main Top, Captain of the Fore Top, etc. These ranks denoted their action stations. The crew was appointed to various parts of the ship under their individual commanders. In this way the musketry fire could be controlled and directed. It is not difficult to realize the tremendous waste of powder and shot that would have resulted in every man firing as and when he liked. On certain ships, and on certain occasions, the positions were put in charge of a midshipman which accounts for such titles as midshipman of the mast, etc.

The coopers were responsible for the numerous iron bands and rivets throughout the ship. It should be remembered that the masts were composed of several pieces of wood which were bolted together and then bound with iron hoops.

The roles of the remaining ranks are, I think, too obvious to require enlargement.

In times of peace the whole crew were entered as volunteers; in time of war, the extra pay paid by merchants to seamen dried up the source of volunteers so that resort was made to the press-gangs. The story of these would require more space than is available so suffice it to say that they were, in theory at any rate, supplied with warrants known as press-warrants which were issued by an officer. This system was instituted by Edward III, in 1355, and can hardly be said to have been abolished till the introduction of compulsory service. I have no doubt that the methods adopted were outrageous but the idea was sound. If men are wanted to man the ships to defend the country, and none will come forward voluntarily, then they must be obtained compulsorily and I much prefer it that way to the ludicrous system of arming, with white feathers, females (who could not, or at any rate did not) feel disposed to do any more useful work than to hand them to men in mufti. It was degrading to have allowed such a thing to happen, and an insult to many of us who returned from the other side of the world in 1914 to play our part and, let me add, at our own expense.

Before passing on to the Royal Marines, let me complete these few remarks on the Royal Navy by saying that a regulation pattern uniform was introduced in 1748.

The very earliest history of the Royal Marines, and origin of the term itself, is outside our scope. To those who, like myself are interested in all military origins I would recommend a study of the life of Cardinal Richelieu (1585–1642) who, I think, first formed a body of men from whom one would be justified in supposing the idea of marines originated.

Marines, as we know them today, might be said to have originated with the 130 companies raised in 1755 on the recommendation of Lord Anson. They were placed under the command of the Lords of the Admiralty and given headquarters at Plymouth, Portsmouth and Chatham. In 1805 an additional division was formed at Woolwich. They were granted their style of Royal Marines by George III who gave them precedence immediately after the Royal Berkshire Regiment (the 49th) and immediately before the Queen's Own Royal West Kent Regiment (the 50th).

In 1804 the Corps was divided into Marine Artillery and Marine Infantry. These two divisions were united in 1923.

The right to wear the wreath of laurel in their badge was granted for their services during the seige of Belle Isle, in 1761, and in 1827 the globe was added. During the Crimean War the Marine Infantry was given the extra title of "Light" and the bugle was added to the badge.

During the early part of the period with which this chapter deals the role of the Marines was, and here I quote an account of the time, "to annoy the enemy by a fire of musketry from the tops and decks". Marines could not be ordered aloft by a naval officer so we must presume that they were ordered up there by their own, or volunteered. I can imagine all went off pretty well on a calm day, but an inexperienced rigging-climbing trigger-happy bunch of Jollies (as they were familiarly called) up aloft in anything like a swell, or rough sea, must have been equally annoying to the home side as the visitors.

However, be that as it may, let us pass from surmise to fact and say that Hannah Snell served as a marine on board H.M.S. *Swallow*, one of Admiral Boscawen's squadron, during the seige of Cuddalore in 1760. She achieved what appears to be the life's ambition of every sailor—she opened a pub, at Wapping. Some people seem to have all the luck!

The first known Marine recipient of a medal—or perhaps it might be more accurate to say the first name of a Marine in the medal rolls—was Corporal John Kelly who served on H.M.S. *Nymphe* and was present when she captured the French frigate *La Cléopatra* on 18th June, 1793.

Now, having dealt with sailors and marines, we come to soldiers. Do you know the origin of the word?

The term soldier is now applied to all men in the Army but was at first only indicative of those who drew pay. It is thought to have come from "solidus" a coin at the time of the Roman Empire, which may have represented the daily pay of a soldier. At that time all males between certain ages were automatically what we would now call soldiers so that I doubt whether the similarity in the name of a coin of the time was any more than a coincidence.

My view is that we are making a better guess at the origin of the term when we connect it with the retainers of Philip Augustus, who at the end of the twelfth century was the first monarch to retain his mercenaries, hired for war, in times of peace and thus, perhaps we may be right in thinking, originated what we now term a standing (or regular) army. These men were called "soldyours" (which meant stipendaries, or those who worked for pay) and I consider that this is more likely to be the origin.

The first mention of the word "soldier" that I can trace in our military history occurs in the wardrobe account of Edward I (1272–1307) wherein soldiers are variously classified as "soldier scutifiers", "soldier constables" or simply as "soldiers". The pay for all these classifications was the same—one shilling per day.

While armour was in general use, soldiers were distinguished by scarfs and badges, on the latter of which were the arms of their leader. Something like a uniform was worn in the reign of Henry VIII when the men's upper garments were white; those in the personal service of the king wore the Cross of St George on their coats. When, however, an army was raised in 1544 the soldiers were equipped with blue cloth coats with red edges. White cloaks with red crosses were worn during the reign of Queen Mary. In that of Elizabeth I the infantry wore a cassock and long trousers, both of grey. The cavalry wore sleeveless red cloaks down to the knees. Grey coats and breeches were the uniform just prior to about 1700, soon after which, red became the general colour for the coats of British infantry.

Horsemen, or what we would now call cavalry, are almost as old as history, but the first record I can find of them being subdidvided into formations with anything like modern titles occurred in 1324 in which year I find that Edward III divided his cavalry into small bodies, each of which was commanded by an officer called a constable and his unit a constabulary. I agree that this is an expression, and a unit, which we now associate with the police, but the words constable and constabulary are still in use. In reading the accounts of the war with France during the reign of Queen Mary, I found mention of the word "troops" but this may have been the term in use at the time the author was writing and not at the time of the campaign about which he was giving the details. Grose, in his discourse on the attack of St Quentin (1557) states that a body of cavalry was distinguished by the appellation of troop; a name subsequently given to a half squadron, or the eighth part of a cavalry regiment.

The first mention of light cavalry that I can trace occurs in the writings of Marshal de Montluc who served in the armies of Henry II of France (who recaptured Calais in 1558). He mentions a general of light horse which had a strength of 1,200. We have never used the term as such though dragoons were light cavalry trained to act mounted or on foot and were used for patrolling, or to form the major portion of an advance guard.

According to historians, the word "dragoon" comes from the Latin "draconarius", the name given to the standard-bearer who carried a standard, or colour, with the figure of a dragon thereon. My own view is that it was probably derived from their firearm—the dragon. Père Daniel states that they originated in the French armies at the end of the sixteenth century. They appear to have been introduced into the English Army before the middle of the seventeenth century though the oldest regiment, the Royal Scots Greys, was not formed till 1681.

Hussars were also a species of light cavalry which originated in, in fact constituted, the national militia of Poland and Hungary. They were introduced into the French Army by Louis XIII (1610–43), under the name of Hungarian Cavalry. In my opinion the word owes its origin to the fact that Matthias, King of Hungary, 1458–90, ordered every twentieth house to furnish one paid mounted soldier, and the inhabitants of the other nineteen had to club together to provide the pay of the man serving. The word "huzz" was Hungarian for twenty, and "ar" meant pay hence the man furnished and paid for by every twenty houses was known as a huzzar, which we spelt hussar. If that is not the correct origin it is a very good story and I am sticking to it.

Lancers were introduced into the English Army in 1715 to correspond to the Polish Lancers in the French. The lance was considered the ideal weapon with which to attack infantry.

The introduction, and finally the increased use, of artillery deprived the cavalry of much of their advantage though they continued to be an essential part of an army.

To deal fully with the origin of artillery and the many interesting improvements which it went through during the first few hundreds of years since its invention would take too long but, I will give a quotation from the Bible which shows that artillery was not new even then. In this connection we must remember that artillery existed before the use of gunpowder—at any rate in Europe. The quotation to which I refer is from 2 Chronicles, ch. xxvi, v. 14 and 15, wherein it says, "And Uzziah prepared for them throughout all the hosts shield, and spears, and helmets, and habergeons, and bows, and slings to cast stones. And he made in Jerusalem engines, invented by cunning men, to be on the towers and upon the bulwarks, to shoot arrows and great stones withal."

In 1481, Edward IV feared an invasion from the Scots so wrote round to his barons exhorting them to resist with "Bombardos, canones, culverynes, fowelers, serpentynes et alios canones quoscumque, ac pulveres sulphureos, saltpetre, petras, ferrum, plumbum, et omnimodas alias xtuffuras pro eisdem canonibus necessarias et oportunas." I have no idea what all this means but imagine that it was the old way of saying, "If the Scots come chuck everything at them including the kitchen stove."

Uzziah was not the only one to have "cunning men" as we had them in the period 1940–44. At that time the Home Guard was training to throw oil drums over hedges with a thing called a fougasse; they were also learning how to throw bottles from a Northover Projector. They also had their bombards which, providing all went well, hurled a finned bomb either full pitch, first bounce or skid in the desired, or self-chosen, direction. Their star weapon was a sticky-grenade which was an explosive charge concealed in a glutinous mass on the end of a short handle—the whole looked rather like a thing for clearing blocked drains. A brave fellow—he needed to be—was expected to go up to an enemy tank and stick this thing on it having, we hope, first drawn his V.C. and ticket to Eternity.

We are, however, not so much concerned with the weapons as the men with whom we will now deal.

In the early days of artillery the guns were drawn by civilians under contract and it was not until 1794 that a unit known as the Driver Corps was formed. This was later known as the Corps of Gunners and Drivers and, finally, as the Corps of Royal Artillery Drivers. In spite of the similarity of titles they and the Royal Artillery were separate regiments. The last named corps was disbanded in 1822 and the men were transferred to the Royal Artillery. The rank of driver, owing to mechanization, was abolished in 1925.

During the Peninsular War the artillery was composed of Horse Artillery and Foot Artillery, the latter organized into companies and subdivided into Field, Garrison and Siege Artillery.

The term battalion was discarded in 1859 in which year those of troops was altered to batteries.

At this time, too, when military operations were pending, trains were formed from which we get the various names such as Wagon Train, Supply

Train, etc., and the ranks wagoner, or wagon driver. The non-commissioned ranks in these trains were usually referred to by their single rank, such as sergeant, corporal, etc., but I have also seen sergeant-wagoner used but I would doubt its accuracy.

In 1685 James II commanded the Master General of Ordnance to prepare a Train of Artillery to oppose the Duke of Monmouth on the basis of one gunner and one mattrose to each piece. The latter assisted the gunner in loading, traversing and cleaning the piece. The rank was abolished in 1783. The rank of bombardier and pedardier were introduced in 1686 and their role was defined as assisting the Fire Master who was responsible for all the guns and the training of the crews to man them. In 1712 Mister Borgard was appointed Firemaster of England, the forerunner of the title Master General of Ordnance.

I am so often asked for details concerning some of the ranks found in rolls and on medals of about the middle of the last century that I think it would be of interest and help if I gave a list of the non-commissioned officers of the Life Guards and Horse Guards, Cavalry and Royal Artillery.* I am open to correction as to whether I have got them all in their right order of seniority. I think I am right in saying that some of them should be grouped together. However, I don't think that the point whether a paymaster-sergeant is senior or junior to a hospital-sergeant need worry us very much.

Life Guards and Horse Guards

Schoolmaster	Farrier-Major
Regimental Corporal-Major	Troop Corporal-Major
Quartermaster-Corporal	Bandmaster
Corporal Instructor of Musketry	Trumpet-Major
Armourer-Corporal	Corporal of Horse
Saddler-Corporal	

A Corporal-Major ranks with a Sergeant-Major, and Corporals of the Life Guards and Horse Guards rank with Sergeants in the cavalry and infantry.

Cavalry

Schoolmaster	Hospital Sergeant
Regimental Sergeant-Major	Bandmaster
Quartermaster-Sergeant	Troop Sergeant
Sergeant Instructor of Musketry	Troop Sergeant-Major
Paymaster-Sergeant	Trumpet-Major
Sergeant-Armourer	Sergeant
Sergeant-Sadler	Corporal
Farrier-Major	Trooper

*I acknowledge the kindness of Messrs Lock Ward, & Co. in allowing me to copy the following list of ranks which were taken from *Our Soldiers and the Victoria Cross* which was published in, or about, 1860.

Royal Artillery

Brigade Sergeant-Major	Hospital-Sergeant
Brigade Quartermaster-Sergeant	Paymaster-Sergeant
Battery Sergeant-Major	Collarmaker-Sergeant
Battery Quartermaster-Sergeant	Sergeant-Wheeler
Farrier-Major	Sergeant and Staff Clerk
Wheeler-Major	2nd and 3rd 3lass
Farrier-Sergeant	Battery-Armourer
Assistant-Instructor in Gunnery	Corporal
Trumpet-Major	Bombardier
Collarmaker-Major	Shoeing Smith
Orderly Room Sergeant	Trumpeter
Staff-Clerk 1st Class	Gunner
Bandmaster	Driver

Royal Artillery ranks now include Regimental Sergeant-Major, and Quatermaster-Sergeant; Corporals are now Bombardiers and Bombardiers and Lance-Bombardiers. A rank also found in the Royal Artillery is Master Gunner (in three classes). A Master Gunner First Class, is the highest ranking Warrant Officer, with the exception of Conductor (R.A.O.C. and R.E.M.E.). A Master Gunner, Royal Artillery, must not be confused with Master Gunner of St James's Park, who is a high ranking officer (usually of General's rank) with a distinguished record of service. A past Master Gunner of St James's Park was Field-Marshal Lord Roberts, V.C.

In the case of the cavalry the first three ranks were warrant-officers; the first six in the artillery.

I do not think that it is necessary for me to give all the ranks in the infantry as they were much the same as they are now except, perhaps, for the Colour-Sergeant who was, as the name implies, the sergeant of the colour party. Some ranks now to be found are Signalman (Royal Corps of Signals), Craftsman (R.E.M.E.), Gunner, Sapper (R.E.), Fusilier, Rifleman, Trooper (Cavalry and Royal Armoured Corps), Guardsman, Conductor, sub-Conductor, Superintending Clerk, Instructor-in-Gunnery, Instructor-in-Musketry, Bandsman. Unusual ranks are Worker or Fore-woman to be found on medals to the Queen Mary's Army Auxiliary Corps for the First World War. The Royal Air Force have, of course, their own ranks. Some of these are Warrant-Officer, Flight-Sergeant, Sergeant, Corporal, Leading Aircraftsman, Senior Aircraftsman, etc. A comparative table of officer's ranks in the three Services is given on the next page.

It is not suggested that all the ranks mentioned in this chapter or in the next will be found on medals or that the list is complete. Many medals bear the most unusual descriptions particularly those for the South African War of 1899–1902. President, groom, civilian veterinary surgeon, nursing orderly are some of these.

It must be remembered that all these ranks may be inscribed in an abbreviated form, but a little thought will usually elucidate them. One must, however, use one's common sense as one letter may have more than one interpretation. For example, Cpl.A/Sgt. is Corporal, Acting Sergeant,

RANKS OF THE THREE SERVICES

Ranks of the women's services are in parenthesis. The W.R.A.C. commissioned ranks are as for the Army, the Director holding the rank of Brigadier.

ROYAL NAVY	ARMY	ROYAL AIR FORCE
Admiral of the Fleet	Field-Marshal	Marshal of the Royal Air Force
Admiral	General	Air Chief Marshal
Vice-Admiral	Lieut.-General	Air Marshal
Rear-Admiral	Major-General	Air Vice-Marshal
Commodore (Commandant)	Brigadier	Air Commodore (Air Commandant)
Captain (Superintendant)	Colonel	Group Captain (Group Officer)
Commander (Chief Officer)	Lieut.-Colonel	Wing Commander (Wing Officer)
Lt. Commander (First Officer)	Major	Squadron Leader (Squadron Officer)
Lieutenant (Second Officer)	Captain	Flight Lieutenant (Flight Officer)
Sub. Lieut.	Lieut.	Flying Officer (Flying Officer)
Senior Commissioned Gunner, etc.	Second-Lieut.	Pilot Officer (Pilot Officer)

Note. Flying Officer and Pilot Officer are ranks and do not imply that the holder of these ranks is engaged on flying duties. He may be administrative or ground staff.

Owing to their different duties and consequent administrative differences it is difficult to compare non-commissioned ranks. Broadly speaking Chief Petty Officers and Petty Officers of the Royal Navy rank with Warrant Officers in the Army and Royal Air Force, Q.M.S., Staff Sergts in the Army and Flight Sergts in the R.A.F. The R.N. does not appear to have a rank equivalent to Sergt in the Army and R.A.F., but a Leading-Rating ranks with a Corporal in the other services while an Able Rating carries out the duties of a Lance Cpl. (Army) and a Leading Aircraftsman (R.A.F.).

while A/Sergt. is probably Armourer Sergeant, E.R.A. is Engine Room Artificer, L.A.C. Leading Aircraftsman, P.O./A. probably Petty Officer, Air, A.B. Able Seaman.

Enough has been said to show that one should not be surprised at the most unusual "rank" on a medal. In the past medals were even presented to prominent persons who obviously took no part in the campaign. Waterloo medals exist inscribed to "The Master of the Mint".

In the collections of Her Majesty is an Abyssinnian Medal named in the usual way for this medal to "H.M. Queen Victoria".

The next arm of the service about which I must say a few words is that of the engineers.

The early history of the Royal Engineers is another which is so full of interest that it is impossible to do more than skim through it.

Prior to 1772 military engineering was done by civilians—mostly, I regret to say, foreigners who came and went as they pleased. The inconvenience of the Chief Engineer signing on elsewhere in the middle of a campaign prompted a Lieutenant-Colonel Green to institute a Corps of Military Artificers which, in 1771, was established by a Royal Warrant as the Soldier Artificer Company which consisted of a sergeant-major, three sergeants, three corporals, sixty privates and a drummer. The strength was increased in 1775, and in 1786 it was divided into two, the additional men required being enlisted as labourers. An early record of these men states that the hearty good will with which they invariably worked was so impressive that they were allowed to enter, or leave, barracks without a pass and to wear whatever dress suited their inclination. The same account goes on to say that, "It was common, therefore, for the non-commissioned officers and privates to stroll about garrison dressed in black silk and satin breeches, silk stockings, drab beaver hats and scarlet jackets tastefully trimmed with white kerseymere." The sergeant-majors of my time, seeing a man with his uniform tastefully trimmed would have shot him, pleaded justifiable homicide and probably got off!

In 1787 the Corps of Royal Military Artificers was formed, with which the Soldier Artificers Corps at Gibraltar was amalgamated in 1797.

In 1812 a Royal Warrant authorized the establishment of a school at Chatham to teach military field work, and in the next year the title was changed to that of Royal Sappers and Miners. Up to 1856 the officers came from the Royal Engineers which had existed as a separate body since 1683. The Royal Engineers and the Royal Sappers and Miners were amalgamated into the Corps of Royal Engineers by a Royal Warrant dated 17th October, 1856.

I have left the officers till now because it will be easier to go from them on to the various departments which dealt with the health, pay, and feeding of the army.

In their order of seniority the officers were, Field-Marshal, General, Lieutenant-General, Major-General, Brigadier-General, Colonel, Lieutenant-Colonel, Major, Captain, First Lieutenant, Second Lieutenant, Cornet or Ensign.

It puzzles many that a lieutenant-general should be senior to a major-general, but the reason is quite simple if one knows the origins of both ranks. A lieutenant was a deputy so that when the general was away the lieutenant-general, being the general's deputy, took command. The same remarks apply to the ranks of colonel and lieutenant-colonel. We never adopted the rank of lieutenant-captain and merely left it that if the captain was away his lieutenant would take charge.

The use of the term brigadier-general continued in our army till about 1880 when major-generals were given command of brigades. It was re-introduced during the South African War (1899–1902) and continued till about 1921 when it was abolished and that of brigadier established.

Ensigns were commissioned officers below the rank of lieutenant in infantry regiments. One was appointed to each company and the juniors were responsible for the Colours. There is no such rank in the Royal Artillery, Royal Engineers, Royal Marines and the Rifle Brigade as that of second lieutenant was used.

The word cornet is derived from the Italian "cornetta" denoting a small flag; hence, in both the English and French armies, it was applied to the officer who had charge of the regimental standard in a cavalry regiment. He ranked immediately below a lieutenant so that he corresponded to an ensign in the infantry.

I do not wish to get too involved with the whole composition of the Army at the time with which we are dealing so it must suffice for me to say that it was composed of combatants, non-combatants and civilians. We could get involved in endless arguments as to the difference between the last two categories. Rightly or wrongly I propose to use the following description. A combatant is someone in uniform who fights; a non-combatant is someone in uniform who doesn't fight—like a doctor; a civilian does not wear uniform and does not fight. We are not concerned with their status as regards their liability to be shot at by the enemy as the rules concerning the taking of pot-shots at padres, officially known as the Hague Convention, was not internationally recognized till 1907.

Non-combatants and civilians had no executive power whatever, which means that the youngest cornet was senior to an Inspector-General when it came to giving orders to the men. Both these two categories had, however, military equivalent rank which was respected. It is, really, the same sort of situation as exists in the Royal Navy today between, say, an engineer commander and an executive lieutenant. The rules of common sense apply. I should say that the medical service completely reverse the situation as regards those committed to their change. In other words, what a medical officer says in the hospital, and in certain cases elsewhere, must be carried out by all ranks whether senior to the doctor or not.

Let us take four of the departments and see what the equivalent ranks of the members were.

Medical Department

Inspector-General	.	.	Ranked as Brigadier-General
Deputy Inspector-General	.	.	Ranked as Lieutenant-Colonel
Staff Surgeon, 1st Class	.	.	Ranked as Major

Regimental Surgeon . . .	Ranked as Captain
Staff Surgeon, 2nd Class . . .	Ranked as Captain
Apothecary	Ranked as Captain, but junior of that rank
Assistant-Surgeon . . .	Ranked as Lieutenant
Deputy Purveyor	Ranked as Lieutenant
Medical Clerk	Ranked as Ensign

Commissariat Department (Civilians)

Commissary-General . . .	Ranked as Brigadier-General
Deputy Commissary-General, with three years' standing . .	Ranked as Lieutenant-Colonel
Deputy Commissary-General, under three years' standing . .	Ranked as Major
Assistant Commissary-General .	Ranked as Captain
Deputy Assistant Commissar-General	Ranked as Lieutenant
Deputy Clerks	Ranked as Ensigns

War Department (Civilians)

Storekeeper, Barrackmaster, 1st Class	Ranked as Major
Deputy Storekeeper, Barrackmaster, 2nd Class .	Ranked as Captain
Barrackmaster 3rd and 4th Class	Ranked as Lieutenant
Clerk	Ranked as Ensign

Veterinary Department

Veterinary Surgeon, after 20 years' service . . .	Ranked as Captain
Veterinary Surgeon, after 10 years	Ranked as Lieutenant
Veterinary Surgeon, during first 10 years . . .	Ranked as Cornet

I have made no mention of the pay and clothing of the Army about both of which a few words are now necessary.

The first Paymaster-General, Sir Stephen Fox, was appointed in 1668. He was, and had to be, a rich man for he paid the Army out of his own pocket and periodically rendered accounts to the Treasury, after adding a percentage to the sums advanced. In addition to the interest on the loan he was allowed a shilling on every pound he paid out by way of payment for his expenses. Little wonder that the first two holders of the office netted about half a million pounds profit each!

For many years the pay of the men was issued to the colonel who ran his regiment as economically as possible so that he could pocket what was left. A favourite way of making money was to show more men on the books than could be paraded. On the principle that out of all evil comes good, we find in this system the origin of pensions because it was the custom to allot the pay drawn for a certain number of non-existent men per company to a fund out of which payments were made to widows and occasionally—very occasionally—to men who were discharged for wounds or old age. The idea that men who were so stupid as to get wounded should draw a pension was looked upon as pure sentimentality. In the times of the Georges the nett annual pay of a soldier, after deducting his compulsory payments, was just short of a pound per annum from which, if he had any sense, he saved up for his retirement however it may be caused.

The system of the colonel paying the men and pocketing what he could out of the sum given him for the purpose had the effect of making the commanding officers pay more attention to the accountancy side of their job than the parade with the result that the efficiency of the service as a whole suffered. This the paymaster-general, a civilian, could not allow so he appointed paymasters to every battalion and regiment and thus relieved the colonel of some of his work and almost the whole of his income! The principle was abolished in 1856 and the pay duties were transferred to the Secretary of State, as were those of the Board of Ordnance.

Prior to 1854 the soldier was clothed by his commanding officer who charged him for his original issue and then deducted 2d. a day off his pay for replacements. Those who have read military histories of the period will have come across the term "off-reckonings" and may have wondered what they were. Sums were deducted off the men's pay for food, clothing and other necessaries. These totalled together were known as off-reckonings and were the items from which a parsimonious commanding officer made his profit. In other words, the cheaper the cloth, the cheaper the food, the cheaper all the necessaries could be bought, the more for the colonel whose only restriction was that the uniform had to be of a pattern selected by the Clothing Board.

The Commissariat was responsible for obtaining the food for the men, providing for the horses as regards food and stabling, and the transport. Till 1836 the expenditures were supervised by other civilians known as Controllers of Army Accounts who were little better, if at all, than those they presumed to check.

The barracks and quarters came under the Barrack Department, later War Department, as did other property which is the reason for the initials W.D. found on stones and boards on the perimeter of Government property used for military purposes.

And now, finally, I come to a department whose members have shown a devotion to their duty both in battle and out which has been the admiration of all who have witnessed it—the Royal Army Chaplain's Department.

In the light of the present day, much of the early accounts of the connection between the Church and the Army seem amusing so, in giving them as I found them, I am not intentionally poking fun.

The first mention that I can trace of a clergyman in the Army dates to the Feudal System under which the Church had to do its share the same as anyone else. In some cases one might almost say that it fell harder on them than the rest of the population which was, subject to sufficient payment in lieu, allowed certain exemptions. The clergy, however, were often

F

compelled to attend in person so as to give the appearance of spiritual blessing on the campaign.

There was, at any rate so it seems to me, a far more subtle reason for insisting that the monks and clergy were well represented, namely, because they were the engineers and often the only persons capable of reading and writing. This accounts for the fact that so many of the early records of military campaigns were compiled by monks. The gentry were far too busy with their own amusements, and the rest of the population in trying to live, to bother about education or any of the arts so that in practically every early campaign one finds that any job requiring skill was done by the monks.

In fairness to history, I cannot refrain from mentioning the financial side of the clergy's attendance at wars.

We know that the spoils belonged to the victors and that they were shared out, supposedly anyway, after the battle according to the services rendered. If, therefore, the clergy could claim to have provided a goodly part of the force both in men and material they claimed a goodly share of the spoils which helped to pay for the abbeys and church expenses generally.

In many cases the job of finding men for the forthcoming war was given to the church which was allowed to confiscate the property of those who did not turn out to fight. In addition to providing the men it also had to supply the horses, waggons and food, which it did by ordering the requisite stuff to be brought to the churchyard where, in theory at any rate, it was bought and resold (plus profit) to the king either directly or through his commissioners.

I'm afraid that if we must stick to the truth we find that the clergy did not do too badly out of our early wars, in fact, to put it bluntly, they did very well.

The first Chaplain's Department was formed in 1662, the same year that Parliament accepted the Reformed Prayer Book.

The present Department was formed in 1858 and the clergymen of the Church of England were designated by classes and chaplains of the other denominations were also given commissions.

The classes and their equivalent military ranks are as follows:

Chaplain-General to the Forces		.	Ranks as Major-General
Chaplain, 1st Class	.	.	Ranks as Colonel
Chaplain, 2nd Class	.	.	Ranks as Lieutenant-Colonel
Chaplain, 3rd Class	.	.	Ranks as Major
Chaplain, 4th Class	.	.	Ranks as Captain

Certain differences arose between the Army chaplains and the local clergy as to the rights of the former to conduct marriage and burial services which were resolved by the Army Chaplain's Act, in 1868, which gave the Crown the right to nominate certain churches and districts, such as garrisons and camps to be extra-parochial.

Until 1946 the attendance at church parades was compulsory but now a soldier, like a civilian, is free to worship when and where he likes.

The first clergyman mentioned on a medal roll was Thomas Morgan who served on H.M.S. *Alfred* at the battle of the Glorious First of June, 1794.

MILITARY RANKS

In many cases the sequence from the institution of the various ranks to the present day is extremely hard to follow as the duties which they now perform bear little, if any, resemblance to their original. In others, except for minor differences in the titles, we have corresponding ranks and, where I think the original functions will be amusing to the reader, I shall give a few extracts from histories written centuries ago.

War, in the course of the last five or six hundred years, has gradually become more scientific and the different functions which the commanders could do themselves had to be delegated to others who in their turn found that they wanted assistants. From the need of assistants the problems grew till each required a special branch of the Army to deal with them. The head of each branch was given the title of "General" prefixed by the style of "Master" and the nature of his particular responsibility such as Quarter-Master General, Wagon-Master General, Scout-Master General and so on. To avoid confusion with the special rank of general the heads of the different branches will all be dealt with separately at the end of the chapter.

The rank of general was loosely used to signify a person in supreme command, or charge, so that, for instance, the quarter-master general was the man responsible for all the quartering though he was not a full general as regards army rank any more than was the post-master or barrack-master. He was, as now, usually a major-general which is the junior rank of general in our army today though we have at various times had brigadier-generals as I shall show.

FIELD-MARSHAL

The term is said to have been derived from two Saxon words, "marach", a horse, and "scalk", a servant. A marach scalk was the person responsible for looking after the horses in the royal stables. The term "maris calcus" is found in early Teutonic history during which time he must have been an important member of the household for he is one of the few who have the amount of the fine to be paid for his murder specifically mentioned!

The chief command of the Army was formerly held by the earl-marshal and two such, De Montmorency and Fitzosborne were appointed by William I.

The title of earl was introduced by William to replace that of ealdorman which the Saxons had used. It remained the highest in the country till 1337 when the Black Prince was made Duke of Cornwall on 17th March. Incidentally, the title of marquis was first introduced in this country by Richard II who conferred it on Robert de Vere, Earl of Oxford, making him Marquis of Dublin to rank between the dukes and earls. The title has never had any military connection though in Saxon times dukes, then called duces, were, so Camden says, commanders of armies.

The office of earl-marshal was made hereditary in the family of the Duke of Norfolk by Henry VIII but it must have been disassociated from the Army at some time prior to this because Lord Brooke was appointed by Henry VII to be marshal of the Army.

The senior rank in the French Army is that of Marshal of France the first of whom, Henry Clement, was appointed by Philip Augustus in 1204, the year in which he recaptured Anjou from us. Until 1270 there was only one Marshal of France but in that year Louis IX (Saint Louis) created another prior to starting out on the Seventh Crusade. Francis I appointed another to help him during his many wars between 1521–44.

The early French armies also had a rank known as a Marechal de Camp who combined the roles of providing the food and fodder and commanding the reserves. I suspect that the French word camp was confused with champ, meaning field, and it is from this that the Hanoverians obtained their feld-marchall which they introduced in 1735.

The first field-marshals in the English Army were John, Duke of Argyll, and George, Earl of Orkney, who were appointed by George II in 1736.

In early Scottish history there was an officer known as the Earl Marischal of Scotland who commanded the cavalry. This rank was like that of Earl Marshal of England in the Howard family, hereditary to that of Keith. George Keith, like my ancestor, backed the wrong side in the Rising of the Fifteen and the title was forfeited from him and his heirs.

GENERAL

The rank is of French origin and dates from about the same time as the formation of the first European standing army which was formed by Louis XI who was King of France at the time of our Edward IV.

In the cause of strict accuracy one must admit that the rank of lieutenant-general is older than that of general and that of captain-general older still.

The latter rank originated with Guy de Nele who was appointed by Philip de Valois in 1349 when instructing him to command the district of Xaintonge and to see that the defences of all castles and fortified towns were in good order.

In 1635 the rank was given to the Duke of Savoy by Louis XIII prior to the departure of the Army to Italy and, as he was senior to Marechal Crequi who was also present, we may assume that it was the senior military position in the French Army.

It was introduced into this country by Henry VIII who, in 1521, when he abolished the office of Lord-High-Constable appointed a captain-general to be commander-in-chief of the Army. The title is mentioned in the list of the army that served before St Quentin in 1557 and also that of lieutenant-general as being his immediate subordinate. The rank of captain-general does not appear to have remained very long for we find that during the reign of Elizabeth I the senior military officer was a lieutenant-general though she probably had the rank of commander-in-chief or some other senior to him.

In the army raised to recover the Palatinate in 1620 and again in that of Charles I the commander in each case was styled a lord-general with a lieutenant-general as his second-in-command while the third senior officer was called a sergeant-major-general. The latter somewhat long-winded title was abolished by Cromwell who appointed twelve major-generals in 1656 which constitutes the first occasion I have found mention of the rank as we know it.

The sovereign is Captain-General of the Honourable Artillery Company and, in January, 1951, King George VI assumed the title of Captain-General of the Royal Regiment of Artillery. The title is still retained in the United States by the Governor of Rhode Island and Governor of Connecticut.

Any rank which contains the word "general" is now usually associated with the Army so that it is amusing to recall that in the French Navy of the period about 1640–1720 the rank immediately below that of vice-admiral was lieutenant-general. In the reign of Elizabeth I the naval officer in command of a squadron was a general. Those who have studied the period of the Commonwealth will remember that Blake was given the ranks of admiral and general though appointed for a purely naval mission.

The actual rank of general appears to have come about by the process of abbreviation and, perhaps, the continued absence of the sovereign. The word lieutenant signified the same as vice which means acting instead of. If there was no chance of anyone senior to a lieutenant-general being present it became absurd so, if my contention is correct, the senior officer became the general and his immediate subordinate became a lieutenant-general in the same way as a vice-admiral in the Royal Navy is the immediate subordinate to an admiral.

BRIGADIER-GENERAL

According to the French historian Père Daniel (1649–1728), those in command of several regiments were given the title of brigadier by Louis XIV who was King of France 1643–1715. The rank, sometimes referred to without the word general, was introduced into our army in 1685. Those in command of the cavalry and infantry were then known as Brigadier-General over all the Horse and Brigadier-General over all the Foot.

The use of the rank continued till about 1880 when major-generals replaced brigadier-generals as commanders of brigades. It was reintroduced soon after the Boer War and continued till 1921 when it was abolished and that of brigadier established.

The term brigade used to apply to formations of artillery, engineers, and infantry. The first and last are well known but few probably know that a brigade of sappers consisted of eight men which in turn divided into two demi-brigades whose task was to dig a single sap. The length of a sap is not stated and neither was it during the First World War when we poor benign infantrymen dug them by the mile!

COLONEL

The derivation of the word is uncertain. I have seen it stated that it may have come from the title given to a person appointed to form a colony but I think it far more likely that it came from the French and Spanish coronel which are, in their turn, a corruption of the Italian colonello, the leader of a colonna, or column.

The first use of the word that I have been able to trace was in 1545 when Francis I conferred the rank of colonel-general on officers commanding considerable divisions of French troops. The expression "division of troops" bore no relation to the present military unit known as a division. The word "division" was used in the same manner as we would now say a "body of troops", in other words, it had no specific meaning as regards a particular number or formation. When reference was made to considerable divisions it meant a large force.

A French historian, Brantome (1527–1614), states that the rank of colonel was given to the head of the Albanian Corps prior to the use of that of colonel-general by Francis I. To trace the accuracy of Brantome's assertion we should have to study the history of Albania between the years 1443–78 when, under George Castriot (Scanderbeg), it revolted against Turkish domination.

The first mention that I have traced of the rank being used in England was in the regulations made by the citizens of London who, in 1585, proposed to appoint colonels having authority over ten captains. Both colonels and lieutenant-colonels are mentioned in the accounts of the army that was raised to oppose the threatened invasion in 1588. Prior to these dates the commanders of bodies of troops equivalent to a regiment bore the general title of captain.

In Ward's *Animadversions of Warre*, published in 1639, mention is made of the ranks of colonel and sergeant-major as will be seen in the following extract which reads rather amusingly at the present day.

"The office of colonel is very honourable, and a place of great confidence in the army, wherefore he ought to be a grave and experienced soldier, religious, wise, temperate, and valiant. He has under his command two special officers, his lieutenant-colonel and sergeant-major; his office is, in time of war, to see his regiment complete and to order his divisions and to draw them into form of battle: his place in battle is various according as he shall be commanded by the general, but most usual, he takes his place before the right wing of his own regiment ordering his officers as he shall have directions from his superior in authority. He is to be forward in showing a good example to his officers, that his worth and valour may not be blemished. His eye is to be duly upon his own officers and soldiers, to rebuke them that are negligent and cowardly and to animate those that are forward.

"He ought, in time of skirmishing and battle, to pry and take serious notice of the enemy battalions, how they are ordered, and what advantages are to be gained. He must be cautious and circumspect how the enemy plays his game, and he himself is to be wary and cunning in playing and managing his own."

Among others of his duties that are mentioned is the following which will strike a chord in the minds of those of us who can remember that anachronism in what called itself a free country—the compulsory church parades.

"Every sabbath he is to have sermon in his tent, forenoon and afternoon, and every officer of his regiment is to compel his soldiers that are free from guard to repair thither. No butler shall draw beer in the time of divine service and sermon."

In any case any young soldier reads this remark and yearns for the good old days when privates were waited on by butlers, I should say that the word signified the person who looked after the wine, or served it. A butler was what we would now call a barman who serves any and all of the drinks available in the bar in the same way that the butler served those in the butlery. The modern military expression for a butlery is a wet canteen and I am afraid I do not know whether those who serve therein have any special names.

PURCHASE SYSTEM

I think that it is here that I should say something about the system by which lieutenant-colonels, captains, lieutenants and ensigns could buy and sell their commissions.

When the system was first introduced it was a means whereby the sovereign could raise money and there is no doubt that the ethical side of the business never received a moment's consideration. War required money, and armies required officers, so why not let the latter requirement help solve the problems of the former? On the principle that the sovereign could do no wrong, we will leave out mention of what happened at the top and start with regimental colonels. They had, until the reign of George I, a very neat way of raising money. They were allowed to appoint their own officers but there were no rules saying that appointments could only be made to those over a certain age so that unscrupulous colonels appointed their young sons as ensigns and then sold the appointment. There are records of cases where the lads ranged from twelve years of age to sixteen, so that a large family—especially of boys—had financial prospects not available to the modern officer.

George I was the first monarch to investigate the corrupt practices which the system had generated. Before going further I should remind the reader that service pensions or any cash payment for disability, whether brought about by sickness or wounds had not been generally introduced so that the sale of commissions was used as a reimbursement in much the same way as retiring doctors sold their practices. The value of commissions varied, even in the same arm of the service, according to the financial state of the unit and where it was stationed.

Lieutenant-colonels and to a lesser extent captains, were responsible for their own accounts; some were in credit; some just balanced; while others were sadly in debt. The cash value of the commission varied according to the state of the account, if any, that went with it. All were, of course, subject to the laws of supply and demand, and to the human factor which sells to the highest bidder.

George I forbade the sale of commissions at a higher figure than was paid for them, and also insisted that all sales should have his previous consent. A

Board of Officers was convened in 1720 to go into the whole matter and a fixed scale of prices was instituted which remained in force till 1765. From that day till the system was abolished in 1870 constant revision took place though the actual alterations made were very slight. As I think it will be of interest to see what some of these figures were I shall give them for each rank from lieutenant-colonel to ensign in 1840.

In my time it was possible, when ordered abroad, to exchange with another officer of the same rank who would otherwise have to come home. These exchanges required official blessing and were often accompanied by a cash inducement. In those days infantry regiments had one battalion abroad and the other at home and it was usual for an officer to stay with his battalion though the chance of an exchange did occasionally arise. In the case of the Royal Artillery, Royal Engineers and the other services it was not so difficult to obtain exchanges as there were more officers on the move.

LIEUTENANT-COLONEL

The lieutenant-colonel of a regiment was, in addition to being the colonel's lieutenant, or second-in-command, the officer responsible for training as the following extract from Ward's *Animadversions of Warre* indicate.

> "A lieutenant-colonel of a regiment is a person of high consequence and great dignity, being the second person in the regiment. He is to command the captains to draw out their companies into the field and to see them exercise. He is to exercise every company of the regiment himself at his pleasure. He is to have his ear open to the complaints of poor distressed soldiers and see them righted. He is to take note of all quarrels and disputes among the officers and endeavour to reconcile them otherwise to lay his command on them and confine them to their lodgings until the colonel understands of it."

As the origin of the rank has already been referred to when dealing with that of colonel we need not cover the same ground again.

The price of a lieutenant-colonel's commission was, in the Foot Guards, £9,000; Life and Horse Guards, £7,250; Dragoons, £6,175; and in the Infantry of the Line, £4,500.

MAJOR

Ward, in his work already quoted, mentions the rank but not its origin. The duties which he enumerates amount to the same as those of the second-in-command of a unit today. He states that the major was responsible for passing on to the commanders of the companies the orders of the commander. He was, so Ward states, responsible for the supply and distribution of the ammunition and for visiting the guards both by day and night.

The rank was originally that of sergeant-major and in course of time the prefix was dropped—not altogether to our benefit as I found in the last war when asking for a billet for myself. I was told by the landlady that she had a very respectable house and took in nothing less than sergeant-majors!

The purchase price of a major's commission was, in the Foot Guards, £8,300; Life and Horse Guards, £5,350; Dragoons, £4,750; and in the Infantry of the Line, £3,200.

CAPTAIN

The word is derived from the French "capitaine" which came from the Latin "caput" meaning head.

In military parlance the title of captain was used by both the French and ourselves to signify someone who corresponded with the present rank of general in that he commanded an army. In some cases we find that it was given to the commander of a fortress, or garrison, quite irrespective of its size or the number of defenders. Père Daniel relates that it was once applied to all military men of noble birth in which case it was an inheritance and nothing to do with military service.

The first English use of the rank in any form which could compare with the present took place in the reign of Henry VII when it was given to officers commanding the Yeoman of the Guard.

The following extract from Ward's book, written in 1639, is both amusing and interesting—especially if one remembers that the place of the captain to which he refers is now taken by the major commanding a squadron, battery, or company.

"He is to train his men how to march and counter march and to advance forwards and backwards by files.

"A captain ought to march into the field in front of his company and his lieutenant in rear. When marching out of battle the captain's place is to bring up the rear, the lieutenant to lead the company.

"He ought to have one wagon at least to carry his baggage and conduct his sick soldiers. He is to be as little pestered with luggage of his own as possible lest it should hinder the march.

"He must indear [sic] his soldiers to be prodigal of their lives to do him service and to be familiar and eloquent in persuading and disuading his soldiers and to stir up their valours to undergo pain and peril."

There are many more details mentioned the last of which is as true today as that on which it was written. It reads:

"Lastly a captain ought to carry himself in such a way that his soldiers may both fear and love him. Too much familiarity breeds contempt and too stern a carriage breeds hatred."

Among the duties that I have not mentioned are those concerning the closing of the canteen and insisting that all lights are put out. There is also a most detailed account of how he should ensure that there is fire and movement in battle both when advancing and retiring. After reading the last account one realizes that the principles of war do not change—only the methods of their application.

The price of a captain's commission was, in the Foot Guards, £4,800; in the Life Guards, £3,500; in the Dragoons, £3,225; and in the Infantry of the Line, £1,800.

LIEUTENANT

I have already shown that a lieutenant was the deputy for his immediate senior in whose absence he takes command.

Ward uses the following strange wording to describe the duties of a lieutenant.

"A lieutenant is an officer with high credit and reputation, and he ought in all respects to be well indoctrinated and qualified in the arts military, and not inferior in knowledge to any officer of higher authority; for an unskilled captain may better demean himself with an experienced lieutenant than an unskilled lieutenant can fadge with a skilful captain."

The meaning of the old term to fadge is hard to describe when applied in the military sense. The best way is, I think, to say that it means that a good captain and good lieutenant would stand a better chance in battle than a good captain and bad lieutenant. The statement seems so obvious that it is difficult to see why Ward troubled to mention it. The word may have had a meaning of which I am unaware but it would seem obvious that two good officers have always been better than one good and one bad.

Today, with the system of time promotion in force, a captain is second-in-command of a company commanded by a major. Today, again, subalterns with less than three years' service have restricted powers of punishment and, of course, a commanding officer may restrict those of any subaltern at his (the commanding officer's) discretion.

In 1840 lieutenants in the Foot Guards held the rank of captain. The Royal Regiment of Artillery, the Royal Corps of Engineers, the Royal Marines and the Rifle Brigade did not have the rank of ensign so that subalterns in these regiments were distinguished as first- and second-lieutenants.

The price of a lieutenant's commission was, in the Foot Guards, £2,050; in the Life Guards, £1,785; in the Horse Guards, £1,600; in the Dragoons, £1,190; and in the Infantry of the Line, £700.

ENSIGN

The word is derived from the French "ensigne" which came from the Latin "signum" meaning a flag.

Ensigns were commissioned officers immediately below lieutenants in infantry regiments. One officer of this rank, which was abolished in 1871, was appointed to each company and the two juniors in each regiment were responsible for the colours.

Ensigns held the rank of lieutenant in the Foot Guards. In the Royal Artillery, Royal Engineers, Royal Marines and Rifle Brigade, as already stated, there was no such rank and that of second-lieutenant was used.

The regimental ensign, or colour, was the rallying point in battle so that the history of the rank of ensign is interwoven with that of banners which are dealt with elsewhere in this book.

The price of an ensign's commission was, in the Foot Guards £1,200; in the Infantry of the Line, £450.

BARBER, SURGEON, APOTHECARY
AND PSYCHIATRIST

In the olden day the arts of shaving and surgery were considered sister professions. In France, for instance, in 1340, there were barber-chirurgeons and barbier-perruquiers and it was not till many years later that they were separately incorporated.

Grose, in his *Military Antiquities*, states that an officer styled a medicus was present in the army of Edward II when he fought the Scots, presumably at Bannockburn, in 1314. This is the first mention that I have found of a doctor, as we would call him today, being present with an English army in the field. The term does not signify whether he was a surgeon or physician but it does give more faith in his anatomical knowledge than that of barber. As his pay was only sixpence per day I doubt whether a great deal of faith was placed in his skill. He was grouped in the same class as army followers which included shoemakers, tailors, barbers, physicians and, what must have been the crowning indignity of all, washerwomen.

A surgeon is mentioned as having been present during the siege of Calais in 1346 with a salary of a shilling a day so that either his talents were being recognised or, even in those days, doctors had joined one of the more-pay movements which are the curse of this country at the present time.

I would give Henry V the credit for thinking of the possibility that anyone but himself might require medical attention in the field as he instructed Thomas de Morstede, whom he appointed surgeon-in-chief to the Army,* to obtain the services of twelve other surgeons for the forthcoming campaign in France.

In the reign of Elizabeth I a small sum was deducted from the pay of every man to augment that of the surgeon. This sounds like the origin of a sort of military health insurance but, with the proportion of one surgeon to something like 10,000 men, it is doubtful whether the soldier got good value for his money even if he was lucky enough to find a doctor.

Baron Dominique Larrey (1766–1841) was the originator of what, for lack of a better expression, I will call a field medical service. He was Napoleon's chief surgeon and went with him on the Egyptian campaign. It was he who introduced what were known as "ambulances volontes", or flying ambulances. This is a confusing expression in modern parlance because, even after the construction of a good runway, I cannot imagine a bullock drawing an ambulance getting up sufficient speed to become air-borne—at any rate not for long. Lassey's account of his experiences and the organization which he formed can be read in his *Memoires de Chirugie Militaire et Campagnes* published in 1814.

The system of field ambulances and field hospitals was introduced into the English Army by Sir J. McGrigor during the Peninsular War.

When the standing army was established in 1661 it was the custom to appoint apothecaries and hospital mates to either of the two fighting services as circumstances demanded. I fancy that the apothecaries were more

---

*The senior surgeon attached to the Royal Household is known as the Royal Sergeant-Surgeon.

psychologists than anything else as I find that the most popular prescription was a diet of ale, claret, potted chicken and geese. I know nothing about dietetics but this strikes me as far more nourishing than the "number nines" that the successors to these fellows considered so essential to the health of the Army during the First World War.

The Medical Staff Corps was formed in 1855 and shortly afterwards a school was opened at Chatham, and later one at Netley, for training junior probationary officers in military hygiene, surgery and medicine.

I first heard of the doings of psychiatrists (generally referred to as trick cyclists) during the Second World War. I wonder whether they organized the indoor games, known as intelligence tests, which seemed to have been instituted to prove that all officers were imbeciles and the other ranks subnormal and wrongly employed. I recall a poser which my driver answered first time and the garrison commander said was impossible!

I am still not convinced that a few trick, and family questions, reveal more to them about a man than does active service. My regimental sergeant-major had my views on these tests, and a better description of them than I could ever hope to give either verbally or in print. Perhaps the classification given him as a result of his test fired him to more vitriolic oratory. I never dared to ask what "the gypsies" had told him!

CORNET

The word is derived from the Italian "cornetta" meaning a small flag, hence in both the English and French armies, it was applied to the officer who had charge of the regimental standard in a cavalry regiment. It was also used to denote the rank of an officer commanding a troop. His seniority was immediately below that of a lieutenant so that he corresponded to an ensign in a battalion of infantry.

I have failed to pinpoint the first use of the rank though I found mention of it in histories dealing with the military events of the sixteenth century.

SERGEANT-MAJOR, COLOUR-SERGEANT AND SERGEANT

I regret that I cannot trace the first use of the rank of sergeant-major to denote a warrant-officer.

It originally signified the third senior general and later the officer who acted as liaison between the colonel and the regimental officers and thus performed the duties now done by the adjutant.

The following extract from Grose's *Military Antiquities* will strike a chord among many soldiers and, I venture to say, raise a smile. Referring to the sergeant-major he says:

> "He is to be a good scholar and witty but must be quick of apprehension and furnished with able memory. He must have a paper book with pen and ink to set down all orders and commands that he may not err or vary one tittle from what was delivered to him."

Later, when referring to the relationship between the sergeants and the sergeant-major he says:

"They are to repair to him to take word from him and they are to acquaint their captain and other officers.

"All inferior sergeants are to stand round about him and he is to deliver the word privately in the ear of the sergeant which [sic] stands on his right hand, and he is to secretly whisper in the ear of the next and so on from one to another around. The last man is to give it to the sergeant-major again. If the last man give it wrong, then he must give it all over again.

"He is to have a swift nag to carry him about the quarters and to visit his guards for his business lies very confusedly in the army.

"He is visit all outward guards both in the day and night. He is to show such of his officers as are to pass upon watch where to place their sentries."

In the foregoing account of the duties of a sergeant we have early recognition of the importance of repeating back all verbal orders. Perhaps that ancient yarn about the runner who was given a message which ran, "send reinforcements; the general is going to advance" which he converted into, "Send three and four pence; the general is going to a dance" originated about this period.

I regret that I never saw any of my sergeant-majors mounted on swift nags galloping about barracks. The language of some of them was quite fruity enough without the further encouragement of a few falls though the spectacle would have been one well worth watching.

The regimental colours were guarded by four or six sergeants who were called colour-sergeants.

The origin of the rank of sergeant in anything like the sense in which we know it today is very hard to trace. One must remember that it was also used in law so that the added difficulty arises of distinguishing the legal from the military use of the word.

I would say that the military rank originated in the militia because when it was re-established by Charles II he appointed sergeants from his regular forces to train militiamen. Whether they were known as sergeants before, or on, appointment I cannot say but it is in histories of the militia that I first saw the rank mentioned. The appointments were made on the basis of one sergeant to every twenty militiamen so that I see here the origin of one whom we now call the platoon sergeant.

CORPORAL

The word is derived from the Italian "capo" signifying a head; the rank denoted a person who commanded a small squadron or party. In histories dealing with the Army during the reigns of Elizabeth I and Mary I found that the duties of a corporal consisted of superintending the marches of companies and to command skirmishing patrols.

Another account gives his duties as being similar to those now performed by the corporal of the guard. An extract reads as follows:

"He is to warn all his squadron, or part of it to the watch and appoints when, where, and for how long each of his men is to stand sentinel, and he is bound to teach them how to behave themselves when sentinels, and is to visit them frequently; but if he finds any of them asleep, he must not leave him as he found him, but he must bring him to the corps de guard, and there make him prisoner till further order."

LANCE-CORPORAL

The rank is derived from "Lance-spesata", denoting a broken or spent lance. A cavalryman who had lost his lance or had become dismounted served with the infantry until he could be rearmed or remounted.

During this period he was considered to be the guest of the corporal whom he helped and thus got the name of aide-corporal.

It was the usual custom for the corporal to pay his aide but some did not. Here, perhaps, we have the origin of that distinguished rank now known as acting-unpaid-lance-corporal.

SOLDIER AND PRIVATE

The origin of the word "soldier" is somewhat obscure and seems to be generally considered to have been derived from "solidus" which was a coin at the time of the Roman Empire. This may have been the daily pay and thus the recipient is named after his daily wage. In Book 3 of the account of the Gallic War a reference is made to "soldurii" but it does not say that they were paid, and neither is there any means of telling how they obtained the name.

The first mention that I can trace of a word which sounds like the one used today is in Froissart's account of von Artaveld's army of Ghent (1339) in which he says that a special guard of sixty "souldyers" was employed at a salary of four Flemish groats a day.

In accounts of this period men who served for pay were known as soudoyers or souldyers, that is, stipendaries.

So many of our military terms originated on the Continent that I somehow feel that the word "soldyer" must have been in existence some while before 1339 as I find in the wardrobe account of Edward I frequent mention of the term "soldier" and I do not think that it would be wise to deduce that the term "soldyer" was derived from our "soldier". I prefer to think that it was the other way round in spite of the fact that I can trace the mention of a soldier before that of a soldyer . . .

In the time of Charles I the word "private" was used to denote the lowest rank and it was followed by name of the arm of the service, i.e. private trooper, private dragoon and private foot-soldier.

It is interesting to note how the title of the lowest military rank changed during our early history as the following particulars, which were taken from pay rolls of the time, will show.

1557	Private Soldier.
1598	Private Man.
1659	Souldier [sic].
1689	Private Trooper (Horse).
	Private Soldier (Foot).
1714	Private Man (Mounted Regiments).
	Private Soldier (Dismounted Regiments).
1797	Private (All Arms).

CAPTAIN OF PIONEERS AND PIONEER

The duties of the Captain of Pioneers are described in histories dealing with the fourteenth century as being similar to the present-day engineer officer who accompanies a reconaissance party. He went forward with the High Marshal to examine the site of the next camp to see whether the approaches were suitable for the passage of the transport and to make them so if they were not. As soon as the camp was formed he received the marshal's orders with regard to any fortifications and entrenchments necessary and then supervised their construction.

Having obtained the full information of all the manual work required, he obtained his labour through the lord-lieutenant. Here perhaps, we have the origin of the engineer working parties which have always been such popular attractions with the infantry—especially when out of the line for a rest!

The dictionary says that the word pioneer comes from the French peonier, or pion, signifying a foot soldier. The original French translations of these words signified a person working off a sentence for an offence. As the punishment usually consisted of heavy manual work there is a sort of distant connection, though it is hardly flattering to the Captain of Pioneers to be, according to the literal translation, the head convict.

The role, or definition, of a pioneer underwent several changes for I find that he was, later, described as a skilled miner or carpenter, almost what we would now call a tradesman. At another time he was one of the nine lucky ones who was not executed under the system of decimation for some such offence as mutiny, treason or cowardice.

When the title was used to describe one undergoing punishment it signified a man who had to continue as a labourer until such time as he performed an act of gallantry. As his work could hardly be expected to give him a chance to show his bravery, it is reasonable to assume that he was employed by the Army for life.

TRENCH MASTER

This rank is a contemporary of the last. The holder was responsible for the maintenance of all trenches, fences, barricades, and all the other items that were made, or dug, to protect the Army.

I came upon the rank, or title, in the Portuguese Army during the First World War. I have no knowledge of the organization of that army, but I remember that on one occasion I was referred to the trench officer for the usual particulars required by a unit when relieving another such as location of the stores, arcs of fire, and danger spots, etc.

MASTER OF THE REVELS

This title has only a slight military connection though one must remember that entertainment played an important part in the king's affairs. The Master of the Revels, sometimes referred to as the Master of the Tents, or Master of the Masks and Revels, was a permanent officer in the royal household. He was responsible for the care of the tents and pavilions belonging to the king which job also included the finding of a suitable site for their erection. His duties did not extend beyond the royal entourage. In the less serious periods he had to organize the entertainments and act as what we would now call a master of ceremonies.

The rank was first introduced by Henry VIII and I found mention of it up to 1674 but not since then.

In addition to the foregoing ranks there were several appointments which included the word "general" such as adjutant-general, quarter-master-general, and so on.

There are three civilian offices today, which include the word, that come readily to mind. They are the attorney-general, solicitor-general, and the best-known of them all, the postmaster-general. The first two have always been law officers with no military connection but the last-named owed his origin to military necessity as will be shown later. As a matter of fact the judge-advocate-general is also a civilian, but we will deal with him, too, in his correct place.

All the military offices which include the word general infer that the holder is a senior officer but do not specify his particular rank. For instance, the quatermaster-general could be a lieutenant-general or major-general and the same remark applies to the adjutant-general.

As the holder of one particular office is not necessarily senior to that of another they will be dealt with in alphabetical order.

ADJUTANT-GENERAL

This office was introduced sometime in the sixteenth century and took priority immediately below that of sergeant-major-general. The duties then assigned to him seem to be extraordinary diverse including, as they did, the compiling of the daily situation reports, visiting the outposts and the supervision of all measures taken to guard the Army against surprise.

As a matter of strict accuracy I must record that it was not in the reading of our early military history that I found the first mention of the appointment but in the story of that remarkable man Ignatius Loyola who, in 1534, started his society in Paris. In 1540 he received a papal bull authorizing him to further his creed all over Europe.

He appointed an adjutant-general, having himself been styled general by the Pope, in every country in Europe and charged them with appointing their own subordinates and the sending out of emissaries to further the work of the Society in the areas for which they were made responsible.

I think that the roles of the early adjutant-generals were a bit too different from now to make the connection easily recognizable. The first adjutant-general appointed with a role similar to that of today was a civilian, E. Roufosse Esquire, in 1673. In 1686 two were appointed, one known as the Adjutant-General of Horse, and the other the Adjutant-General of Foot who acted as the connecting links between the general and their particular arm of the service.

BARRACK-MASTER-GENERAL

This title originated in 1714. In 1793 the title changed to Superintendent-General of Barracks with Colonel de Lancey as the first holder. On 30th

May, 1794, that is in the next year, the name was changed to Barrack-Master-General. The title existed till 1806 when it was abolished and the care of barrack property, and the building of new barracks, was entrusted to four commissioners, one of whom was a soldier.

JUDGE-ADVOCATE-GENERAL

The Judge-Advocate-General, though a civilian, is the chief officer responsible for the administration of military law. He holds his appointment under the Great Seal.

Military law, or military jurisprudence, is something to which an English soldier becomes liable in addition to the civil code, though he cannot be tried under both for the same offence. In most foreign armies the soldier is only subject to the military code quite irrespective of the nature of his offence or where it was committed.

The administration of military justice is, except for comparatively minor offences which are dealt with by regimental officers, supervised by a member of the staff of the judge-advocate general at courts martial.

Under an Act of Parliament, known as the Mutiny Act, the Crown has a right to convene a court martial to try all soldiers of whatever rank. This right is delegated to general officers commanding-in-chief commands and certain districts. It is also given on somewhat rare occasions to officers who have received a special warrant to convene such courts and confirm their findings.

The object of military law is not to inflict another burden on the soldier but to ensure that he has the fairest possible trial and that his rights as a citizen are fully maintained.

The officers who compose a court act as both judge and jury in that they decide either guilt or innocence and, in the case of the former, pronounce the sentence. They are primarily soldiers, not lawyers, so that they cannot know all the legal snags which might arise. To ensure the strict administration of justice, both military and civil, the judge-advocate general is represented at all courts by one of his deputies whose duties are to advise the court on all points of law when asked, and to keep his eye on the proceedings to see that the accused is safeguarded against any miscarriage of justice and is given the greatest possible latitude to state his case. He is, if I may use the expression, an umpire who has no say in the form of the examination and cross-examination providing they are fair and legal. He has no say in the actual findings and sentence of the court providing they comply with the law.

The officer who convened the court will review the whole proceedings and may confirm or lessen the sentence but he cannot increase it.

As I have found a certain confusion among cadets between martial and military law, I had better explain that the judge-advocate general has nothing whatever to do with the former. Martial law gives the military authorities certain powers which they do not normally possess, but it in no way affects the administration of military justice. It may affect the seriousness of certain offences and entail more severe penalties, but it does not affect the judicial procedure while those offences are being tried. The object of the presence of a member of the judge-advocate general's staff during a court martial is precisely the same whether the country is at peace or war, or under martial law. Martial Law is proclaimed by an Act of Parliament, not by the judge-advocate general!

The term advocate is derived from the Latin "advocare", to call in aid. In Roman times the advocate gave his services free and now, from the soldier's point of view, his attendance is the same.

The first mention that I have traced of a judge-advocate general being appointed to the Army is in 1625 when one went with it to France.

MUSTER-MASTER-GENERAL

This office is also mentioned as Commissary General of Musters. His immediate superior was the Commissary General who gave him his orders as to when, where, and how many men to muster. His subordinate officers were called Commissaries of Muster.

The office originated in the arrayors who raised the armies for the Norman kings. The first order delivered to individuals was dated 1322 and was addressed to Thomas Lencedekne and Reginald de Botereux by the Plantagenet king Edward II.

Whether known as an arrayor or muster-master-general his duties were the same and continued to be so in practically the same form till the title was abolished by George III in 1818.

His first duty was to call out the Army, or a particular unit, for inspection to see that the numbers on parade agreed with the rolls, and then to check that the men whose names appeared were the actual ones on parade.

His next duty was to see that the men paraded were fit to serve and to ensure that replacements were found for those who had to be discharged. In addition to the men he had to examine the horses, and all the other items which the particular unit was responsible for producing.

He rendered his report to the Commissary General who paid the captain of the company accordingly.

A somewhat similar role was performed by the Commissioners of Array. The difference being that the commissioners were really the early forms of press gangers in that they forcibly enrolled extra men, and commandeered all the other extras required such as horses, carts and anything else to which they took a fancy.

There were also other commissioners who carried out what were known as arbitrary levies for raising money. These were done at the same time and it was these which produced the cash with which the Commissary General paid the captains of companies.

These early periods, interesting though they may be to the historian, were entirely devoid of niceties. Men and money were wanted so both were obtained and it was more than a man's life was worth to argue.

As the foregoing remarks have inevitably left the impression that the men were paid at the time of the muster I must add that those who were considered to possess an income of £20 a year received nothing. In any case, the period of reckoning did not start till the man had crossed his county border. One can well imagine that few knew where this was so, for simplicity's sake, no pay was given till the men reached the port of embarkation!

POSTMASTER-GENERAL

I have added the word "general" to this office for the sake of convenience and to show that there is a decided connection between the present Postmaster-General and the early postmaster who owed his origin to military necessity.

It will be necessary, and I hope interesting, for us to wander from the purely military sphere to trace the origin of this office.

The word "post" is derived from the French "poste" which in turn came from the Low Latin "posta" which signified a place where horses could be hired. From places where horses could be hired for pleasure they gradually developed to those where some were kept for private hire and others for official use. The horses at these establishments were called post-horses, and those who ran the establishments were known as post-masters. Postes were first established in France in the thirteenth century for the conveyance of official correspondence and the use of officers of state. It is amusing, but strictly accurate, to say that officials travelled by posts—not post. The reason for this is obvious because one horse could not travel a distance of, say, two hundred miles as speedily as the journey could be done on relays of fresh horses.

In course of time a coach was provided which, needless to say, was known as a stage coach—the word stage having replaced that of post. It is of interest to note that as late as 1840 the hire of a stage coach was 11d. per mile plus a further 3d. per mile for the driver. The equivalent charge in modern cost of travel is seen very clearly if one realizes that the farm labourer of those days earned enough in a week to travel barely five miles in a public conveyance which, on normal main roads of the period, was unlikely to average more than eleven miles an hour at the most. In addition to the bare cost of hiring the coach and driver there were the post-boys and turnpikes, or tollgates, to be paid. In a book written about this time I note that the author says that the average journey can be made at a cost of 1s. 10d. per mile all inclusive. With this information we need not wonder that our ancestors did not travel unless they had to.

The reader will be familair with such expressions as, "the king summoned his barons", or, "the king called a council", but I doubt whether he ever stopped to think how he did it. The first thing he did was to issue a writ which is a written document summoning a person, or people, to attend at a certain place and time. It can also signify an order to do a particular act but we are not concerned with this definition at the moment.

Having written, or got someone to write, the writ he gave it to a nuncio, or messenger, to deliver it to the person concerned. The first payments to nuncii are to be found in the Close-Rolls of King John. The first to be mentioned by name that I have traced was Domini Regis de Hastang who was paid from the wardrobe account of Edward I.

Though I have no proof that they were originated by Edward II, there are records to show that posts did exist from which horses could be hired. In 1481, during the war with Scotland, Edward IV established posts twenty miles apart by the use of which it is stated despatches could be carried at the rate of an hundred miles a day. By the end of the fifteenth century, or the beginning of the sixteenth, it was customary to mark a despatch "haste poste haste" from which, obviously, we get our present similar expression.

I have been unable to trace any use of these early posts as purely military institutions but I have, I hope, shewn that the existing civilian ones were used by the sovereign for military purposes.

It is true to say that the Royal Writs had to be taken to different parts of the Kingdom and reasonable to suppose that this was done as expeditiously as possible so let that be the excuse for studying the system of posts and postage up to the time of the appointment of the first Postmaster-General.

A statute of Edward VI, passed in 1548, fixed a penny a mile as the hire charge per mile for each post-horse. In 1581 Thomas Randolf was appointed Postmaster of England as superintendent of posts, but there is no mention that he was responsible for the carriage of letters. The fact that the elements of a transport system were in being means *ipso facto*, that there were the means for the carriage of letters.

We are so accustomed to receiving letters posted in the United Kingdom on the day after posting that it is worth recalling that the first order concerning the time a letter should take was made in a Royal Proclamation in 1636 which decreed that a service should be instituted between Edinburgh and the City of London to run night and day to enable a letter to be sent and a reply received in six days. As the total distance by modern roads is something like 770 miles, this, together with the time taken to deliver the letter and get the answer, is not bad going. I should imagine that the courier was a bit bored, and probably sore, after his round trip!

The connection between the civilian-run posts and the military is by inference till 1644 in which year an entry in the Journal of the Commons reads, "The Lords and Commons, finding by experience that it is most necessary, for keeping of good intelligence between the Parliament and their forces, that post stages should be erected in several parts of the kingdom, and the office of master of the posts and couriers being at present void, ordain that Edmund Prideaux, Esq., a member of the House of Commons, shall be, and is hereby constituted, master of the posts, messengers, and couriers." In 1649 the Common Council of the City of London proposed appointing its own postmaster, but was forbidden to do so by a resolution of the House of Commons which declared "that the office of postmaster is, and ought to be, in the sole power and disposal of Parliament".

The most complete step in the establishment of the postal service as we know it today was contained in an act of 1656 which was passed "to settle the postage of England, Scotland, and Ireland". One of the enactments contained therein was "that there shall be one General Post-office, and one officer styled the Postmaster General of England and Comptroller of the Post-office".

The act deals exclusively with the carriage of letters and packets and in doing so divorces the Postmaster-General from military matters.

PROVIANT-MASTER-GENERAL

This officer, who is mentioned in the histories of the fourteenth century, was responsible for obtaining the proviants, which we would now call rations. In addition to obtaining them he, with his staff, had to see that they were distributed to captains of companies. All mills, slaughter houses, breweries, fisheries, and all places where food and fodder could be obtained came under his control.

His assistants were known as proviant's secretaries, proviant's clerks, wagon-makers, smiths, and, at one time, the wagon-master and quarter-master came under his jurisdiction.

When on the subject of proviants, it is worth recalling that some captains paid their men by the system of "pay by provand". This meant that the men, instead of receiving pay, were given huge chunks of cheese or sacks of flour. The proviso on these occasions was that the man should carry away his provand. The unscrupulous captains—that is the majority—took good care that the load was too big for one man to carry. By this means they could claim unbounded generosity and pocket the cash!

The office is easily confused with that of Commissary General. As no two of them are mentioned in an account of the same campaign it is reasonable to suppose that they were the same people though historians have ascribed slightly different roles to them.

The original term for ration was portion which varied according to rank. The unit of distribution was that allotted to the trooper or soldier. Whatever they got the ensign received four times as much and so it went on up to the rank of colonel who received twelve portions.

In one old history I read that each man received a "pottle" and I wondered what it meant. I subsequently found that it was a measure holding four pints. The daily ration was one of wine or two of beer.

In one respect at any rate the soldiers of today, except teetotallers, can claim that the Army is not what it was!

QUARTER-MASTER-GENERAL

The chief responsibility for billeting the Army rested with the marshal who, as Grose says, acted as quarter-master-general. He met the representatives of the companies (later, when so called, the regiments) who were known as harbingers, or harbergers, and allocated to them the buildings which their unit was to occupy.

The office of quarter-master-general is comparatively modern for, until about the beginning of the nineteenth century, the duties of finding billets were divided between the quarter-masters of horse and foot-quarter-masters, as the latter were so quaintly described.

Billeting in the early days was a much more complicated business than it is now and so, even at the risk of a digression, some explanatory remarks are necessary.

There are many allusions in history to the ways in which the church helped the military and none were more important than over the matter of finding accommodation and supplying the other needs of an army on the move.

Though the armies lived on the country it was still necessary to carry around a certain amount of stores. It is obvious that the same pair of horses could not be expected to drag their load hundreds of miles without rest and re-shoeing. In winter, or in the event of a sudden change of weather, more horses would have been necessary.

The church was made responsible for the army's requirements. Nuncii were sent forward with writs telling the priest what to have ready in the way of accommodation, stores, horses and wagons.

It is difficult to realize some of the very real problems which armies on the move some five or six hundred years ago had to solve. Maps were non-existent so guides were wanted to show the way from one halting place to the next. The armies lived on the countryside it is true, but what if there were no crops? To commandeer everything in sight is a short term policy and might, especially if it became necessary to come back that way, lead to defeat.

How, then, to live on the country and at the same time disorganize it as little as possible?

The solution, brought about by economic necessity and not any kind-heartedness, was to make the inhabitants move the army by stages.

The church, as I have said, was warned to have provisions and accommodation available and also so many draft-horses and, if also required, re-mounts. These horses had to draw the vehicles to the next halt and then return. In this way, in addition to free haulage, two other problems were solved. The first was the provision of fresh horses and the second that of guides.

INDEX

INDEX